Bob Lawrence

MY
WILD life
BOB LAWRENCE

*To my wife Sue
who has put up with it all!*

First published in 2000 by
R. P. Lawrence

ISBN 0 9537999 0 5

Page and jacket design by Chris Madeley Graphic Design, Shropshire.
Front jacket photos:
    Tiger - Chris Madeley.
    Author - S. Rowen, Capener Rowen Ltd.
Rear jacket photo courtesy of Graham Scott, Suzuki Rhino Club.
Typeset and printed in Great Britain by Bewdley Printing Co. Ltd., Kidderminster.
All unattributed photos; the Author.

MY WILD life

CONTENTS

Foreword

There are many dates, times and places in my life firmly etched in the memory. One of them is the Christmas Party 1998 but not simply because it was one of the most enjoyable ever. After a year of increasing unease, that morning an immediate post-Christmas operation had been ordered for a biopsy. It wouldn't, though, spoil Christmas for anyone for no one was told. Ultimately, even then, only three or four people would know. Both this development and the interminable wait for the results concentrated the mind wonderfully. I kept my mind busy through those winter evenings producing the bulk of this narrative. I reflected on my supreme good fortune in life and the wonderful people I've been privileged to know and work with who have sustained me, however unwittingly, through thick and thin. I bear few any animosity, for I have been shown little or none.

My children taught me the mysteries of the word processor. Then the first draft went off to Bill Campbell, of Bill Campbell Television, with whom I was working at the time, wrapped in a Tesco carrier bag. When it arrived back one lunchtime in a Bewdley pub, resplendent in a *Sainsbury's* bag, I knew he was impressed! Chris Madeley, one of my 'old boys' (1974/78), now Chris Madeley Graphic Design came next and, together with Bewdley Printing, provided priceless support and endless encouragement without charge, but changed nothing of the original. If the writing came easily, selecting the photographs was a nightmare - even after doubling their page allocation. Every picture tells a story and there are tens of thousands of them. Chris helped with this, too. Indeed his tireless enthusiasm, boundless energy and sheer professionalism did more than anyone to get the project out of the carrier bag. A special thanks also to all my friends who contributed photographs, no one asked a fee. Like everyone else involved, they kept my book secret and didn't tell my long-suffering wife Sue to whom my tale is dedicated.

Bob Lawrence
March 2000

Opposite Page:
Southern White Rhino, West Midland Safari Park.
Since the park opened, 98% of the world's rhino population has been wiped out.
(Photo Author)

West Midland Safari Park
A Brief History

*The original entrance to
the Park was through the Lodge gates off the A456. (Photo Author)*

The site of the safari park can be readily traced back to the 18th century. The trail begins with Samuel Skey (1726-1800) who began his business life as an apprentice grocer in Bewdley. He made his name, however, through the manufacture of dyestuffs and sulphuric acid, amassing a considerable fortune in the process. He appears to have been a man of considerable enterprise. When he encountered planning difficulties (the site of his intended family home was 'entailed land'), he spent £500 getting an Act of Parliament to repeal this. In 1775, he then 'swapped' some farms he owned at Bromsgrove for the 270 acres of land from Lord Foley upon which he built Spring Grove House and the small estate which burgeoned around it. He later bought Dowles Manor, Bewdley, where he was buried.

*Opposite Page:
'Animal Magic!' Old hands, old friends. John Drysdale and I combine to choreograph this striking pose.
(Photo J. Drysdale)*

Completed in 1790 and landscaped by Capability Brown, this sumptuous house had excellent views to the north towards Trimpley and Habberley as well as most of the estate to the south, including the lakes. Both natural and man-made, these were largely fed from the natural springs bubbling up through the underlying sandstone from which the area derives the name 'Spring Grove'. In recent years, however, the water table has dropped to such an extent that these springs are largely dormant and the lakes are now fed from a borehole sunk behind Pets Corner.

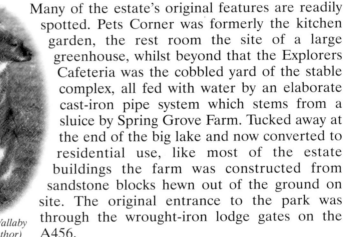

Bennett's Wallaby
(Photo Author)

Many of the estate's original features are readily spotted. Pets Corner was formerly the kitchen garden, the rest room the site of a large greenhouse, whilst beyond that the Explorers Cafeteria was the cobbled yard of the stable complex, all fed with water by an elaborate cast-iron pipe system which stems from a sluice by Spring Grove Farm. Tucked away at the end of the big lake and now converted to residential use, like most of the estate buildings the farm was constructed from sandstone blocks hewn out of the ground on site. The original entrance to the park was through the wrought-iron lodge gates on the A456.

The painter John Constable visited the house frequently between 1811 and 1835 whilst courting his future wife Maria Bicknell, a relative of Samuel Skey. Several sketches still exist of the estate which were drawn during these visits. The estate remained in the Skey Family until 1871 and in private hands until 1970. The last private owner was Major Harcourt Webb, founder of the well-known firm of Webbs Seed Merchants.

The West Midland Safari Park was opened in 1973 by the Chipperfield Organisation. In 1984, the park was taken over by private owners and has been improved and enhanced every year since. Spring Grove House itself was extensively refurbished as a Banqueting Suite and now caters for wedding receptions, dinner dances, conferences and Sunday luncheons.

Sitting comfortably? I'm going to tell you a story……

CHAPTER 1
In the Beginning...
(To Mum and Dad who supported me for so long)

The football had hung in the air for an eternity. Brand new, it glistened sparkling white against a vividly blue August sky. I can remember it as if it were yesterday. It was a final full dress rehearsal for the coming season a mere week hence. Competition for every place was fierce. Young, strong, full of running, the youthful naivety that gives one a sense of invincibility even after eighty hours toiling in the harvest fields each week, coupled with the fourteen mile walk to and from work each day (or even perhaps because of it) made for uncompromising opposition. A captain's arm-band and a cup winner's medal still warm in my kit bag from the previous season completed the euphoria. My little world lay at my feet. I leapt imperiously, rising head and shoulders above all and sundry, the goal looming large with a panicking goalkeeper the most superfluous of obstacles. I made contact readily but the nudge in the back meant an awkward landing. Marginally off balance, one foot touched the parched ground fractionally before the other. The sudden pain in my pelvic region was appalling. Through the nausea, distant voices urged me to take the resulting penalty - it was expected of me. Aghast, we all stared incredulously as the ball trickled feebly and ineptly goalwards for an apologetic keeper to retrieve. The legs had gone.

Days later, stinking of liniment, I stepped out gingerly for the season's curtain-raiser. It was impossible. "We need you out there," implored the trainer as I exchanged my precious number

Opposite Page:
'At the end of the Day', six week old Lion Cub.
(Photo Author. 1977, Zenith Camera and Praktica Lens)

West Norfolk Primary Schools' Sports Association

This is to Certify that

Robert Lawrence

was the winner of

the bean-bag relay (boys under-12)

at West Norfolk Primary Schools' Sports

held at **Barroway Drove,**

on **July 17th, 1961.**

H. H. Tyrrell
——————
Chairman

Chariots of Fire! Preparation for the rigours of life ahead!

four shirt with that of the sub. I gasped just with the effort of untying boot laces as I did the following week and the week after that. I was never to kick a football again.

The pain was excruciating. Keeping down food was often impossible as my lower spine burnt relentlessly within me. The family doctor prescribed aspirin. Agriculture college loomed large - the final year of four, the practical year - and I could do practically nothing. Wasting the initial three years by not completing the fourth wasn't an option. My education had been a big enough farce already. As part of the first CSE intakes, we'd been assured that a Grade 1 was effectively an 'O' level. However, once attained (and I passed nine, a record number from the Nissan hut at my humble secondary modern, a quarter of whose pupils were on probation!), they weren't the expected prelude to 'A' levels. Before we could sit them, we had to have 'proper' 'O' levels. Similarly, the four year OND in agriculture at the Kent Agriculture Institute was supposed to equate to an NDA. It wasn't and never has been.

The attraction of college was, of course, the sport. American style, the lectures were squeezed between working the black economy to pay my way, the football and the cricket. Four games a week, together with all the associated training and travel. They were the days of my life, played out amidst idyllic picture postcard scenery. The village greens, oases of tranquillity amidst the hustle and bustle of the orchards and hop gardens in this, the Garden of England, tucked away beneath the North Downs and the little black and white pubs overlooking the pond. Memories all the more poignant now that so little of it survives. Memories, too, like putting down ten overs, four maidens and taking six wickets for sixteen begrudging runs, including an unforgettable caught and bowled. The ball had been hooked and was either going for six or taking the umpire's head off. Diving full length, I caught it one-handed off the tip of his nose. He hauled me to my feet, hugged me (with total impartiality!), then gave the disbelieving batsman, their captain and county progeny, out! With the temperatures into the eighties, the home side sought to get back into the match by changing our tea-time menu for a searing hot, dubious-looking curry. Noting their preference for the original salad, the locked loo and the squealing from some suspiciously hungry pigs up the road (we weren't agricultural students for nothing!), I went hungry, strode out to hit the winning runs and was smuggled from the pavilion on the floor of the minibus to avoid the lynch mob. Tragically such an alien concept today in modern education, sport bonded us into a formidable unit in either football or cricket. The course intake of just fifteen could field strong sides in both sports - the girls did the scoring. We lived, played and worked around the clock, together. A typical day might begin at 5a.m., if it were our turn to do the milking, and end at 3a.m. the next day after a long trip to an away game in the next county, very much the worse for wear if we'd won. A quick shower and it was milking time again. It wasn't unknown for those with reduced staying power to fall asleep in the shower, their buttocks blocking the outlet, flooding out the entire block and half drowning anyone with the temerity to actually be in bed at such an hour. Suddenly, I was out of it. The prospectus took the course far and wide at home and abroad. I alone remained.

Although the solitude was familiar to this born again asthmatic, the inactivity was galling. I'd been bedridden as a minor, not starting school until I was almost eight, after a six month 'kick-

Six a side Cup Winners 1970. I'm on the left. (Photo Kent & Sussex Courier)

Sporting Swansong. Kent Agriculture Institute Hockey side 1970/71, but time had run out for No.4, third from right, back row.
(Photo D. Wood)

start' in a sanatorium. After that came the then-fashionable tonsil removal, shingles and chicken pox for good measure. It was an anonymous upbringing, too, being the headmaster's son in a traditional rural village. The social stigma caused by this accident of birth meant being ostracised by all and sundry, second only perhaps to the sons of the local bobby and the vicar. Whilst the former didn't have children, the latter did, but more than justified his popular image. That just left me.

The college physician pursued my difficulty more vigorously than the family doctor at home. Physiotherapy, traditional at first, then latterly specialist underwater treatment proved equally fruitless but, suddenly, a lifeline appeared - hockey! Although devoid of the strength in my legs to scarcely kick a ball, the bulk of the goalkeeping kit hid a protective corset from the inquisitive and my cricketing instincts stood me in good stead. Replacing the incumbent, my record made me the best goalkeeper the college ever had. It got me through the winter.

Spring turned to summer with no progress, physically or academically, but summer brought exam time. Ironically, within an hour of completing my final paper, the game was up. The consultant was calm, reassuring, utterly professional and well-versed in conveying the catastrophic, albeit, he said, never before to one so young. It was no consolation. Forget the football, cricket, hockey, the farming and the motorbike - "A desk job, perhaps," he added kindly, "with a suitable chair." Five vertebrae were disintegrating, he went on, waving X-rays at the light box. So much for the aspirin. There was no choice. A spinal fusion - a combination of steel pins and bone grafts to rebuild the spine and hold vertebrae L1, L2, L3, S1 and S2 together - was the only option available. Twenty five years before the world heard of BSE, I was to have bone granules from a German cow implanted within me. "Come back next week and my chaps will fix you up," he said, from a million miles away. 'Fixing me up' meant lying on a bench, having plaster of Paris poured over me from head to toe and remaining perfectly still like a battered sausage until the mixture had cooled. They then simply cut horizontally around my deep-fried torso until they were able to split it open and free me from this pharaoh-like incarceration. Thus moulded to my every inch, it was lined with wool to await its day.

The day was a lifetime coming. Summer seemed interminable, but then everything did. College finished and I awaited my appointment with destiny. Three times I was given dates and on each we were met, walking down the garden path, by the telegram boy. The bed had been taken by an emergency admission (although I was rapidly disintegrating into one myself). Finally, in September, I made it to the ward. Ironically again, as I lay there shaven, scrubbed down and light-headed under the pre-op medication, the post arrived. Unable to touch it myself, the theatre sister, a girl from my own village and the wife of the player who had picked me up from the ground the year before, read the letter from college. Under much parental and tutorial pressure stressing the futility of what I'd been expected to achieve in that last year, the college had passed me out by the lowest permissible margin. The second letter said the football player's insurance I'd paid was invalid. The money had been misappropriated and never reached the broker. A year later, a whip-round to make up for it produced £23. Under these conflicting emotions, they wheeled me away at breakneck speed along the labyrinth of corridors connecting the Nissan huts of this wartime burns unit and across the final, open hundred yards in the rain, beneath an umbrella. "Promise you'll be there when I wake up?" I enquired of my soaked, friendly neighbourhood theatre sister. "Of course," she said. And she was. Eight hours later, her voice roused me back in Ward 7. "Have they done it?" I asked her incredulously, fearful of another false dawn for I was numb all over. "Yes darling, you were marvellous!" she said, taping my letters to the plaster. She tightened the restraining straps about my incarcerated form, moistened my lips with a sponge, my cheek with a kiss and rushed for the last number 88 bus home to our sleepy little village way out in the sticks. I was left strapped in my casket on a trolley in the dark, alone. I was 20 years old.

The following six weeks vie strongly for the worst of my life. The lengthy delay between fitting my plaster cast and placing me in it meant it no longer fitted. The bone graft began to fuse after ten days. At that point, I was turned over face downwards in order that the bottom half could be raised and the stitches taken out. The cause of the discomfort was there for all to see - except me, of course. My knobbly pelvic bones, prominent now by weight loss, were worn clean through the flesh into the plaster itself. The bleeding had fused me to the cast. A short-lived fresh dressing was all the relief possible. The scars remain to this day. Encased again in my casket, I was turned over again like a tombola machine. It was as far as I was to move for six weeks. Every movement, such as it was, proved agonising. The maximum morphine dose permitted was barely sufficient for me to recognise my mother at times. There were few other visitors. Back complaints are, after all, a common prescription for malaise. The football team were too nervous about the possible repercussions to put in an appearance, whilst my college colleagues were scattered to the four winds selling cars in Canada, working on North Sea oil rigs - anything, in fact, except farming.

Days later, still straining every sinew to master the art of eating off my chest whilst prostrate, a dreadful crack came out of my plaster. Heard clearly by a nurse across the ward, her bell brought the orderly fussing in. "Can you feel the needle?" he enquired, fretting with my toes. It could have been a six inch nail for all I knew. I couldn't feel a thing. Despite the anxiety, I remember feeling surprised at the ease with which I was falling asleep that night. Then the angels came. Clad in long, white flowing gowns, their faces masked and heads covered, they bore me swiftly and silently away into a halo of intense light like a latter-day extraterrestrial. How long they hovered over me, working swiftly and efficiently without ever appearing to utter a word, I'll never know. Only the compassionate eyes and the occasional caress served to allay any sense of panic. Suddenly, it was down to earth again - breakfast time in my cast on the trolley, carefully positioned in the ward to avoid the draught from the cracked window, a leaky roof and an impeded view of the nurses' changing room. "You must have been dreaming," laughed the sister when I asked what had been going on. Maybe, maybe not, but I could move my toes again.

Walking unaided, if indeed I was to, would take a month, they said. Three weeks was the record set by a hitherto very fit PE instructor. Come my time, I was winched from my mould and refitted with a corset. I hadn't slept for days, furiously practising around the clock the physiotherapy and mentally preparing for the ultimate test of mind over matter. I *would* walk. Lifted upright for the first time in six weeks, the NHS brandy for the expected rush of blood from head to feet wasn't needed. Indeed, given the choice of drinking NHS brandy and walking, there was only one option! I placed one foot in front of the other, then did it again. Caught off guard, I was through the door before the nurses could prevent me. The orderly called the sister, she the doctor, the doctor the consultant, who came out of the operating theatre to join the astonished throng around me on the lawn. I still remember the exuberance of feeling the breeze on my cheeks again. I needed help to get back, but I'd done it. Three days later, I was on the platform at Tonbridge station as my girlfriend alighted a train, en route, she thought, to see me in hospital. The poor girl nearly fainted as I emerged from a cloud of steam to touch her shoulder. And then I went home. Nearly thirty years later, I can still touch my toes. The surgeon's legacy was priceless.

Still in a plaster straight-jacket, however, I kicked my heels for another winter. We had no television, car or 'phone. The distant girlfriend eventually found other attractions and returned an engagement ring. So, come the spring, I took a gamble, kick-started my motorbike and sidecar and set off on the longest journey of my life to date - to see my sister studying at Birmingham University. A minor brush with the law saw a probationary period, which I opted to serve as a cricket groundsman at a Birmingham cricket league ground. I'm sure that if I'd been fit to play I'd have escaped retribution altogether, but I resisted all the offers of a game. Even for me that would have been pushing my luck, but the £2 per week wages tax-free were priceless. As I arrived home from this one evening, my sister said she'd seen on TV that a safari park had opened nearby. Why didn't I apply for a job?

The decision was made the following day. An NHS doctor checking on the long term sick took one peek down my corset, gave me a sick note for a further six months and began to talk about green insurance cards. Suddenly, I was disabled - officially. I tore the lot up and went for the interview. I was offered a job on the spot - they had no one else with a college education! It was accepted. I changed doctors to get signed off, then again when I was advised to have more surgery, and began work. It was in the open air, amongst animals (many of whom I scarcely recognised), albeit just opening the front gate. And then there was the money, £20 of it for every six day, seventy hour week. After years of penury, living on a £7 per annum student grant less the mandatory £4.50 students union subscription and latterly £16 per week sickness benefit, it was a fortune. As a child, I'd kept mice in the coal shed, rabbits in the back yard and had a dog, but I'd never been to a zoo in my life.

CHAPTER 2
The Twilight Years
(To David and Olive Chorley who made everything possible)

T hus began what in retrospect was my apprenticeship, as bizarre and unintentional as it was instructive. It was a classic induction in how not to do virtually everything. I paced myself meticulously. Work, eat, sleep. Travelling to and from Birmingham daily left little time for anything else anyway. Seventy to eighty hours a week astride a motorbike or a cast-iron unsprung tractor seat wasn't therapeutic on my reconstructed regions, so my old corset proved invaluable.

The new beginning nearly ended as abruptly as it had begun. Within a week, I'd been promoted from opening and closing the front gate to a driver and given a £2 per week rise by virtue of my college education. That much of it had been spent on the playing fields in the Garden of England did not feature much in the discussion! In a fit of pique, another driver, jealous of my advancement, tried to run me over in a tractor. There was still some footwork left in my scarred torso and I received only a glancing blow as the instinctive body swerve deflected me sideways from the reach of a Ford 4000 tractor. I lay in the verge scarcely daring to move for fear of discovering injury. Finally it sank in, I was okay. The hospital advised a week off and certainly the cuts bled for a day or so, but I wouldn't be denied. The culprit, a director's son, was untouchable, but I now knew to watch my back for the place was in a state of virtual anarchy.

Opposite Page:
'Tyger, Tyger burning bright' The Tiger by Night.
(Photo Author. 1975, Zenith Camera and Praktica Lens)

Just weeks later, my tractor broke down amongst the lions, its tank full of sugar. Someone did receive their marching orders for that but, for the most part, anything went. Leather-clad, pistol-toting neurotics strutted around as if on the set of a spaghetti western, not the least adverse to letting fly whenever the mood or the drink took them. The victims were often the hapless occupants of Pets Corner, summarily executed for lion food. Then there was the taxidermist, the Irish one, the one who always complained that business was dead. I thought that helped! His subjects were dressed out on his lawn after dark so his neighbours wouldn't notice (presumably the darkness hid the smell too!), then the remnants were born off to his 'partner', the night porter at a hospital, who 'lost' them in the incinerator. Scenes reminiscent of Custer's last stand were enacted despite the belated realisation that even blanks could be deadly at close quarters, as many a shattered windscreen could testify. Few records remain of this era for few were kept.

The park was steadily destroyed by man and beast alike. Acres of semi-mature woodland were felled by bored staff simply for something to do. Two hundred year old oaks were first defoliated by giraffe, then barked and uprooted by elephants before becoming scratching posts for rhino. Five foot high chain-link on four inch posts was expected to contain rhino, ostrich and eland - notorious jumpers - and, ridiculously, keep out foxes. They seldom read the script, however, and steadily ate through the exotic fare within. Doubtless with this ever present threat uppermost in their mind, the East African Crown Crested cranes graced the skies, baboons the bordering woods (watching over the occasional errant eland or two grazing beneath them), ostrich our neighbour's fields, whilst tigers swam in the lake. Not surprisingly, perhaps, this caused the sea lions to run amok - on dry land! It was a shambles, but, in an age where lion cubs graced pet shop windows in Birmingham (elephants and chimps their back yard) and could be purchased quite openly and legally by anyone with a council house garage big enough to hold them (you still can in Northern Ireland!), it seemed par for the course. Not then a Zoo Licensing Act (1980) or even a Dangerous Wild Animals Act (1976), Health and Safety at Work, COSH or risk assessment. I doubt anyone had the intellect to apply it anyway. Although we seemed the very epitome of the need for regulation, we weren't alone. There were others far worse. In the meantime, the sole definitive safety instrument was the local police sergeant. If he said a tree was too near a fence, then down it came. He passed similar judgement on fences, animal housing, firearms, even the boats on the lake - all in the name of safety - something that policing rural Worcestershire had ill prepared him for.

My role in this lunacy was to watch over a twelve-acre reserve containing twenty four lions, keeping them away from cars with open windows (if I couldn't prevent the windows from being opened in the first place), from soft top roofs (a common feature on cars then), from their occupants (who were seldom averse to getting out of the vehicle) and from the four gateways manned by pedestrian gatemen. One of them I always remember was a Pakistani boy, a veritable magnet for the lions who, inexplicably, were mesmerised by him and stalked him constantly. If they came too close, he'd cast everything aside and flee on foot - into the bears! For a entire year, until mercifully he left, I'd called him Abdul, only to belatedly discover his name was Abbas. Wherever you are Abbas, I'm sorry.

I always remember the first pearls of wisdom I received from London Zoo regarding one's visitors. 'Treat 'em like idiots and design all your signage and protocol accordingly'. Not what you're taught in today's 'Welcome Host' seminars, of course, but I first began to follow this logic on the day I caught someone wandering around in the lions. The sign was eight foot by four foot, the entreaty to stay in your car red on white. The problem was the gentlemen was short-sighted and had to get out of his car to read it! The same sign would continue to present problems over the years. Twenty years on, the warning to keep your window closed in the lions was quite sophisticated, bilingual in fact. The English read well, as did the Punjabi, but the Hindu! What the translator had written was 'Keep your windows OPEN!' It took three years for anyone to spot it, though.

You soon learnt the warning signs. The Japanese always want to get out and pose by anything, so, if you see a camera, be on your guard. The screaming child was often a prelude to it being hung out of the car by the scruff of the neck amongst the lions, like a sacrificial lamb, to relieve itself in mid-air. There was also the case of the lady who threw her baby out of the train. Why? There wasn't a sign to say you couldn't! Others were less subtle, like the gentleman who raced into the park on a motorbike. He took some catching in a tractor. Again, to be fair, there wasn't a sign to say you couldn't, but honestly! From the ridiculous through to the sublime. One morning, we watched helplessly as a pedestrian visitor pushed a wheelchair through the rhino. On occasions like this you daren't move. You wince at every squeak of every tyre, at every plane that flies over, every time they pause or speak, but both parties appeared oblivious to the presence of the other. Only when a decent gap had opened up between the rhino and the wheelchair, could I quietly freewheel into position between the two of them and block the rhino's view of the interception and rescue. To do all this, I had a tractor, a single barrel shotgun, two blanks and occasionally a thunder flash of truly volcanic proportions. There were no two-way radios. The shifts were all day. There were no breaks.

I soon discovered that I worked for an American company, Hardwick Inc. of New York, who leased the property from the then mighty Chipperfield organisation. Jimmy Chipperfield (a confidant of Idi Amin) managed the park for the Americans and supplied the animals. So who, then, did I really work for? Like everyone else, I found the demarcation line vague and elusive. The Chipperfield Circus winter quarters was also on site with a further influx of staff - a motley collection of miscreants and animals who roamed the park at will adding to the interference and confusion of priorities. The Americans were purely businessmen and saw it purely as a business venture. They had no animal experience, knowledge or acumen and the Chipperfields ran circles around them. What Jimmy Chipperfield thought of it he kept to himself, though I can make a pretty good guess from his unprintable asides in off guard moments. My signed copy of his autobiography published in 1975 devotes barely two pages to Bewdley though, at the time of its writing, the arrangement was still supposed to be working. It explained a lot of things, not least the chaos. Managers and their assistants, wardens and their deputies came and went with bewildering frequency, each as inept, inexperienced and bemused as their predecessor by the conflicting loyalties and shifting priorities. Most left broken men. There were mutinies, desertions and, most tragically of all, suicides. Fearing my departure too at one point in the mayhem, the company secretary, a down-to-earth farmer's daughter, contacted the then manager, Richard Luck, who was at HQ in Miami at the time. He ploughed a relatively lonely furrow in the contemporary sanity stakes and was readily persuaded that herein lay a kindred spirit. "Hold firm," came back the message, "Things will improve." There was no time-scale attached.

Much of this was inevitable with such a fledgling organisation, but we were the latest in a line of parks (and the last to open in England), so there were precedents which might have been heeded. Most of the other safari parks had similar management arrangements, so many of the teething problems should have been foreseeable and therefore preventable. The fundamental difference was that arrangements elsewhere were with the Lords and Ladies of the manor i.e. the incumbents as at Longleat, Woburn and Knowsley near Liverpool. With us, the landlords were also the Chipperfields, with our decision-making forum effectively absent in the States. One thing, however, persisted for many a year. Though we were frequently berated with 'company policy', no one ever knew what it was.

It was, then, a bizarre and surreal world into which I was now thrust, the hours long, the pay poor and the pace of life so frantic that we seldom ventured off the place. Soon I was to become totally enveloped within it. We frequently remained open until after dark for some reason, then we began locking up. It was often gone nine, frequently 10.30p.m. before I arrived back in Birmingham, and I still had a cricket square to maintain. Many's the time I've slaved beneath the city's street lights, stripping down motorbike engines or clutches into the small hours in order to be back on the road for 7a.m. There was, though, relief of sorts at hand, a chance to reduce the day to manageable proportions. A derelict cottage on the estate, currently used for stabling circus horses, was there for the taking. I needed local accommodation and so too did 'H', another warden, who was getting married to the girl in Pets Corner, the start of a long tradition in such matters! It took endless wrangling but eventually we got our way and what a way it was! We mucked it out with pitch forks, then hosed it down. Once dried out, we repaired the windows and threw some paint at it. Whilst doing this, we uncovered a light switch. To our astonishment, the lights flickered on. You still needed the tilley lamp to read and you couldn't boil a kettle and watch TV at the same time. I slept in the box room, the marital suite wasn't for me. So, it was one last trip to Birmingham for all my worldly possessions, which fitted comfortably into the sidecar. It wasn't much but it was home.

At the insistence of our American cousins, we were constantly urged to spice the park up with live entertainment. Participation in 'It's a Knockout' was compulsory after work, then there were the steel bands, the sky divers plunging into the sea lion pool, volley ball, camel rides and all manner of stunt men. There were attempts to stay open in the evenings, the skateboard park, the parrot shows, hot air balloon meetings and RAC rallies through the park. Most of this went down like the Titanic. The British are far too laid back to get whipped up into a frenzy, American style, over such things. It did land me in some bizarre situations, though. One Boxing Day, a visiting stunt man used two of us in his 'Wall of Fire' routine. He'd just escaped the polite applause after being 'buried alive' in a bonfire of cardboard boxes from the gift shop, which Dave Chorley had soaked in petrol, when he waved us both over. He spread-eagled himself face down on the ground and instructed us to rope each wrist to our landrovers (the only two we had working that day) parked thirty feet apart. On his command, we were to drive at an unspecified speed parallel to each other with him suspended between us, ensuring we pulled him through the fire. We stared at him in disbelief. If either of us slowed, stalled or hit a pot-hole, at the very least we'd pull his arms off. As the slow handclap began, the 'agent' nodded - yes, he *was* serious. My team mate was Tilley, a Sri Lankan. His teeth flashed his usual cheery smile as his vehicle was bump-started. I attempted to match his lurching pace! So, we dragged our hero, kicking and screaming, across the bumpy ground through the frozen mole-hills, the goose droppings and the dog faeces and into the fire, before wrapping him around a tree as we attempted to cast him off! Fortunately, the next show was cancelled - we'd run out of cardboard boxes.

Entertainment 70's style. The elephants roam the amusement area while the band plays on.
No one looks very impressed! (Photo Author)

Sophie and Louise with author. (Photo P. Smith 1974)

The staff numbers in those heady days were high, partly because of the appallingly inept construction of the park. The lion 'houses' were simply railway freight boxes. There was no mains water in the reserves - all the drinking water had to be carried to the lions in dustbins in an open-topped tractor and trailer. There was no electricity bar one extension lead (buried in the ground!), no drains. Like traditional farming, it generated a system requiring huge numbers to service the basic necessities. There was little supervision and while the cats were away the mice would play - cricket! By early afternoon, with scarcely a car in sight, the lions invariably asleep during the heat of the day, the boredom drove us mad - literally. So, after a gap of three years, I once again picked up a cricket bat. Untroubled by the lions, the pitch, my back or the bowling, save for the occasional ball that reared off a length from hitting the odd bone splinter from the lions' meat, I rolled back the years, often carrying my bat throughout the afternoons until it was time to put the lions away. One soon adapted a style of play to suit the arena. You learnt to ignore the odd distant bear behind the bowler's arm and the avian muggers feeding off discarded carrion. If you skied the ball into a tree, it was likely to awake the lions slumbering beneath it. A salutary lesson in keeping the elbow up and therefore the ball down if ever there was one! The opening bowler had lost a yard or two of pace, but a few lions' teeth marks on the ball gave it extra bite and I could extract considerable turn! The man in the gate tower ('Jungle Jim') kept watch for the powers that be, and the score! At dusk, armed only with the bat and the stumps, the field panned out into a huge slip cordon. 'Long on' worked the lion house hatch and we walked the lions in for the night, on foot. Surely mad dogs and Englishmen had nothing on this.

The tower man's job proved inexplicably popular, so, one afternoon between innings, I resolved to check the score. The attraction for this spy in the sky soon became obvious. With the 'keep the windows closed' protocol strictly enforced (unless you were playing cricket!), car occupants became insufferably hot and descended into various stages of, or even total, undress. Indeed, 'making it' in lion country became a popular if not rather expensive pastime. A rocking vehicle would often attract the attention of a curious lion. Inevitably, they quickly discovered that simply biting through the tyre was sufficient to stop all the noise! The tower meantime offered a perfect bird's eye view of the proceedings! Anxious to avoid any embarrassment, we changed to a less lecherous operator, only to be inundated with insurance claims as car after car was hit by the moving gates he operated. It transpired that the replacement only had one eye! His replacement, in turn, proved only to have one leg which presented obvious difficulties in getting into the tower. So came back 'Jungle Jim', all forgiven. Nearly twenty five years later, however, I would repay Jungle Jim's vigilance and discretion. Some routine medication had been incorrectly prescribed and, having taken what should have been a normal dose, Jim collapsed like a sack of potatoes. He didn't even have time to reach his radio. Ultimately, it was the crescendo of car horns from the ever lengthening and frustrated traffic queues that alerted us to the problem. And what a dilemma. The one way system was blocked bumper to bumper in both lanes, the gates were all shut and the man who should have had his finger on the button was lying pole-axed in the middle of the complex, fifteen feet in the air and surrounded by twenty lions. We climbed the gate to release the clutch mechanism from the inside, forced the tower door and placed Jim in the recovery position while an ambulance did a cross-country dash through the rhinos, wildebeest and monkeys to reach the scene. Standing astride him, we worked the gates, unblocking the traffic to allow our exit, while the medics worked furiously as Jim's usually tanned, swarthy appearance turned ever more powdery and ominously white. The tower, maximum capacity five, groaned and swayed precariously under twice its designed load as we lowered the stretcher down past the lions. They stood in silence, curiously muted, as one of their mentors was borne away. He survived.

There were, of course, in the meantime, real perils involved in living on site. That autumn, the police received a tip-off that someone intended to break in and release the tigers, no doubt like latter-day mink. Our house was within sixty yards of the tigers so we slept with borrowed two-way radios on our pillows and loaded guns besides us in case we were needed, but the nights passed quietly enough except for the newly-weds! Then came a further threat, this time to shoot the lions one night. Incredible though it may seem twenty eight years on, we were told that, if shot at, we could return fire! Rumour had it, reliably it transpired, that we were only insured for £3,000 per head and, as we whiled away the small hours amongst the lions, there was much debate over this. Would it cover a shoot-out? Deciding discretion to be the better part of valour, we packed only rice cartridges. If there were to be any retribution, much better for it to be exacted by the lions themselves. Fortunately, it was never put to the test.

Christmas Day, 1973, my first at the park, was as bizarre as any contemporary event of those manic days. Enveloped in swirling freezing fog, my principal fellow keeper and companion at the time, Phil Smith, and I sat in the landrover in visibility of ten feet, looking and listening for sight or sound of our lions, which we hoped were out there somewhere. We fretted, ate our cheese sandwiches at lunchtime, listened to the queen and cursed our luck at drawing this of all the short straws. In those days, before we had two-way radios, the main form of communication was via Old Bill. A legend in his own drinking time (which was most of the time!), this rascally old drunkard did sterling work as the bus driver, boat captain and mechanic. As he nursed his fleet of geriatric brown and white spotted coaches around the park, he also became a postman, collecting and delivering written messages to and from the staff. While he was doing this, unwitting customers would be queuing to board one of the three reject lifeboats for a trip around the lake to be stoned by the errant chimps residing on the island. Frequently, he would arrive at the boat quay to find more than one full complement of passengers and would cast off with a boat in tow to save time. In his spare time he would repair the vehicles. Today, however, there had been a catastrophic system failure. Breaking the ice, Bill had cast off, first getting lost in the fog, then breaking down and becalmed. It wasn't, therefore, until 2p,m. that someone got a message to us saying that the park had closed. We stared incredulously. "You mean we've been open to the public?!" Fortunately, upon investigation, it transpired that the lions were as fed up as we were and, far from spending the remaining daylight hours seeking them out in this unremitting murk, they were already in their house. Recovering the by now stone cold sober Old Bill wasn't so easy. He'd been hollering himself hoarse for hours trying to attract attention, adding to an already infinitely forgettable Christmas for his hapless passengers sitting there being showered in ice by the sea lions. Someone tried to placate them by offering a free return visit, an offering drowned by the chattering teeth. This humble observer of lions slipped away under cover of the fog leaving the smooth talking to others. By late afternoon, I was home.

Industrial action on the railways that winter meant no Christmas post. No presents or cards, save one. Incredibly, the solitary card to seek me out came from one Pat Puxley, the student nurse allocated to my case in hospital. The nurse who had laughed and teased one Sunday afternoon as she shaved my bottom bare on admission. The nurse who'd stuck a spoon between my teeth as they'd prized the pelvic bones protruding through my flesh from the plaster. The nurse who'd ghosted through the fire doors by night to sit with me through the small hours and keep me sane. The nurse who'd helped pull me upright for the first time and whose knuckles I'd squeezed white as I'd dragged first one foot then another forwards. Seldom could such a colossus have hidden within such a slender frame. 'Good luck and good health' said the message from the mantelpiece as the Christmas Fayre for one man and his dog poured from a few tins. By 8p.m. we were both asleep before a roaring log fire. With demand peaking, there wasn't sufficient power to run the TV and it would be another ten years before the telephone reached this outpost.

Boxing day dawned clear, bright and raw cold as I bump-started the warden's landrover. As few in our hierarchy had the strength of their convictions that Christmas opening would yield rich dividends, I found myself the most senior person on site. After barely six months, I was in charge! The original intention was to remain open throughout the year but the 1973 Arab-Israeli conflict nipped this in the bud. The flow of visitors dropped to a trickle, eight cars a day, as petrol ration books were issued, even to those of us who had motorbikes and side-cars. Though not ultimately needed, the damage was done - the park would go into mothballs after the New Year holiday. The staff? I was one of just eight animal keepers retained when the park closed on January 6th, 1974.

On the 12th February 1974, petrol prices rose 50p a gallon. It was not auspicious but I had no need for petrol, even the two gallons a week my ration book would have allowed. We quickly settled into a carefree and idyllic lifestyle far removed from the idiosyncrasies amongst the higher echelons. It was still a struggle to physically keep body and soul together, at times hovering on a knife edge, but I was well looked after. 'H' and particularly his wife Lyn rose to the occasion magnificently at times although, on one occasion, they were reduced to literally carrying me into hospital for want of knowing what else to do with me. I insisted, however, that they waited - I was not stopping. On another occasion, another of the girls went into Bewdley and dragged a doctor back to the park to treat me. But, with the daily routine now more informal, at least we could all pace ourselves.

A local lad, Phil Smith, and I fed and cleaned out our fifty-odd lions and tigers, kept out of the way and were left alone. We rarely saw a soul. We spent hours a day sharing a camp fire up on the hillside with our pet loves, the bears. They'd join our circle, warm their paws, eat our sandwiches and drink from our flasks before dozing off with their chins across our feet. We fought and played with them, too. A particular pair of brown bears made an outstanding wrestling 'tag' team to while away the winter afternoons. Lions, too, made frequent playmates. One pair of lionesses, Sophie and Louise, accompanied us everywhere either on foot or in the back of the landrover however the mood took them, much to the consternation of the unwitting or the unknowing. One trainee driver quite correctly refused to leave his vehicle one morning until we'd cleared the coast, or so he thought. He finally jumped out, oblivious to Louise sleeping soundly on the cab roof. The slamming door awoke her and, in a display of rare petulance, she jumped down and bit him firmly in the backside. "Bitten by a lion," I told the nurse quietly in casualty, not wishing to attract attention. "Name? Address? Religion? Next of kin?" she asked methodically, without even looking up. Suddenly, the pen paused in mid-air and began to shake. She looked around in blind panic. "Bitten by a what! Where?" The wound was easily, if not delicately stitched, the ego and the nerves less so. He wasn't able to drive for a month. If we'd had the slightest first-hand inkling of the fearful savagery they were capable of, we'd have turned grey overnight. But we didn't, and the baptism of the innocents continued. We survived.

Others were less lucky and accidents began to happen when we reopened. The public seemed incapable of understanding the essential pre-requisite for safety. Keeping windows closed meant just that. Not half closed, nearly closed or almost closed but completely closed. A gap of a quarter of an inch was sufficient for a bear's claws to penetrate. Once a grip was gained, the window was removed with consummate ease along with anything else between it and the object of his attention. One day, as I drove a victim to hospital with her cheek bone glinting eerily in the sun from the remnants of her face, it belatedly occurred to me that if these slow, slumbering, sleepy giants could catch fish from running water they were more adept than us, quick and very dangerous indeed. If I saw one of my staff employing our antics of old today, they'd be out before they could say 'whitehunter'.

Sadly, the bears had other unforeseen party tricks in their inventory. Their sheer destructiveness in particular knew few bounds. Come hibernation time, they quickly discovered that the warmest place to burrow was beneath the tarmac road, through solid sandstone at that. They could burrow further through this in one night than a JCB could in a week! Usually the extent of the excavations only became apparent in the spring when the park reopened and vehicles began using the roads. The results were often as spectacular as they were calamitous, especially if the bear was still in the hole as the road swallowed you up! Other subterranean perils awaited the unwary in the underground pump house serving the bears pool which they often requisitioned as a dormitory. The more subtle would notice the absence of the residential frogs and nesting birds when the bears were in residence and fight shy of it. Fools rushed in to activate the pump switch. Invariably, in the darkness, they found themselves pressing a cold white nose instead! Another singularly novel way of keeping warm was the astonishing early improvisation of solar energy employed principally by the Himalayan bears. They invariably slept in the trees in 'nests' built from branches - and lined with the wing mirrors they'd gleaned from passing cars during the summer, over 250 of them in one instance! Perhaps, ultimately, they were even more subtle than we gave them credit for. Their antics made their situation untenable and they ended up spending the rest of their life and times in a park in sunny

The ill fated dolphin show. c.1976
(Photo Author)

The games we played! c.1974
(Photo Kidderminster Times)

My first lion cub. c.1975
My dog wasn't impressed!
(Photo S. Lawrence)

Spain. So, too, did 'Twinkle' the wildebeest bull. Anyone who has seen footage of the spectacular annual migration of the wildebeest across Africa might raise an eyebrow or two at the prospect of the species gracing Pets Corner! Nothing is more calculated to turn the male of any species into a despot than to hand rear it, which is exactly what Mary Chipperfield had done before dumping it on us. It was a familiar trick. Every new zoo got everyone else's misfits (not just animals either!). He was a godsend by night, totally eliminating the need for a nightwatchman for no one could go near the place, but by day his antics were a nightmare. One day, he got my future wife pinned between his horns in a corner. She froze, neither daring to move or speak (a rare feat!) for one and a half hours until someone chanced by and drove him off with a broom handle. Far from enhancing Pets Corner, he was soon incarcerated for everyone's peace of mind. His only exercise consisted of occasional walks, tied to a landrover! He simply had to go, along with his principal companion in crime, a hand reared camel bull. Again placed in a public area, his attempted and quite unmentionable manoeuvres on the unsuspecting public rapidly made him a social outcast.

Meanwhile, the latest manic scheme was the first attempt to theme the park. Quite simply, it meant thatching everything that didn't move, rather badly. To obtain the raw materials required, all the staff were dispatched daily to a reed bed beside a river somewhere in Warwickshire. Or rather, to a pub beside a reed bed beside a river somewhere in Warwickshire, from whence they very occasionally returned with some rather unsuitable bullrushes. Having slept off their hangover on them in the back of the pick-up all the way home, they were rarely suitable for their intended purpose. Phil and I refused to go - and got away with it. Amidst the anarchy we went our own way. Theoretically, at least, by day we conserved, by night we hunted. We shot rabbits in lion country, roosting pigeons from before the eyes of the startled baboons sleeping in the trees, and punted for duck on the sea lion lake. We learnt the lie of the land like the back of our hands in all conditions. It was to prove a priceless asset in pursuing escapees in the years ahead.

Spring drifted into summer as we confounded our critics and reopened, once again offering our visitors a safari park environment which, according to our guide book, offered 'a unique opportunity for conservation, breeding and scientific study'. But then it did only cost 20p! The book was a spartan offering, illustrating but ten of nearly fifty species on the inventory. This, however, was a dubious definition. A tank of fish in the ill-conceived underground aquarium was categorised as a species and there were fourteen of them! The remaining thirty five listed species included *the* guard dog on the monkey gate, *the* tortoise, *the* turkey, *the* cockatoo, *the* macaw, *the* guinea fowl, *the* llama, *the* guanaco and *the* pony! In order of numerical importance, the remaining species were baboons (95 when they were at home!), lions (39 or 40, no one was quite sure), crested cranes (39), mice (30), flamingos (22) and guinea pigs (20). The latter represented our first significant breeding success for, within two months, there were 30! When you further deducted the goats (7), chickens (6), cows, donkeys, sheep (3 of each) and the two chicks, the African experience wore even thinner. The grand total (including the fourteen fish tanks!) came to 447 animals. Nevertheless, as the guide book further assured the discerning visitor, this 'contributes towards the conservation of threatened species of African wildlife'! And you could see all this for just £1.50 per car. In order to change a tyre on one car, though, I had first to empty it - of 22 occupants! Even 'Mr Jim' (Chipperfield), as he was affectionately known in the business, was forced to admit publicly that the pricing structure was wrong.

The revenue on reopening was desperately needed by the parent company, whose global ambitions were haunting them in their own back yard. They were building what is now known as the Six Flags Safari Park (it was then the Great American Adventure) in New York State, the biggest safari park outside Africa. The costs were out of all control, spiralling by the week, and it bled us white. Every night upon closing, every penny we'd taken that day was transferred out of the country to be swallowed up in that vortex. The influx of visitors had little effect on our isolation for we had little direct contact with the public and little time to explore. I occasionally drifted back to Birmingham, from whence I'd come, to browse amongst the bookshops but missing the infamous pub bombs by a mere half hour muted my enthusiasm even for this and I seldom bothered again. Like early settlers, when someone

*The day we met or, the way we met! Sue rides past on 'Crink' the African elephant.
1974 (Photo Author)*

*'Mad dogs and Englishmen' we walk the lions (circled) in at night on foot! 1973
(Photo Author)*

arrived with an animal from another park, we besieged them to discover what was going on 'out there'. Little did we realise it, but we were making a few waves ourselves. The ostrich we hatched were, I'm reliably informed, the first successful hatching in the country. Hot on their heels the following year came a puma born to one of our pumas on loan to London Zoo, after artificial insemination.

One day in 1974, I paused to photograph a girl riding past on an elephant. I've still got the picture. I was soon to be introduced to her grandparents, the ultimate test of acceptability. It meant an eight mile bus journey in jacket, collar and my only tie through the beautiful countryside (virgin territory for me at the time but now our home) and a three mile walk to the farm to face the inquisition. I passed. In 1977 came the wedding pictures. Twenty five years on, over half of Sue's life has been spent with me and almost half of mine with her and we're still together. I cannot imagine a power on this earth that would dissuade me otherwise. Neither of us can manage without the other - and we can both still ride an elephant! Curiously, we now live on the neighbouring farm in sight of her family seat. From the onset, both sides of her family welcomed me, took me in and treated me as one of their own. Sue would continue to work at the park until our first child was imminent, alternating between this and her principal passion in life, her Welsh Cob Section C ponies. The link today is still there, but tenuous. She only helps out directly in emergencies and on bank holiday weekends, but indirectly, of course, I couldn't maintain my commitment without her support. In the meantime, Christopher is old enough to take up the cudgel and continue the dynasty. He's already begun his apprenticeship like his father before him, as a gateman. Nicola isn't far behind.

Another Christmas came and went, unnoticed by some. At the Christmas party on Christmas Eve, the gardener had fallen under Old Bill's influence. Rapidly becoming paralytic, we'd borne him off back to Bewdley and put him to bed. He awoke two days later having missed Christmas altogether! His assistant gardener, meanwhile, had swept down the hill out of the park and straight across the dual carriageway without stopping. If he was trying to create bedlam, the timing was impeccable. He escaped the ensuing pile-up lightly really with just a broken leg.

Unfortunately, when I visited him in hospital he didn't know which one, but he was a little confused. The police had just paid him a visit too and charged him (and subsequently convicted him) with dangerous driving. He'd been riding his push bike! Falling on hard times financially during his convalescence, he resorted to crime, stealing from people's gardens and the like. As you may have gathered by now, he wasn't over endowed up top. He was caught red-handed one morning cutting cabbages, in a policeman's garden!

Meanwhile, the mayhem at the park continued, the turnover at the top as rapid as ever. We had an English manager plucked from the middle of Africa, an Englishman from our German park, an Italian, a Spaniard, a Scotsman, a Sri Lankan and an Argentinian all operating under an umbrella of overseeing American vice presidents from the Miami office who themselves came and went with bewildering speed. All had their own ideas and all implemented them by cutting staff numbers! Our positions within the company varied almost monthly as did our means to perform them. Eventually, in 1974, along came an Englishman from Spain as manager, David Chorley, his Irish wife Olive and babe in arms, son Darren. As the attrition continued, soon there was no one else left and so he passed the warden's epaulettes to me. For better or worse, it gave the park what it needed above all else, stability and continuity, for we both stuck it out. The scale of the undertaking can be gauged by the fact that Dave and I could or had to run the park with basically no more than the help of a secretary in the office. Today, a meeting of the directors and the departmental managers will see over twenty people in the room with another layer of fledgling supervisors below that. I alone now have three deputies with five senior keepers supporting them. Given the volatility and instability of the world in which we moved, neither of us could conceivably have imagined in our wildest dreams that, twenty four years on, we'd be sitting in that same office one breakfast time sipping champagne, I celebrating 25 years' service and he his 60th birthday within a few weeks of each other. It was still far from plain sailing. From Bewdley we reported to the Italian who ran the German park, assisted by his three wives! And to think I had trouble remembering if I was a Man of Kent or a Kentish Man! There was always the occasional missive direct from America which required handling with the utmost diplomacy to avoid treading on the many toes, but it was order of sorts.

By 1975, we were all again effectively reduced to the ranks as an American vice president, a genuine and likeable enough chap, descended upon us to exert daily influence. By the autumn of 1976, he had returned home at the end of his tether. He'd given it everything and it hadn't worked. His biggest mistake was to save money by not making and running a TV advertising campaign. Such things cost a fortune, not making them costs even more as he found to his cost. He'd been desperately unlucky, too, particularly with the weather. Forever to be associated with an unprecedented drought, 1976, his last year, had in fact blown in tempestuously. A ferocious storm in the first week of January destroyed much in the park causing untold thousands of pounds of uninsured damage. The boats sank at their moorings, roofs and caravans simply disappeared and hundreds of yards of expensive chain-link fencing, much of it newly erected, went down. As Dave, Johnny the American and I toured the park in the darkness doing what little we could to contain the damage, scores of Capability Brown's two hundred year old trees fell about us like ninepins. If we'd been able to see them coming, we'd have been petrified. As we crested a hill the 95mph winds hit us head on, stalling my American Jeep dead in its tracks. An ill wind in fact, an omen of prophetic proportions. And so it proved.

Come spring, we experienced the park's first snowfall. Then the infamous drought set in presenting us with horrendous food bills for essentially the animals remained on full winter rations. Contrary to popular belief, such weather isn't conducive to good business. In a heat wave, it's noticeable how business begins to tail off after ten days or so as people, confident of the conditions, plan alternatives like venturing on long trips to the coast or stay in the garden for comfort, to sunbathe or to simply do nothing. People certainly don't wish to sit cooped up in a car for an hour or so in a safari park with people shouting at them to keep their windows closed, for in those days that was the regime. Business fell by half. There was an ill-fated attempt to introduce a sub-standard bird garden and the replacement of the infamous baboons with rhesus monkeys leased, it subsequently transpired, from a company which bred them for research. A giant-sized clanger if ever there was one. The only weekend when visitors were on a par with projections was ruined by a huge bush fire which resulted in the park's evacuation. Finally, everything hinged on some income from the last bank holiday of the year at the end of August, plugged for all it was worth by a hastily strung together TV commercial. Bang on cue, the drought broke. Torrential monsoon-like rain on the baked ground flooded everything, including the car parks. It was an unmitigated disaster. It summed up the year nicely, such is the effect of things on our lives over which we have no control. Dave and I could only sit and watch helplessly all summer as we rollercoasted into oblivion. At 1976 values, we'd lost £250,000 that fateful summer. In a sense, Johnny was lucky. Hurt though he was, he could walk away. Dave and I were stuck with it.

Johnny's successors were Canadians, which made a change. At least, though, they were animal-orientated coming from the company's park near Montreal, Quebec, possibly in belated recognition of the park's suppressed strengths. From the onset, many local people had been of the view that the animals were but a poor subterfuge for an amusement park. Logically, with the amusement area occupying barely three sparse acres of a 195 acre site, the criticism made little sense. The view probably gained more credence because the area occupied an inordinate amount of the hierarchy's attention, notwithstanding what all the customer surveys said. Why did they come to the park? What did they enjoy most? What would persuade them to return? The animals, of course. The response? Put another ride in! Amusement-style attractions are two a penny but, as I never tired of arguing, what was the one thing none of them had or was ever likely to have? A major animal collection. Used sensibly in tandem, the two themes would complement each other perfectly.

As animal men, there was instant rapport with the Canadians which was fortunate, for their final solution was the last chance saloon for all of us. The Chipperfield Organisation was brushed aside as we sought to control our own destiny. The idea was to dismantle the traditional safari park concept doing away, in

White rhino and elephant 'interact' in their new paddock 1977.
(Photo Author)

Sister-in-law Patsy on a winter feed round in 'Cheap 1'!
(Photo Author)

My wife Sue, with two of our Welsh Cobs.
(Photo K. Webb, Kidderminster Times)

Diet Pepsi! Sue bottle feeds a Pere David Deer Calf.
(Photo J. James, Birmingham Post and Mail)

particular, with the drive-through predator reserves. Instead, the carnivores would now be viewed within a fixed exhibit - still from the family car, still at very close range, albeit now through a fence. The elephants and rhino, too, were to retreat into compounds behind barriers to save the prohibitive cost of fortifying a mile long perimeter to contain them. This hybrid between the traditional zoo and safari layouts was deemed a 'game park' by the Canadians. The advantages were enormous. It was much safer, more informal and more comfortable as, the monkey area apart, there was no longer any need to keep windows closed in hot weather. Crucially, though, the need to employ a small army of gatemen and supervisory patrols disappeared overnight. The only problem was that there was no money to accomplish the master design. The new order had to be created making use of what we had. Accordingly, we spent the first half of the winter meticulously dismantling miles of fencing, carefully saving every post, every yard of chain-link, every bolt and nail. Then, at Christmas, we began putting it all back up again in a radical new departure from anything seen hitherto in British parks. The park was divided up into geographical areas, African, Eurasian and American, with the indigenous animals from each continent grazing freely around the exhibits containing lions, tigers and wolves respectively. Once I'd formulated the new layout and our Canadian mentors were sure I knew exactly what was required, they largely left us alone. I remained in the field, Dave watched over what passed as purse strings and twice weekly we reported back on the cumbersome great telex machine that occupied much of the office. It was do or die, we had to be ruthless. Anyone or anything unable or unwilling to adapt to the new order simply went.

And so we slaved around the clock seven days a week, throughout and including Christmas and New Year's day, snow, wind, darkness, hell and high water to achieve our survival; rebuilding the park as it's been seen by millions in the form it's in today but with the flexibility to constantly adapt and change with the times. The collection changed as dramatically as the park's appearance. We cut the lion population from a peak of one hundred and twenty down to fifteen on the basis that once you'd seen one pride you'd seen them all. As already mentioned, the bears went to reduce the annual burden of repairing the roads they habitually

Construction problems! Winter 76/77.
(Photo Author)

'....vastly expanded opportunities for interaction between animals and visitor were the new order....' (David Taylor, International Zoo Veterinary Group) (Photo Author)

dug up every winter to hibernate beneath. The bear fence provided enough raw material to build winter accommodation for all the African antelope, which remains to this day. And so it went on. In their place, the space they'd occupied was taken up by a huge influx of new species within the geographical groupings, many of them never seen before in an English safari park. It created enormous interest and a phenomenal work rate during the relocation. I took the opportunity, too, to get rid of other things on the premise that if we couldn't look after them properly we shouldn't keep them at all. Out went the chimps, the sea lions free-ranging about the lake, the penguins in their diminutive paddling pool, the pumas and leopards in their tiny cages in Pets Corner, amongst others. They were not compatible with the safari theme. On the broader front, out went the concessionaires to give us total control of the business operation. In came the then revolutionary 'all inclusive' pricing structure and the much frowned upon (by the purists) sale of animal food for the public to feed the animals.

At last all was ready. Folklore has it that March comes in like a lion and departs like a lamb. Nowhere is it more possible than here for, sometime during the month, tradition has it we reopen two weeks prior to Easter after the winter recess. There remained just one thing left to do. Having flogged the staff mercilessly all winter, all that now remained was to get rid of them. Therein lay the greatest saving of all. From a peak of forty eight staff, the master plan could operate with just eight. My tractor fleet was cut from six to one, my ailing landrovers from twelve to one. Some replacements were needed but, in the absence of funding, we simply built our own vehicles (nicknamed 'Cheaps'!) at an average cost of £200 per unit. Anxious to see the miracle with his own eyes, the company president flew in from America. Notwithstanding the financial stringency, he flew on Concorde. His entourage, including ominously (in American tradition) his lawyer, toured the park in silence. Then David Chorley and I were summoned to the office. "You gentlemen are a credit to the company," he began. The sighs of relief drowned the bullshit although somewhere amongst it I vaguely heard that I was to do very well out of it all. Eventually, some months later, my salary shot up by £10 per week, before tax.

Where two worlds collide?
The main animal complex (left) is
separated from the Amusement Area
(right) by the Hippo Lake (centre)
(Photo Author 1997).

In Anthony Smith's 'Animals On View', a guide to the wildlife collections of Britain first published in 1977, the author expressed satisfaction that the owners of the West Midland Safari and Leisure Park appeared to have decided that their destiny lay with the animals. In many ways an odd offering (its foreword justified the book on the grounds that so many new zoos had sprung up in recent years, then listed no less than 33 that had recently closed[!] including 7 dolphinariums), the safari park section listed nine parks, excluding those in Ireland and the odd attraction here and there like Stapleford Park in Leicestershire which had tried to cash in on the 'drive through' euphoria by opening an odd field or two of lions and monkeys. Now but six remain, including the Highland Wildlife Park which was in the original list but which scarcely compares. Jimmy Chipperfield deserved all credit for his innovative adoption of the safari park concept. It revolutionised both the keeping of and people's perception of how captive animals might be kept. But, as I told him to his face one memorable night on BBC's 'Man Alive' broadcast live from London, the idea was stagnating. We hadn't begun to realise the park's full potential. You could have heard a pin drop in the studio as I contradicted 'Mr Jim'. Certainly the make-up girls had some difficulty with his facial coloration! Afterwards he declined the post programme party, dismissing me as an 'anti' before sweeping away into the night in his white Rolls Royce. We were, though, by now thoroughly independent and I knew that such temerity wouldn't cost me my job the following morning.

At 1977 values, the park made a profit of £22,000, a triumph for the rebirth. The future was still by no means rosy but we'd turned it around and begun to build a solid future. That year, we became the first safari park to be allowed membership of the Zoological Federation of Great Britain and Ireland. The British Veterinary Zoological Society visited, too, as people began to take notice of the changes. The last chance wasn't wasted. That winter's work was to make everything else possible. Incredibly, though, it still wasn't enough for some. One evening after dinner, one of our Canadian cousins was to take me aside - was I prepared to take over from Dave? Many times over the years I've wondered if it were but a subtle test of loyalty but, once the incredulity subsided, the answer was only ever going to be a resounding 'NO'. Instead,

I opted to serve my mentor all my days. In 1984, the Americans' crazy bubble finally burst, the 'empire' evaporating into the Miami mist. We were the only profitable remnant and David Chorley snapped it up from the receivers into private ownership. Without him, there wouldn't be a West Midland Safari Park.

CHAPTER 3
Of Ships and Boats and Planes
(To the unsung heros - the keepers)

S tepping from the cargo hold was like walking into an oven. As we'd docked the previous night, the sky had been split asunder by the most ferocious thunder storm I'd ever seen. Thankful to have our feet firmly on deck, we'd watched spellbound as the planes overhead continued to land at the international airport as if oblivious to the meteorological mayhem. Overhead now, on a May morning back in 1975, the sun bore down relentlessly on the smouldering docks in Newark, New Jersey, USA as I stepped from the aft loading ramp of this Cunard container ship, lowered now after its transatlantic crossing with six giraffe. So this was America. The land colonised by those with mindboggling names (watch the credits at the end of a movie), who swear by the law suit, who live out of brown paper bags. The land whose material wealth is the envy of the world yet spawns a crime rate the like of which the herculean efforts of the then contemporary Kojak, Starsky and Hutch combined couldn't even dent. This, though, was the least of my worries for it was also the land that seemed unaware that we were coming! You could have imagined that we'd dropped from one of the previous night's aircraft for no one was expecting us. There was no welcoming party, no import licence, no crane to load the giraffe crates onto the non-existent trucks and, more ominously, no food left. To comply with quarantine regulations, we had to dump all unused foodstuffs at sea prior to entering harbour. This in itself made subsequent delays unacceptable. Just as were we beginning to realise that our travellers cheques were irredeemable, one of the

Opposite Page:
Top left: White rhino in Bewdley, 'Brutalis' in Ongava, Namibia and,
bottom, white rhino in the Namibian bush. (Photos Author)

curious multitude of officials now gathering about us noted that the crates were in excess of the state's bridge limit. We knew that with Watergate bursting on an unsuspecting public and with New York state, Mayor Koch and all, on the verge of bankruptcy, government administration was in disarray, but this was ridiculous. The trip had been 'planned' for over a year.

The previous spring, the giraffe had been isolated at Bewdley in a purpose-built quarantine for the then regulation sixty days. With MAFF (Ministry of Agriculture, Fisheries and Food) vets watching our every move, we'd taken blood samples every fifteen days and undertaken TB tests to the satisfaction of officials on both sides of the Atlantic. The giraffe were in their crates on board the lorries when news came of a dock strike at Liverpool, the port of embarkation. There was nothing for it but to offload everything and await developments. We waited in vain. Industrial peace didn't materialise until it was too late in the year for a reasonable chance of a smooth crossing. There was little choice but to return the animals to their winter quarters and try again next year. With fingers crossed, the whole tedious business was repeated the following spring. Again, the ministry vet waxed lyrical in the Veterinary Journal making a considerable name for himself in the process but, more importantly, sixty three days later with quarantine tests completed, a quick trip up the M6 saw us in Liverpool docks. With an ease which made nonsense of the previous difficulties, we were loaded aboard, swallowed up into the bowels of the modern container ship.

Life on the SS Atlantic Conveyor was both luxurious and formal in the finest Cunard tradition. Although only a container ship, we dressed for dinner, were waited on by uniformed stewards, took formal strolls on deck before afternoon tea and, still being single, Sue and I had to promise to keep to our individual cabins! Fitted with stabilisers, then a modern innovation, the ship could cope admirably with rough weather and cross the Atlantic in just eight days even allowing for brief calls in Greenock and Halifax, Nova Scotia before reaching New York. There was scarcely time to explore this great vessel given our work and the speed of our journey but the logistics of life were enormous - 3,500 sports cars on one deck alone. In view of the vessel's fate (sunk in the Falklands war), it was particularly poignant to note the many

Falkland Islanders among the crew and see the photographs they all proudly carried with them of home.

Quartered at the stern, three decks below the waterline, the giraffe travelled well. Not so my future wife. Notwithstanding the smooth voyage, she had no sea legs whatsoever and it was with great relief that she joined me on dry land. Having been so involved with the project from its inception, it was disappointing not to be allowed to accompany our charges on the final leg of their journey, but we were not allowed anywhere near the quarantine station. As officialdom finally awoke to our presence, our problems mounted. Someone or another the third, junior, solemnly announced that we constituted a threat to the quarantine integrity of *the* United States and demanded all my clothes and possessions. Wasn't it a trifle hot to stand out in the midday sun stark naked? And besides, the young lady? We weren't even married yet! The realisation that Sue had also been in contact with the giraffe instilled a touch of decency into the proceedings. I offered my oldest pair of trousers up as sacrifice. As long as the incinerator belched smoke, protocol would be seen to have been observed. Our ordeal over the giraffe continued theirs - another thirty days solitary was required before they could get on with the rest of their lives. When it was over, these giraffe had become the most expensive ever. The eighteen month operation had cost an astronomical £46,000 per animal. At today's values, however, we'd pay no more than £12,000 per head! The ultimate destination was the Great American Adventure Safari Park, now known as Six Flags, which our parent company was instrumental in building. At the time, it was alleged to be the biggest game reserve outside Africa but then it would be, wouldn't it! The park was big, neat and impressive and staffed by many ex-pats whom we hadn't seen since their Bewdley days. The animal facilities, built in the heady pre-inflationary 'money no object' days, were probably twenty years ahead of anything other than the top veterinary university hospitals here. The attention to detail was a trifle mindboggling back in 1975. If the grass appeared in danger of burning up in the hot sun then someone somewhere pressed a button and every square yard was soaked by invisible sprinklers. Fast food was common then, too. One pre-frozen, pre-packed, pre-wrapped block of processed meat per carnivore was delivered daily.

The Americans appeared acutely conscious of their lack of credibility in the eyes of the world with the enveloping Watergate scandal and went out of their way to make us welcome. Strangely, though, my most memorable first impression of America came on leaving it in time to return for the inevitable bank holiday weekend. The flight left at dusk, climbed steeply and banked over New York revealing a sight which quite took my breath away. At night New York is ablaze. Lights of every conceivable shape, colour and size, both stationary and mobile, pierced the darkness below as far as the eye could see. It seemed odd to me, in retrospect, that such an artificially created spectacle could make such an impact on someone who had spent his life in the countryside witnessing natural wonders, but it did. The lights twinkled and flashed, beckoning after the aircraft, it seemed, as if to lure us back. They soon did.

Outward bound the following year, our Laker Skytrain en route to Montreal via New York had encountered violent head winds and simply threatened to run out of fuel! Twenty five years later at 8,000ft. over the Namibian desert, I recalled this as I watched the red light on the instrument panel of our little six-seater which the pilot was endeavouring to cover with his left knee. When it began flashing, I could see that it wasn't the seat belt light but the fuel warning and remembered Olive Chorley's experience on a similar flight some years earlier. Taking off, she'd noted the lack of visibility due to the rain before realising that rain doesn't smell like aviation fuel. Having topped up the fuel, someone had forgotten to replace the cap on the tank and it was streaming down the fuselage! Our red light, though, proved a genuine instrument error. Not so our Skytrain. The flight had begun with the steward still demonstrating the safety drills when the plane had stood on its tail and reared near vertically into the heavens. As the steward flew near horizontally past my shoulder, I wished him well with his emergency drill - he would need it when he hit the rear bulkhead! We put down to replenish at a military airfield outside Montreal just miles from our destination, the company's park at Hemmingford, Quebec, but we weren't allowed off. Everything was customs bonded. We did get there eventually via New York and Montreal again twenty four hours later. Canada in the 'fall' is not to be sneezed at and we toured at will after our business at the park, not least to get away from our otherwise idyllic log cabin whose fridge was stocked entirely with yak meat! Reluctantly leaving on the first leg of the journey home, the short haul to New York, I'd noticed an unhealthy noise in the engine atop the fuselage above our seat. The steward noticed it, too, and called the cabin crew. We'd just been served coffee and told we'd be over New York in forty minutes when a loud bang over my head punctuated the announcement. The plane nose-dived, the seatbelt light flashed brightly and suddenly we were due to land in ten minutes. There was to be no waiting for a landing slot at this, one of the world's busiest airports. There was mayhem below as aircraft of all colours, shapes and sizes veered off the runway we were plummeting towards and onto the grass. This time, though, the flashing lights were all blue ones, lots of them, all down the runway which was turning white. I didn't open my eyes until we were in the terminal building. Some wise crack said we'd nearly gone straight through it. Sue didn't notice a thing!

Despite the traumas, these trips were invaluable dry runs for some testing times ahead. Part of our then parent group's global strategy was to build a park in Japan. The grand design already extended to parks in Canada, America, Spain, Germany and, of course, us in England. As the Japanese park neared completion, an enormous world-wide operation was launched to stock it. We were tasked with the co-ordination of all the movements through Europe, an operation costing hundreds of thousands of pounds. The logistics were enormous. The 12,000 mile, five week sea journey across some of the world's most inhospitable oceans had to be self-contained. Every conceivable item from food, bedding and veterinary equipment to spare nuts and bolts for crate repairs had to be anticipated because Japanese quarantine rules were prohibitive. Once a ship had sailed, the animals were effectively in isolation. There could be no stops anywhere en route. It was not unknown for this rule to be breached and the recipient country to refuse the shipment as a consequence. The hapless animals then become refugees being shuttled from port to port, often from country to country, in an attempt to find someone to accept them.

At Bewdley we quarantined ten more giraffe, ten camels and ten wildebeest, having constructed further new quarantine facilities and crates from scratch. All this, of course, in addition to the everyday life of the park. This included shipping an elephant out, three days' TV filming, hand rearing at home the first wolf cubs to be born in an English safari park (and the subsequent photographing of them with the Wolves football team!) and demonstrating the use of a dart gun to a group of researchers going out to Africa. Finally, after three months of planning, building, ordering supplies and consulting complex shipping schedules, the animals were loaded aboard their travelling crates before a posse of newsmen. Everything down to the last broom handle had been stowed away in a convoy of six articulated lorries for departure at first light when disaster struck. The skies opened and a storm of tropical intensity burst upon us. We struggled like men possessed to rope down the protective canvas. The gale sucked the breath from our lungs rendering speech impossible while the hail stung our flesh raw. It was an unequal struggle. When it finally stopped, two inches of rain had fallen in two hours, the canopies were in tatters, the crates awash, the animals wretched, not to mention the mess the park itself was in. We parked on a slope to drain out while we toiled through the night replacing bedding and rigging fresh canvas. Dawn broke brightly so we delayed departure to enable the sun to dry us out. Finally, at lunchtime, the convoy eased its way out of the park. Dave Chorley, Phil Smith, Billy Collins and I followed by car. En route, we wrote the car off in an accident somewhere along what is now the M40 but, driving on regardless, we caught up and arrived in Tilbury together, on time.

Overseas travel on such business gives the somewhat erroneous impression of a swashbuckling, free-wheeling, jet set lifestyle that simply doesn't exist. Every international airport and container port the world over looks much the same and Tilbury at 5a.m. on a Sunday morning was no exception - cold, deserted and inhospitable. By 10a.m., however, our charges were on the 'feeder service', a sleepy little coaster, for passage across the North Sea to Rotterdam. So small was it, in fact, that there was barely room for Phil and Billy who were to accompany the animals on this first leg of the journey. Dave and I then flew from Heathrow to rendezvous with our consignment as it docked alongside its parent ship, the SS Osaka Bay (then the world's biggest container ship) for the voyage to its home port, Osaka Bay, Japan. We transferred the animals over, the animals immediately behind the

*Sue with month old
wolf cubs.
(Photo J. James,
Birmingham Post
and Mail)*

bridge superstructure with the food crates to each side for protection. We then raised the telescopic uprights on the giraffe crates to the full 15ft. (12ft. is the maximum whilst travelling by road) to give the giraffe headroom and ventilation. Again, the logistics and perspectives were immense. It was hard to countenance as we sprawled across the containers lashing everything down that the flies crawling about below us on the quayside weren't even people but vehicles! The meticulous personal attention to detail was essential. If much of the arrangements are considered common sense, it is amazing how often they turn into common mistakes. We flew back to Heathrow, the plane banking over 'our' ship as it left its berth, to find two suspicious policeman standing over our battered car, convinced it had been involved in a bank robbery. Having resolved this, it simply remained to drive the 140 miles home and tumble into bed. We'd been away for seventy two hours, had one meal and four hours' sleep. So much for jet-setting.

Once recovered, there were seven baboons and two pumas to go to our German park at Hodenhagen and a busman's day out to Woburn to collect four bison for Bewdley, neatly sandwiched between the birth of two giraffe. All done hurriedly, for overland from Spain were coming twelve rhino and five elephants. The same intrepid foursome met them rolling off a cross channel ferry at Poole, Dorset. The attendant, one who had been everywhere and seen it all, had none nothing. Cleaning out was evidently an alien concept. Unable by now to move, the rhino were jammed in their own filth like sardines in a can. In vain, we hacked at this compacted mess, even turning pressure hoses on it to flush the crates out - to no effect. Clearly they could go nowhere like this but they couldn't stand still either. They were due aboard a ship in Southampton by 9a.m. the next morning, an ocean-going container ship that would sail regardless. Once locked into the shipping and bureaucratic schedules, there is no going back - nor can they stand still in their 'adopted' country even if there is somewhere to put them. The journey along the coast took an eternity. The elephants kept undoing the viewing ports in their crates. The view from the cab wing mirrors was full of elephant trunks. In fact, the truck resembled a giant octopus. Notwithstanding a police escort, motorists persisted in flagging us down. Did we know we had elephants in the back?!

So it was much later, in the dead of night on a secluded wharf in Southampton, that we rendezvoused with a truck which had hurtled southwards through the night under police escort with an empty rhino crate. With the aid of a crane 'borrowed' from the port authority (and their fire engine!), we engaged in a potentially deadly game of rhino tag in the darkness. The empty crate was placed end to end with one containing a rhino as we endeavoured to effect a transfer. The one ton crates leapt and buckled in the darkness as the irate rhino tossed them about like confetti. Taken unawares, David Chorley was flung far enough to crack ribs as he stood atop them operating the doors. Twice, splintering crates sent people scattering as a breakout threatened. Twice, though, I pitted my American jeep against the rhino snorting through a hole in the crate, choking back the fumes of spinning tyres and a molten clutch, for I knew that, otherwise, Southampton beckoned. In four wheel drive, low box at full revs, I could just about hold my ground on a surface made treacherous by torrential rain. Once the transfer was complete, we flushed out the empty crate and used that to start again. Slowly but surely, in the darkness and continuing rain, we worked our way through them until finally the night was won.

We fell into our hotel like zombies at 3a.m., soaked, exhausted and stinking to high heaven. Our rooms had long since been re-let, all that remained was a top floor luxury wedding suite. We took it, albeit merely to use as a snack bar for we had to be on the quayside for loading by 5.30a.m. We gorged ourselves on aged £5 sandwiches and black coffee to keep awake. Fortunately, we had to check out before the staff checked in - rhino manure sits uneasily in five star opulence. The doorman stiffened at the outpouring stench as we left the lift but by the time he'd regained his composure it was too late, we'd gone. Having burnt so much midnight oil, our frustration can be imagined when the dockers kept us waiting till 3p.m. before loading. Then came the long, anxious haul home through the night with an ailing clutch.

Germany came next as we travelled to Hanover, Hodenhagen and Hamburg on successive days to supervise the loading of six bears, ten tigers and twenty lions into their crates and onto their container ship in the now customary pouring rain. At the press conference we had to endure raw fish, stale bread rolls, warm flat

OF SHIPS AND BOATS AND PLANES

lager and the jolly little German reporters. No one, it appeared, had anticipated the language barrier so the entire proceedings seemed an exercise in futility and a burdensome delay. We had to get home - there was a bank holiday pending and there was a problem. The German crates were too small. Some of the lions were left with their tails hanging from the rear of the crate, their fore paws from the front. Clearly, again, they couldn't travel 12,000 miles over five weeks like that. We flew back, having first telexed our carpenters. At home, we had already fashioned eighteen crates for our surplus lions at Bewdley. They would have to make more, quickly. As thousands of cars passed through the park that bank holiday Monday, we crated our lions, stocked a refrigerated container full of meat and assembled the convoy. After work, we headed south under cover of darkness to meet the ship from Hamburg as it docked at Southampton. Once aboard I got to work, the decks having been cleared with some alacrity. With an anxious captain pacing the bridge, his gaze alternating between the tide, his watch and the activity on the deck, we sedated half a dozen lions, stretchered them from port to starboard and placed them in their new crates. There was even time to remove an ingrowing claw on one of them - just. The throbbing beneath the deck, though, was growing more ominous by the minute. The captain had no choice - the tide was turning and ocean-going container ships await no man or animal. The tugs were impatient he had to go. And so did we - the next dry land was Panama and neither Dave nor I had so much as a toothbrush! We grabbed the equipment, said our hurried farewells to Phil and Billy (who this time were staying aboard for the duration) and scrambled over the side to make our landfall via the pilot's cutter. A cable from the ship the following day confirmed that all the lions were awake and none the worse for this unnecessary experience.

Again, prodigious planning meant this shipment too (making a total of over one hundred animals) arrived safely. There was, though, an unseemly wrangle over an additional freight charge for two lion cubs born as the ship navigated the Panama Canal! They too survived. Still, though, there remained a complication. Unusually, when loading the lions in Hamburg, we'd discovered the captain had no weapon on board. It didn't appear prudent to sail without something to hand so we 'found' two shotguns at our

Giraffe in transit at a service area on the M5 whilst the elephant (inset) is bound for Japan. c.1975 (Photos Author)

Crated giraffe on the quayside in Newark, New Jersey, U.S.A. 1975. (Photo Author)

Lions in their undersized crates, Hamburg 1975. (Photo Author)

German park, broke them down and took them aboard in a suitcase. Months later, we had a frantic 'phone call from Germany. The police had been in for a firearms check. If they couldn't account for the guns, someone was going to jail! We quickly purchased two locally which Dave and I rushed to Heathrow, pausing only to assemble two innocuous brown paper parcels. "Contents?" murmured the clerk at dispatch without looking up. "Guns," we said. He laughed like a drain - and put them on the conveyor belt!

How many miles we travelled that summer and how many cock-ups we resolved I'll never know, but we've had our own, too, over the years. The first call I received one Monday morning in July was from the Chipperfield Organisation's Roger Cawley. "We're picking the rhino up tomorrow, Bob. What's the earliest the lorry can be with you? Bob? You still there, Bob?" I didn't have a clue what he was talking about. He went on to say that two of our three rhino who'd been at the park since its inception, for whom we'd cared for twenty five years, had been sold and were leaving less than twenty four hours hence. What were the arrangements? What were the facilities at Blair Drummond Safari Park, Scotland, their new home? Roger took it for granted that I'd checked them first hand and personally overseen everything, but I knew nothing. We decided that he'd make his enquiries while I made mine. The lorry would not be coming to us the next day. Overnight, I drove to Scotland anonymously to see for myself. My staff, reduced to a state of near anarchy, expected nothing less of me. They never broke ranks. No one breathed a word.

Under the Zoo Licensing Act, any collection absorbing a new species needs the approval of their local authority, whose environmental health officers (or equivalent) police the system on behalf of the DETR (Department of the Environment, Transport and the Regions). They will determine whether the acquisition can proceed after considering the facilities and the arrangements for the animals' care. A vet had considered himself satisfied with the accommodation arrangements provided that winter quarters were ready well before the end of the summer. Accordingly, the local authority's 'Food Safety Team Leader' was minded to agree to the move! It was even rumoured that she'd never been to the park, much less seen a rhino. But what was the vet looking at? There was nothing there and it was already the end of July. The plan was to simply dump them out there in the open, one at a time. How would the first arrival react to this strange new place whilst awaiting forty eight hours for its companion? There was nowhere secure enough to contain a rhino if it became agitated. How would she respond to the wrench of separation from her female companion from whom she'd scarcely strayed five yards in twenty five years? Throughout that time, they'd lived in insulated, heated buildings with extractor fans for humidity control. Now, in the autumn of their lives, they were to find themselves outdoors in a harsh, strange, new environment. Roger discovered that they had been sold as a compatible pair that would share any future shelter that was eventually built. They weren't and never had been - they'd always had separate quarters at night. More transparently, they'd been sold as twenty year olds. The international stud book, readily available to all, showed them to be nearer thirty. As absurdity heaped upon absurdity, we reminded ourselves that twice in the previous six months rhinos had escaped during or post transit situations in Dublin Zoo and South Lakes Wildlife Park, Cumbria, and had to be shot. The industry couldn't afford another disaster and we weren't going to be a party to it. Much maligned in other matters, Roger Cawley knew his responsibilities here and that was that. Doubtless our role would come out one day, but there are times in life when you have to stand up for what you believe in and what is right - and this was one of them. After twenty five years we owed it to those animals, all of us.

But there was worse to come. After 'confessing' to the move, the person responsible had another revelation to make as he left for two weeks' holiday abroad. The two rhino we'd purchased in Africa a month earlier were leaving Durban for the UK - the next day! There was no health certificate, no import licence, they weren't insured and they were heading for Felixstowe, an unauthorised port of entry. In fact, as I burned the midnight oil trying to untangle my rhino puzzles I discovered there wasn't an authorised port of entry into the UK at that time at all! Every entreaty brought the same response - the rhino must be on that boat at all costs. But what cost? Whose sense of values were being tested? The shipping line's agent at Felixstowe paled when the costs were spelt out to him in single syllable, crystal clear Anglo Saxon rhetoric. If they materialised, they would be returned at the shipping line's expense on the same boat, or incinerated. Did they have a press officer? Suddenly the Durban end began to talk sense.

Meanwhile, I'd sent an emissary to the home of the chairman of the Tilbury Port Authority, who was on holiday, with a personal message. Could he allow them through? I mentioned that they were an endangered species and part of an internationally recognised potential breeding programme, but didn't dwell on it - he may not have been impressed. However he agreed. So, I kept the 'phone lines hot all week untangling a month's paperwork. Finally, at 4p.m. on the Friday night, MAFF (Ministry of Agriculture Fisheries and Food) agreed they would allow them in. They could sail on Monday's boat. I spent the weekend dotting the 'i's and crossing the 't's but on Monday the lines went strangely quiet. "Did the rhino get away?" I enquired of my South African connection. "What rhino?" My heart sank. "Ah, those rhino." One had developed an injury, never expanded upon. It was not fit to leave the boma, much less travel, I was told. Within two hours, it had deteriorated so badly that it had to be released back into the Umfolozi game reserve, Natal. An entire week had been taken out of my life for nothing. It had been a complete waste of time. Such is the effect of the unthinking on the unknowing.

Our old rhinos did eventually retire to Scotland in November, all three of them this time, together. A proper house had been built. I sent their keeper with them for a week to make sure. The lorry arrived one Saturday and was reversed up to the house. It was bonfire night so we sat with them until 1a.m. when all finally fell quiet. With sedation looming, undue disturbance was best avoided. At 8.30 on Sunday morning I quietly darted 'Alice'. We walked her calmly up the aisle into the trailer and she was gone. Within forty eight hours it was back for 'Maggie'. As we walked her in, the tractor reversing behind to block the way back, the steering arm snapped, bringing it to a halt. With some alacrity, it was removed, welded and reassembled but by now Maggie was reviving and began tossing the trailer high into the air, complete with myself and an intrepid reporter from Radio Hereford and

Worcester who was covering the parting of the ways - live! Incredibly, he kept his cool and continued commentating. What price that tape! By the end of the week, 'Dick' too, the last of the park's original incumbents, had gone - which just left me! Who said they were just animals and had no feelings? Someone in the office of course. Of course they have feelings, so too do their custodians. It was a poignant moment.

That same month, two replacement white rhino found their way onto a boat in Durban bound for Tilbury amidst the chaos we'd come to expect from South African administration. How they came to be there without papers, in total contravention of international law, one can only speculate but after a turbulent journey in torrid weather they made it, just. In Hamburg, the German authorities sought to impound the paperless pair. Quite what they intended doing with them is obscure but I got that sorted out too and they arrived safely. Two years earlier, six other rhino had trodden the same route. Three of them we sent to Knowsley Safari Park near Liverpool, the remainder stayed at Bewdley. When I was at school, the world's rhino population could be counted in substantial six figures. There were 65,000 black rhino alone just twenty five years ago. In fact, that twenty five years has seen 98% of the world's rhino disappear. Ironically, they've disappeared even faster than their habitat has. Today, the total world population of all rhino, black, white and all the various sub-species, (both in the wild and in captivity) is barely 12,000 and half of these are whites. Although this current figure is relatively stable (though some like the northern white rhino are down to 40), there is only one place on earth where rhino truly flourish.

Even in the vast 96,500 hectare expanse of the Natal Parks Board Hluhluwe and Umfolozi game reserves, however, there is a limit to the sustainable numbers and there is an annual auction to sell off the surplus. The money goes back to the park board who, at that time, were encouraging the removal of their surplus more vigorously than ever. They feared that political unrest during the transition to the new black government could have disastrous consequences on their inventory, with a breakdown in law and order encouraging poaching. This, ironically, during the park's centenary year. Established in 1895, these reserves represent

Africa's longest-standing protected areas and were the last bastion of the southern white rhino. Barely fifty remained on earth, all within the newly proclaimed boundary of a reserve which would have a decisive impact on the future of the continent's rhino. By 1960, there were 6,000 and the famous 'Operation Rhino' was launched to safeguard the species by dispersing the progeny around Africa. The rest, as they say, is history. Over 4,000 have been relocated to date, leaving a hard-core nucleus in the parks of up to 2,000 white and 500 black rhino.

It was to here, therefore, that we had turned for our new rhino. Like our own original specimens, over 60% of Europe's captive white rhino population had been imported in the early 70's and, it was estimated, would die out naturally within ten years. Although great strides were being made in rhino management, fresh blood was urgently needed. Despite this, I ran headlong into an avalanche of paper and bureaucracy. With white rhino still a CITES Appendix I species (Convention on International Trade in Endangered Species of Wild Fauna and Flora), I'd anticipated the application to be closely scrutinised. There was a precedent of sorts for our actions as we'd already purchased six whites for our company's private Namibian game reserve which were already breeding, but there was little inkling of the stormy waters ahead.

The application was rejected and there was no formal right of appeal. The government's scientific advisors, the JNCC (Joint Nature Conservation Committee), couldn't see any benefits accruing to the species as a whole as a result of our breeding programme. Curiously, the application floundered principally in the murky waters of Article 111.3 of the Convention, which forbids Annex 1 animals being used commercially i.e. people paying to see them! I found this ruling curious, not least because of the manifestly absurd contradictions implied in it. Without commercialism in this context, no zoo in the world could exist and 10% of the world's rhino exist in captivity. Even we, as the country's biggest safari park, receive no subsidies or grants and are totally dependent on gate receipts. Curiously, too, the rhino in question were being seen daily in their Natal game reserve - by paying visitors! In any event, I failed entirely to see what commercial aspects of the proposed import were more predominant than the survival of the species itself. There had been considerable disquiet at the previous year's auction when specimens were purchased by trophy hunters and shot. The DETR appeared intent on denying us the opportunity of attending those same auctions to bring rhino into an internationally recognised breeding programme. If this criteria had been applied to Pere David deer, Przewalski's horses or the Hawiian geese which we had just bred for the first time, these species would all now be extinct. As it was, at that time we were being told that ten African countries - Angola, Cameroon, Mozambique, Tanzania, Zambia, C.A.R., Ethiopia, Malawi, Somalia and Uganda (plus, it was feared, Rwanda given the turmoil there then) - could no longer boast a single white rhino between them. The latter five didn't have a solitary black rhino left either. All this, of course, caused by poaching, itself a highly commercial activity! It also appeared at the time that John Aspinall's organisation had papers for the import of wild caught rhino. Why the distinction, I railed. Quite what category London Zoo's panda had fallen into, if it wasn't commercial, I couldn't imagine either, I added. Oddly, again, at the time there was supposed to be an agreement whereby the JNCC would liase with the UK Rhino TAG (Taxon Advisory Group) via the Zoo Federation and hence the European TAG (to which all our rhino are assigned) on such matters. It was particularly unfortunate that this wasn't happening on this occasion as the information held here was considerably more up to date than that held by the government's own advisors. Somewhere amongst all this, I was asked to differentiate between the educational and conservation benefits likely to accrue from any breeding. The more I considered it, the less I felt unable to do so in a captive context. Elementary mathematics led me to conclude at the time that with children paying £1.00 per head entry for an average five hour stay, studying over 1,000 animals, that's about 0.1p per animal. That hardly smacks of the dreaded commercialism! After all, as Walt Disney (ironically one of the biggest commercial moguls ever) once said, 'Our greatest asset is the hearts and minds of our children'. It drew no response.

I threw all this at the DETR unremittingly, with supporting documents and the vigorous support of Nick Lindsay, Curator at

Whipsnade, who chaired the UK Rhino TAG. Seven months on, the JNCC were sufficiently sick of me to concede that the import would be likely to benefit the species after all! But, in their view, not sufficiently to overturn the commercial objections. I took the argument to the CITES Secretariat in Geneva. Like the DETR, we too treat each case on its merits. The previous year, we'd become aware of an errant, captive bred, hand reared white rhino bull that was proving impossible to manage, probably because of behavioural problems attributed to the hand rearing. Every other avenue having been exhausted, euthanasia was staring him in the face so we offered him rehabilitation in Ongava, our Namibian reserve. The offer was accepted, the £20,000 transfer put in hand and completed with minimal difficulties. He made the best of his last chance and survives to this day. With regard to his paperwork, no one had mentioned commercialism. I then began preparing to get our MP to table a question in the Commons. While they were chewing this one over, we had a piece of luck. At the 9th Conference of the CITES parties taking place in Fort Lauderdale, USA, the South Africans proposed that their population of white rhino be downlisted to Appendix 2. It was accepted. Ironically, because of the very success of the Natal Parks Board outstanding contribution to saving the white rhino, commercialism was now acceptable. We had to re-apply, of course, and the entire matter had to be refered to the JNCC, just in case they didn't know anything about it. But suddenly it was 'game on', just as quickly as EC Regulation 3626/82 Annex C Part 2 could be amended! The South African export CITES was granted in forty eight hours.

It was the biggest importation of rhino into the UK for twenty years. It had taken me eighteen months to prepare, cost me my life's ambition to go out to see the rhino caught, cost the park £200,000 (including the new rhino house I'd built) and was followed by half a dozen camera crews, including one from The Cousteau Society. Journey's end, though, can bring fresh drama. After one 6,000 mile journey from Africa by land, sea and air, four elephants arrived at 10.30p.m. one Sunday night. As I opened the door of the crate to check them, it fell off in my hands! West Mercia Police, meanwhile, had received criminal intelligence from Interpol of the activities of a gang of rhino rustlers. It seemed that even here they were not safe. Had the animals jumped out of the frying pan into another fire 6,000 miles from home? The plan, a novel one, was to target captive rhino. To add spice to the plot, a rhino head and elephant tusks had just been stolen from the walls of Hodnett Hall, a stately home in nearby Shropshire. The police took it seriously and advised us of our high profile group accordingly. Absurd though it may appear, it didn't seem entirely implausible, albeit perhaps on a par with specialised activities like art theft. With my knowledge, I could accomplish it with some ease and, with rhino horn literally worth its weight in gold, the possibility couldn't be dismissed entirely out of hand. So, intruder alarms were installed about the rhino house and the keepers slept there with their animals. For a while, too, the local bobby's evening beat took him straight through the rhino house - something, no doubt, that cadet training ill prepared him for! Meanwhile, the Natal Parks Board attendant who'd accompanied the rhino had only one thing on his mind. He wanted to go to Worcester! Once there, I quickly found for him the very street and photographed the very house which his parents had emigrated from before he was born. So, his duty duly done, one Jeff Cooke and I shook hands and he departed for home.

Eight months later, these rhino continued to make news. They were still excreting huge, live bot fly larvae! They attracted considerable interest at The Natural History Museum who were studying the effects on such things in the areas where their host animal had disappeared. Inevitably, perhaps, even then their story didn't quite end there. The paperwork turned into a paper chase. Even moving something as innocuous as a deer within this country legally involves extensive paperwork. First there's the drug book as required under the Animal Meat and Meat Products Regulation Act 1991, with a separate entry into a dangerous drugs book under the Misuse of Drugs Act 1971 for the sedative. Then there's the animal movement book as required under the Animal Health Act 1981 and an entry in our own company inventory. Next comes the Animal Transport Certificate as required under the Welfare of Animals during Transport Order 1994. Unknown to but a few, there's then an obscure record for English Nature under the conditions of my licence to move deer under the Deer Act 1991. You then need to ensure you have a Certificate of Competence as required under the Welfare of Animals (Transport) Order 1997. Then, if your wrist isn't aching too much,

A Bewdley Bobby pounds his rhino beat during the poaching scare 1995.
(Photo J. James, Birmingham Post and Mail)

you can drive off. International movements generate even more paperwork (including some of the above on arrival), the object of which is often obscure as it's checked less and less frequently by fewer and fewer officials. Heaven help you, of course, if you are stopped and aren't in order - as the rhino discovered in Hamburg. However, one questions the point of it all when, two years after the arrival of the first trio, the DETR ring up to enquire why the rhino had never arrived! There'd been a change of government and civil servants from the department were briefing the new minister on the intricacies of the monster he'd inherited. The CITES documents, the very essence of international trade in animals, the subject of eighteen months' hassle to attain them, hadn't been checked, stamped or endorsed on entering the European Community. So, on paper at least, after all that, the animals had simply 'disappeared'. Thus was fresh life breathed into the rhino stalls.

Released at last. After a 6,000 mile journey a rhino is released into his new home in Bewdley. (Photo Worcester Evening News)

CHAPTER 4
Creatures of the Night
(To our friends in blue who take the calls)

With a wildlife park locally, any bump in the night, be it a neighbour returning home from the pub rather the worse for wear or his cat in the dustbin, it is automatically attributed to 'something from that safari'.

The 'phone rings. Without waiting to check either the number or to whom she is speaking, a lady launches into an excited incoherent tale of some bizarre bionic freak terrorising the sparrows on her rooftop. Eventually, she has to draw breath and I get the opportunity to enquire politely for details of size, colour etc. Slowly, a picture emerges of a multi-coloured beast with arms, legs, horns and of indeterminate sex. Oh, it also has wings! Then my tactical error..... has anyone else seen it? Speaking to the husband brings a touch of sanity to the proceedings. He, at least, can remember his name, address and telephone number, but (and I knew I shouldn't have asked with his wife at his elbow), if his wife says that she's seen something then he supposes she must have. The supper re-enters the microwave for the third time, with a fleeting consoling vision that if such a monstrosity is at large in darkest Worcestershire then, traditionally, it would be named after me in lengthy Latin prose. 'Sightings' over the years have included everything on Noah's inventory. Laughing hyenas were the latest, but I wasn't laughing - it was too late.

My discreet arrival at the appropriate address is heralded by the woman and her considerable entourage spilling through the front door, down the garden path and into my jeep. The children set

Opposite Page:
Bless my cotton gnu's and side whiskers! The chase into Kidderminster.

about themselves with gay abandon. Lights flash, sirens wail, the radio emits spine-tingling static and the handbrake is released with near calamitous consequences. At least my quarry will have long gone. "It's round the back," gasps the lady, breathless from further breaching the peace by screaming her charges into submission. "Wait here!" I command as she disappears beneath another cloud of cigarette smoke. I vanish, too, into the dense undergrowth that was once a garden. I'm a hero already - I haven't taken a gun! Nothing. After a decent interval, I relay this revelation in a suitably disappointed tone. Undaunted, however, the cigarette cloud insists on showing me herself. Like the proverbial Pied Piper, I'm followed this time by half the entire street.

With the stealth of an elephant herd and the agility of a rhino, we break cover and stare up the empty garden. "There!" she shouts triumphantly, "On top of the fence!" "On top of the fence?" I repeat slowly for want of something better to say. The top of the fence looked like the top of every other fence in the street. "Yes. It was sitting there last night." "Last night?" I echo again, my stomach rumbling uncontrollably at the thought of the liquid paste in the microwave. "Yes," she reiterates, a little uncertain of herself now. "It went that way," she adds helpfully, waving vaguely in the direction of a two hundred acre wood. "Good. My men are out there now," I lie unashamedly, "I'll go and join them." With that, I burst through the smokescreen and flee to the sanctuary of my jeep. But I'm not clear yet. A tap on the window - it's her again. "Have you got any jobs with the animals? My children could help too." I manage to convey the sentiments of 'don't call us, we'll call you' and, with my elbow 'accidentally' on the siren button to preclude further conversation, I flee, never to return.

Shortly afterwards, a new acquaintance, Ian Ballard and his wife arrived for dinner one evening having collected rumours en route of 'big hairy things with horns' in Stourport, a town three miles away. It sounded vaguely familiar! Before we could sit down, the police rang with the same story. Clearly an inventory check was called for but, still unconcerned, we checked the perimeter fenceline. Dumbfounded, we discovered that vandals had cut great swathes through the fence. The American bison and the wapiti, enormous North American deer, had disappeared into the night.

Wapiti Stag. Not something to bump into on a dark night! (Photo Author)

I survey the fence damage. (Photo J. James, Birmingham Post and Mail)

A Bison in the woods. (Photo J. James, Birmingham Post and Mail)

Chaos reigned in the darkness. Attempts to chase them back from Stourport proved futile and nearly fatal. It was all hands to the pumps. Somehow, in the confusion, Ivan the sea lion trainer ended up with me in my puny little jeep, an early model Suzuki LJ80V. Chasing fifteen bison up an enclave between two fences just six foot apart, they were suddenly startled by a flashlight, turned and charged back. Trapped, unable to outpace them in reverse gear, unable even to open the doors to get out, we stared aghast at this heaving mass of bison thundering down on us in the moonlight, fearing that our last moment had come. Oblivion beckoned but, when we opened our eyes, the bison, every last one of them, had cleared the jeep without touching it and fled into the darkness. Their progress was graphically charted by the radio traffic. Dave Chorley was being similarly embarrassed by their momentum, especially as he was on foot! Forewarned only by the shaking ground as the dark steaming mass bore down on him, he turned and ran, and ran as he'd never run before. Ultimately, his momentum took him so far up a tree as they flashed narrowly past beneath him that he proved difficult to locate, much less persuade to come down. Years later, we nearly lost him again on another dark night. The duty warden had rung up to say that a burglar alarm was going off in Spring Grove House but she couldn't find Dave to tell him. His lights were on, the house was open and the TV was blaring, but of Dave and Olive there was no trace. I was out of bed in a flash, dressed and at the park before the police got there. When they arrived, we began our search, just as Dave materialised. He'd been out to dinner and had left the house lit up as a security measure! But what of the burglar alarm? There was no problem, he insisted, but just in case, even the policemen let Olive go in front as we commenced a room to room search! By the time we reached the wine cellar, however, Dave had lost his reticence and was first to the door. We had one hell of an evening!

Having begun near disastrously, the bison operation had faded. We had to content ourselves with sealing off the woods and containing the bison until daylight. My friend, having had the dinner party of his life without getting a bite to eat, left for home at 3.30a.m. but was back at dawn for the round-up. To this day, we rarely sit down to a meal without recalling our first attempt to do so, amongst others. On another occasion, we'd travelled to

Scotland overnight in convoy to collect some deer. At first light, we'd begun loading and eventually set off on the return journey south, e.t.a. Worcestershire 9p.m. The weather worsened, the traffic snarled up and delivery time slipped to 5a.m. the following morning. On arrival, we awoke the recipient's nightwatchman who we presumed would let us in. Instead, he responded by holding us at gunpoint. He was a ghastly man so it presented a heaven-sent excuse to flatten him, but the years of customer relations instilled within me suppressed the natural instinct. Instead, we both merely bit our lips, but talking our way out of it delayed homecoming a further hour. Dying for breakfast, we eventually fell into Ian's parents' farmhouse only to discover that his mum had kindly rolled out the red carpet - the previous night! Roast beef, Yorkshire pudding, Brussels sprouts - the whole works, in fact, had been kept painstakingly warm all night on the Aga. As we worked our way through this strangest of breakfasts, my eye caught the newspaper. Suddenly, I realised what day it was. My father was retiring as headmaster of his village school today - in Kent! While Sue roused the children, I suffered the revitalising agonies of a cold bath before the dash south. We walked through the school door bang on cue, just as his presentation began.

The bison, meanwhile, were a different proposition in daylight and quickly caught, but the wapiti presented a different challenge altogether to the early morning joggers all over the common several miles away. However, I kept my cool for I noted in their aloof gait an uncanny preference for the correct way home. One by one, they appeared over the horizon drifting inexorably homewards. By the time the morning mist had cleared sufficiently for the police helicopter to get airborne, they were all back. The time, I noted, was bang on 10a.m. Feeding time and opening time - old habits die hard. Again, though, the ubiquitous little Suzuki had come into its own. Like so much else, I'd come upon this, the solution to all our vehicle problems, purely by chance. Driving down the motorway one day, I'd become distracted by the spider in my rear view mirror hanging in the back window. It bobbed up and down, swayed precariously from side to side and..... became larger! I quickly realised that it was, in fact, a vehicle! Fascinated, I watched the manoeuvering with which I was soon to become so familiar. A passing articulated lorry would first blow it a yard to one side then leave it bobbing in its slipstream like flotsam in the wake of a great ship. I followed it to the Royal Show, saw its possibilities and ordered one the same day. The LJ80V was small, light, highly manoeuverable and capable of prodigious cross country feats. From the Highlands of Scotland, the crags of the Lake District to the Welsh bogs, I would leave all and sundry trailing on my deer-catching expeditions. The park soon purchased one, too - the one we were in that night, the forerunner in a succession that has lasted, to date, twenty years. Packing five firemen inside it to tackle a bush fire the previous week made me pretty certain that I could get a whole TV crew and an entourage of photographers to the scene that morning, albeit with it resembling a Indian taxi! The man from the Worcester Evening News sitting on the roof (with the residual bison dung from the previous night) ducked instinctively as the police helicopter emerged from behind the railway embankment on its final sweep, dipped in salute and returned to base. A mobile office, a dispensary fully equipped for the frailties of man and beast alike - dart rifle, fire extinguishers, two-way radio, 'phone, water, tow chain, tow ball, bull bar, jump leads, auxiliary lighting, public address system, camera, binoculars and an extensive car alarm - all packed in neatly like sardines, with good reason. One morning saw an irate rhino park me almost upside down on a boulder larger than the Suzuki itself, just as the office called to ask if we were ready to open! Fortunately the radio, now above my head, dropped into my lap as another nudge saw the jeep bounce back upright on four wheels. Yes, we were ready to open! I often get 120,000 miles out of an original engine and gear box - not bad for all the low gear, stop-start, almost city centre type driving within the confines of the park and the long journeys beyond it, often towing a loose box.

Unfortunately, with these fence cutting antics so well publicised, they served to exacerbate the problem. So, instead of causing merry hell in the town at night, it proved much more fun for the local layabouts to cut our perimeter instead. Whether caused by the original perpetrators or simply by 'copy cats', the problem continued throughout the summer and I spent many a night perched with the police in tree hides or other strategically placed observation points before the habit died. Our boundary is four miles long, much of it through distant, inaccessible woodland and it required an operation of almost counter-insurgency proportions to police it effectively, quite literally at times. On more than one occasion, when dealing with holes in the fence, I noticed holes appearing in the jeep - neat, little round ones that went in one side and out the other. Once, they took out the windscreen. It was not a pleasant feeling either for myself or the animals, several of whom suffered, too, with bullets lodged in them.

Not all homecomings were as sedate as the wapitis'. The pursuit of a gnu which chose to migrate into Kidderminster is a case in point. He headed ambitiously straight downhill into town at a fearful pace with us in hot pursuit. The drug of choice to sedate these antelope is deadly to the human operator. A drop the size of a pinhead call kill within two minutes if absorbed. Assembling the dart in the boot of Dave's Cortina estate car travelling down the pavement at 60mph. is not, therefore, held to be therapeutic - but I managed. Horror-stricken, we could only stare aghast as an elderly man, bent double, head lowered geriatrically over two walking sticks, shuffled out of a garden gate in his carpet slippers straight into our path. The gnu couldn't possibly stop his headlong flight, choosing instead to slide on his backside, legs flailing for grip, cartoon style, round one side of the obstacle as we screamed past on the other in a putrid cloud of brake disc. The pursuing entourage in our wake avoided him, too, as he continued his charmed road crossing oblivious to the mayhem erupting around him.

Fortunately, the traffic lights stayed green for both the pursuers and the pursued alike but an abrupt right turn at the bakery, through the hospital car park, saw the town centre looming large. However, Lady Luck smiled on us for the second time that day as he tore into a cul-de-sac by the cemetery. Heads lowered in respect, preoccupied mourners saw nothing as my dart struck home. Within minutes, he was in the boot of the car and we were away, back up the hill past the unheeding pensioner before we heard the wail of the first police car. Minutes more and he was back on the park - in his pre-export quarantine isolation pen!

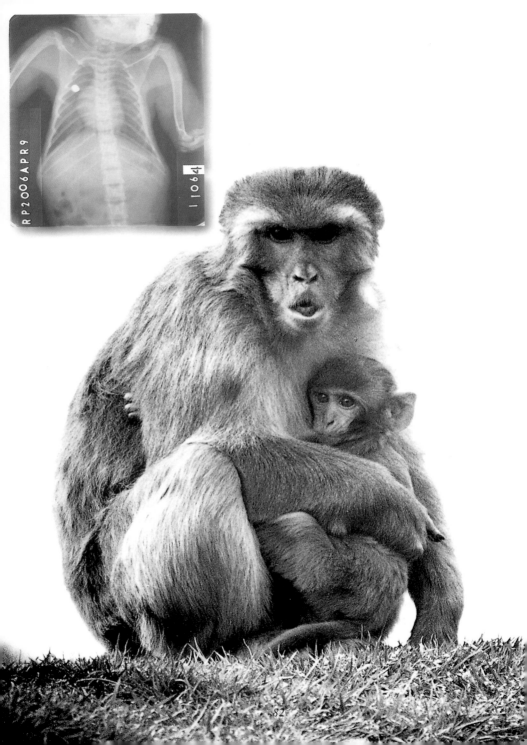

Introductions to the geography of Kidderminster continue to this day. One Saturday morning recently, I was roused from my bed by the local council. It had been a sleepless night. It had begun with a call from the local police. A deer had been spotted on the bypass and, by the way, could they use the park's dog kennels as an overspill? Theirs were full. Then the RSPCA called. Could we house an anaconda seized in South Wales? Then the RSPCA called. Could we house a monkey found living in the cupboard under the stairs in a house in Hereford? Then the RSPCA called - about the two foot alligator seized in a Manchester house. In conjunction with Wyre Forest District Council's Ranger Service, I'd pioneered a scheme whereby some of our rare breeds of cattle from home grazed their newly fenced nature reserves. We'd put some Belted Galloways in the latest one the day before, only for vandals to destroy the fence overnight. They were loose on the outskirts of town, said 'hot and breathless' over the 'phone, and frightened to death. One was cornered and darted in the garden of a council house after a long chase, whereupon it leapt the fence, tore through a wood and emerged in a housing estate on the other side with a park ranger still hanging on for grim death. Between us and the police area car, we bundled her into my trailer and followed the trail back in search of the other, right across the golf course. It was match day. As they teed off, a cow flew across the fairway, then a squad car, then my landrover! The player froze in astonishment, club held high, then swung in exasperation, his concentration long gone. The ball flew between us, bounced off the oncoming ranger's landrover and nearly slayed the constable on foot. Fortunately, my dart was more accurate, striking home above par on the 11th, so this unseemly procession followed the trail of gesticulating golfers across two more greens before we came upon the cow, floundering in a bunker. Bent double as the balls flew above us, we hauled her, too, into the trailer. And it was still barely breakfast time!

Not all such escapades were so easily glossed over. Looking up from his desk one day as his flimsy wooden manager's office began to shake, David Chorley noted that he was being circled at

Opposite page:
Rhesus Monkey with X-ray plate revealing a .22 air rifle pellet in the lung. She survived.
(Photos Author)

a considerable rate of knots - by a rhino! A devout non-believer, he simply pulled down the blinds, raised his eyes skywards - and prayed! If he'd looked up sooner, he'd have seen the cause of his dilemma. A flight of RAF C130 Hercules transport aircraft had soared across the park at treetop height, frightening the rhino out of their skins..... and over their wall! Then there was the sea lion that climbed onto the roof of Dave's predecessor's house and then the one that went off across the fields to the fish and chip shop every night as soon as the smell of fish alerted him that it was open. A sea lion's dexterity in water is scarcely diluted when he comes ashore, a possibility that appeared to have escaped everyone during the park's construction. Night after night, we had our free supper if only we would get down there quickly and get the wretched thing out. Eight feet long, of injudicious weight, stinking to high heaven and, more ominously, with 'fifteen stitches to the bite', he was a formidable deterrent to business when he sat there like that on the serving hatch. We were, though, sick of fish and chips every night - he and the rest of his kind simply had to go. Besides, en route to his happy hunting ground one evening, he'd chased someone's cat right up an apple tree. That, curiously enough, was the last straw, decided the locals. Things were out of hand. In those pre-Zoo Licensing days, the local MP's only recourse was to write to the Home Office - on the cat's behalf! A complaint urged on by a now increasingly vociferous residents' anti safari park lobby. However, while the Home Secretary deliberated, life went on. Having picked up Chorley junior from school the following afternoon, I found myself on someone's front lawn in Bewdley, contemplating the recapture of an East African Crowned Crane. I became distracted, though, by an animated telephone conversation through the open French windows involving a familiar voice. The campaign leader in whose garden I unwittingly stood was being assured by Dave Chorley that security was being tightened! It wasn't. By the time I'd stopped laughing, the bird had flown! It wasn't my first off-park escapade with Chorley junior. When our Italian overlord was in residence, he watched over the reserve gate like a hawk. The second you drove out, he was on the radio in a flash to demand why. If it were this difficult to leave the reserve, you can imagine the near impossibility of actually leaving the park itself. But, with near shoulder length hair, I was desperate enough to sneak out of a

Window cleaning in the Sealion Pool but sealions proved as agile out of water as in it, see below! (Photo Author)

The Sealion on the roof. (Photo Author)

rarely used back exit one afternoon to get to the barber's. Having had a substantial trim, I paid and turned to leave assuming that I'd got away with it. Only then did I notice young Darren staring solemnly at me from the next chair!

Our park in Germany was the natural choice for the sea lion. Devoid of a British garrison town, there wasn't a chip shop for miles. He never strayed again. That just left the others. At 2a.m. one Sunday morning, a police car ran over one in Kidderminster and killed it. Having radioed in to report the fact, it was strongly rumoured at the time that the duty inspector sent another officer out to breathalyse the driver. "Ran over a what!" had come the retort. Our stock with the thin blue line was soon to fall still further. Driving in one night to investigate a neighbour's complaint that our European bison bull had violated his Jersey cow, the driver failed to notice the newly installed and aptly named 'sleeping policeman' laid down, non-reversible steel shutters and all, to prevent vehicles driving *in* the exit road. Unfortunately, the car was being driven by a sleeping policeman who failed to notice his namesake - or the newly erected warning signs. The device ripped off the front axle in this, its baptism of fire. The driver's fate is unrecorded.

Relationships were sufficiently patched up for the police to alert us to a further sighting at 3a.m. on another Sunday morning. We recaptured this sea lion within an ad hoc trap built with the finesse that comes with experience (rapidly dismantled landrover bonnets!) in the fish pond of a palatial residence in Kidderminster. Anxiously watching the closed curtains for signs of detection, we crated this poacher and were home for breakfast by sunrise. To this day, every time I pass the house, I wonder to what they attributed the sudden dearth of fish. After all, herons don't break down the garden fence to reach the pool! The penultimate specimen bolted up the drive one afternoon while his trainer was out. It remained for his wife and I to shepherd him into the ticket office and lock the door. An anxious wait ensued. Until the trainer returned, every visitor had to be admitted free of charge! The sea lion shows, too, remained equally perilous affairs. One sultry spring Sunday afternoon, Manchester United were seconds away from an FA Cup Final defeat at the hands of much unfancied Oldham. 'Pirate Pete', an equally avid fan, was rushing through his sea lion show in order to get to a TV. Then 'we' equalised with almost the last kick of the match. I was swinging from a tree frantically gesticulating the glad tidings to him. Responding to my hand 'commands', the sea lions worked themselves into an increased frenzy, tearing through their expanding repertoire to rapturous applause as 'Pirate Pete' stared helplessly at his watch. Only the final whistle enabled him to regain control. Extra time would have been disasterous!

The last stray fell into a trench being dug by the water board in Bewdley one evening. Fortuitously, it bisected his route to the utopia of the River Severn, umpteen fish and chip shops along its bank and probably freedom for life. The labourers were Irish, working for the water authority on secondment from the gas board under the direction of a drunk foreman for the local council - or something like that. This went some way to explaining the confusion. They'd reported a monkey in the trench! Whilst others returned the monkey box to the park, I tried to explain the difference, quite unsuccessfully. Eventually, the much used Lufthansa crate materialised and, with the help of the heavy-headed navvies, the sea lion was brought to task. I drove him straight to Heathrow the following night without further ado..... until I got there. Having been directed to the freight terminal, by 1a.m. I was completely lost on what appeared to be a perimeter road. Perplexed, I parked in an area of deep shadow and turned off the lights to admire the stars, the galaxy of lights from the airport activities and collect my wits. There had to be a catch somewhere. In complete contrast to all the aerial activity, the place appeared deserted. Surely someone had spotted me? The place was, after all, on red alert at the height of one of the earliest IRA security scares. Then I spotted the shooting star coming straight at me, then the undercarriage, then the puff of smoke as the freighter touched the tarmac. I quietly died a thousand deaths as the estate car rocked in the turbulence. As the noise abated, the silence lay heavy on the runway, punctuated only by the pounding in my chest and the slithering in the crate behind me. Thoroughly aroused by now, the sea lion barked and gurgled as if choking on a stone of fish. Entombed in the car with it, the noise seemed to reverberate like a cannon. Surely the entire world would see us now? I closed my eyes in anticipation of the spotlights, resigned to a life sentence. Still nothing. Fed up with this game of cat and mouse, I turned on the headlights and followed the white arrows they illuminated into the halo of light that turned the freight terminal into daytime. Still no armoured car, no soldiers, no flashing lights, no dogs, no whistles. The sea lion barked again as I sank behind the steering wheel. "What the bleeding 'ell you got there, mate?" said the tap on the window. "Crate's big enough for a bloody missile! Just stick it over there," he continued as I waved the papers beneath his nose, "I'll see to it." "You mean I can go," I spluttered, "Which way?" "Same way you got 'ere, mate. Past all the bloody security!"

The 'fish wars' over, the sigh of relief from the bilges of the 'African Queen', the 'flagship' of our motley craft on the lake, was almost audible. Far from being a leisure craft, over the years she'd slowly begun to resemble a slave galley. There were offset barriers to repel boarding sea lions who'd first soak then terrorise the passengers, mesh screens to deflect stones and other unseemly detritus hurled with uncanny accuracy by the chimps on the island and canvas awnings to prevent the pelican droppings from landing in visitors' laps, or worse. And to think people paid 30p to travel on her! As the final solution culminated, she was stripped of all this and rode much easier, a full 18" higher out of the water. So far, in fact, that even Old Bill couldn't run her aground! The rest of the problem around the lake area was also resolving itself. "What stops these from just flying away?" I'd asked as a naive layman of the flamingo on the water. "Flamingos cannot fly," I was told by the head of a famous circus family going back three hundred years. Clearly, the lessons of history hadn't been heeded because they all ended up one night with the pelicans - in Milford Haven!

Brindled Gnu - in more sedate surroundings! (Photo Author)

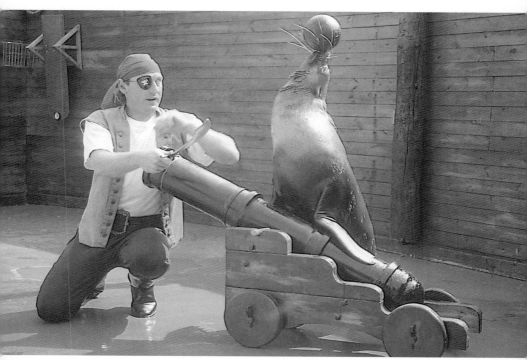

'Pirate Pete' in his tell tale red Manchester United headscarf! (Photo Author)

CHAPTER 5
Animal Rescue
(To Ian Ballard, my companion on many a merry jaunt)

T he words 'sanctuary' and 'rescue centre' are standard parlance in the vocabulary of the animal world. Such establishments are relatively common for no qualifications are necessary to set up or run them. In fact, anyone can do it. Whilst some undoubtedly do fine work, it has been my experience that the worst examples of cruelty, neglect and mismanagement of their occupants' welfare has come from within centres sheltering beneath these banners. Deer farmers come a close second, severely tarnishing the reputation of the admirable majority in the industry. Staffed by well-meaning but misguided people without the knowledge or the resources to undertake their quest in life, they invariably operate with impunity. As 'sanctuaries', it is assumed that they are operating compassionately - not all do so. They frequently seem capable of driving a coach and horses through all the constraints applicable to others because whatever authority they're referred to assumes that, as some sort of rescue service albeit self-styled, they must be 'all right'. This is frequently not the reality. I've encountered deer kept in sheds the year round, deer drowned in a sea of mud, deer hanging dead in fences, dead deer tangled in wire and deer walking about for months with broken limbs. Meanwhile, down the road at the local market, both MAFF and Trading Standards officers (whose task it is to enforce animal welfare legislation) would berate farmers who produced sheep for sale with a limp! I've nothing against deer farming or deer being in kept in secure 'accommodation', but surely The Monarch of the Glen deserves better.

Opposite Page:
Sea King Helicopter over Ramsey Island - the deer airlift begins. (Photo Author)

A case in question occurred in a 'sanctuary' which even boasted local authority tourism signs as a means of attracting visitors. I'd constantly warned ministry vets of the downwardly spiralling conditions for over a year, yet nothing was done. What impressed the RSPCA ultimately was my ability, months beforehand, to predict to the very day the time of the first deaths. I drew little satisfaction, though, from the first three corpses they duly brought me for identification on the day I'd predicted. Prised out of the frozen mud, they were indistinguishable as deer but deer they were, each of a different species. Even when their stomachs were found to be devoid of anything except mud and baler twine, it was not thought sufficient to prove to a court that unnecessary suffering had taken place. Frequently, officials are made to look inept and their reluctance to act with any degree of vigour is frustrating but, from their point of view, they have to be as near certain of a successful prosecution as our ubiquitous legal system permits before they dare act, such are the budgetary constraints. They are handicapped by outdated legislation. Not disposing of an animal carcass is an offence under the Dogs Act 1906. But, it was always felt in this case that, if the land was enclosed for deer and therefore not accessible to dogs, such a charge would not stick. So, carcasses could be left lying undisposed of for all the world to see - 'legally'. And so it went on. Ultimately, we were to shoot dead over fifty deer to bring the problem to manageable proportions. I was only able to find live homes for a fortunate handful. And still the 'sanctuary' emblem remained.

Deer farming became popular in a blaze of hype like so many other enterprises which were to revolutionise the rural economy but, unlike the others, has survived as a viable but much reduced industry. Like the camelids, angora goats, bison, wild boar and latterly ostriches, all promised high returns and, indeed, many did so initially. Each new 'industry' spawns its own bevy of expert advisers and consultants who come crawling out of the woodwork. One year at the Royal Show, I heard a self-proclaimed llama farmer lecturing a film unit who clearly held him in awe. Having kept llamas for nearly six months, he was well versed in their husbandry. They were very difficult to keep alive, he said, extremely difficult to breed (not strong selling points, you'd imagine!) and shearing? Heavens alive, the fleece was such a

Death in the 'sanctuary'.
Top, Red Deer - bottom, Fallow Deer.
(Photos Author)

fearsome prospect that the shears glowed red in your hand! I'd scarcely stick a needle into our seventy or so camelids from one year to the next and the only difficulty I'd ever experienced in breeding was stopping them! I'd never sheared one, however, but I thought that if our expert knew as much about this as he did about everything else, then it shouldn't be too difficult. Sure enough, that evening my friend Ian Ballard and I tried our luck. Within forty minutes we'd sheared three, proved my point and couldn't really see any point in continuing! On the back of these pearls of wisdom, though, our llama 'expert' was hawking his wares for £6,000 per llama! When advising prospective newcomers to these innovative enterprises, I always urge them to ignore the transparently false horizons presented by future livestock sales (for breeding stock for example) in the early days and budget for the basic raw product i.e. the meat, fibre etc. as the bottom line. If it is viable on this basis alone, then go for it. If not, forget it. Those who remembered remain in business while those who didn't, without exception, are gone, very often leaving others to clean up the mess.

When boasting such high returns, inevitably the wrong type of recruit is attracted into these fledgling industries for the wrong reasons - very often people I wouldn't entrust a dog to, let alone a vast herd of animals bought at great expense about which they know nothing. Sadly, too, it is very often people who've invested their all that get stung the worst. Time and again, I've received the eleventh hour request from desperate owners or, more likely, MAFF, Trading Standards Officers, RSPCA officials or others, to bail them out of the direst dilemma. We can represent a 'centre of excellence' service with, for example, unrivalled expertise with reptiles, small mammals and most frequently the capture and/or transport of larger animals for treatment or to a refuge - often back to the park until the problems are resolved.

These calls have resulted in some bizarre events. In the earliest days, a policeman had to be present every time the dart rifle left the park. So, at 5a.m. one Sunday morning, I found myself in a barn, just down the road from where I now live, sedating a heifer

Opposite page:
Ian and I try our hand at llama shearing. (Photo Author)

for a vet to calve. After two hours straining on the calving rope, the duty sergeant and his constable left covered in cow muck and cleansing, stinking to high heaven. The requirement was dropped shortly afterwards. The next call-out for cattle was to a bull which had gone berserk, terrorising an entire village. It proved so unapproachable that I had to commandeer a bulk grain trailer for use as a personnel carrier. This tortured soul vented his ire on our protective steel casing, tossing us this way and that like peas in a drum until I managed to keep my balance long enough to slip a dart into his shoulder. This induction to military-style tactics served me well on the next summons to a farm. The deer here proved impossibly shy of anyone or anything strange until I spotted the farmer's collection of military memorabilia. They didn't bat an eyelid as I darted them from the turret of a Soviet-built T34 tank - 'glasnost' on the farm! I once darted a red deer stag in the middle of Walsall in the dark whilst police held rush-hour traffic at bay. They did so, too, in Greater Manchester when I was asked to bring to book three fallow deer who, quite incredibly, were living unperturbed in the central reservation of a dual carriageway on the ring road. The route, though, was a familiar one. Earlier that year, Ian Ballard and I had investigated a group of wild boar who'd appeared in the grounds of a sweet factory in Manchester, finding rich pickings in the waste deposits. After three trips, we eventually got them, together with sufficient confectionery to last both families over Christmas! Another expedition recaptured an escaped wild boar in Pershore. Then there was the Capybara in Malvern, Muntjac deer in Redditch, Lechwe antelope in Northampton, fallow deer in London and Roe deer in Wiltshire. Every notch on the dart rifle has a story to tell. On another jaunt, complete with some darts I'd adapted especially, I managed to hit and recapture a free-flying, escaped exotic hawk in the sky over Leicester. It took a couple of attempts but, at the third time of asking, I was sure I'd hit it. Then came the message - the eagle had landed and was in custody! A desperately dangerous undertaking for the bird, of course, as I'd warned, but the story went that the RSPB would destroy it if it remained free, to prevent any hybridisation with indigenous hawks. It's amazing what you can hit if you have to and the paucity of the information you're given to go on. "How big is the cow you want darting?" I once asked a farmer over the 'phone. "About the size of a bullock," came the reply, a scenario familiar to many a vet! At a Royal Mail corporate entertainment day, one of the activities we were invited to participate in was archery. I'd never used a bow and arrow in my life and, furthermore, shooting left-handed because of a sore shoulder, I didn't expect to trouble the scorers, so to speak. Somehow, however, the first arrow ended up in the bull's-eye. The second did, too, in a sense, for it went straight into the tail flight of the first! Both rapidly disappeared as decor for the club house, but the Royal Mail tracked them down. They hang on a presentation plaque at home today, still joined together.

On another call-out, I was greeted on a farm by the usual posse of officials - the Police, RSPCA, MAFF, Trading Standards and, on this occasion, the International League for the Protection of Horses, too. Amongst the catalogue of dead, dying and suffering animals, there were horses, too. The trail of despair extended to every room of every shed, every vehicle and anything that could contain animals. The place was overrun. Amongst other things, the angora goats were the worst affected. Their bubble had burst - they were worthless and had been treated as such. Several died as their rescuers carried them away. My task on several visits was to dart some of the horses, some for moving out for therapy and rehabilitation, others simply to enable them to be extracted for euthanasia. A week after my visit, another thirty horses under the same ownership were 'found' in a nearby field in a similar state of neglect. On this occasion, however, a jail sentence was handed out. Like all the cases that I've been involved in, however, there was a history to it well known to officialdom and one wondered just how it had ever degenerated into such a disaster. At the time of writing, I've just returned from darting a horse for the second time in six months. Initially unhandlable, its headcollar had grown into its flesh and we had to dart it, cut it free and fit another, only for it to happen again. This time, the RCPCA commissioned me to effect the capture and they assumed ownership. Contrary to popular belief, the RSPCA don't consider it their main purpose in life to prosecute people. If this is necessary, they consider themselves to have failed somewhere down the line. For many animals in dire straights, they are the quickest and often the only hope of salvation. Often, though, they simply don't have a choice other than to prosecute. Many zoos are paranoid about their

My 'hole in one', an arrow within an arrow within a bull's-eye!
(Photo J. James, Birmingham Post and Mail)

I show my Tanzanian student the secrets of the dart rifle.
(Photo K. Webb, Kidderminster Times)

activities and have a strained relationship, but once I'd cleared the air with them, we've never experienced the slightest difficulty. About twenty years ago, I was staggered to read in a newspaper that the local RSPCA inspector's annual report contained 196 complaints about the safari park. I'd received none. What, then, was he doing about them, I asked? Nowadays, if they ask occasionally to see something, we simply show them. Indeed, trainee inspectors are allowed a guided tour behind the scenes to familiarise themselves with contemporary standards. We've never had cause to regret this 'open house' policy. Certainly, they've never had to uphold a complaint about us.

When the ostrich farming bubble burst, six times in twelve months we were called to remove birds from what, in one instance, were appalling conditions, by people who'd simply given up. Standing in two feet of water or stuck up to my knees in mud in the 'shelter' to the point where I myself had to be pulled out, one couldn't help but wonder how we could presume to 'farm' such animals. The pasture verged from threadbare at best to non-existent. The fencing wasn't stockproof (indeed in places it hung in loose coils on the ground, a perfect potential snare for any bird) and there were no handling facilities. The lucky ones were extracted to be brought back to the park for safekeeping and ultimately stay there, thrive and breed. The unlucky ones were found, long since dead, in the field. When the RSPCA prosecution came to court, myself, the inspector involved, a vet from MAFF, two other vets and several police officers were all called to give evidence - as the owner pleaded not guilty! A sense of reality might have prevented some part of the £2,900 the case cost him in fines and costs (for causing unnecessary suffering and failing to dispose of the carcasses), together with a twenty year ban on keeping ostrich. Or so we thought. On appeal the following year, the convictions were cast aside amidst great confusion over interpretation of the law. Essentially, no one could agree on the status of the ostrich. They are imported under poultry regulations, yet poultry welfare legislation (drafted decades before ostrich were heard of in this country) whilst mentioning obscure species like quail, doesn't mention or specify ostrich. Quite how they or their meat can be classified if it is not poultry is hard to imagine. I'm sure there are many other legal anomalies lying dormant in respect of other

exotic animals that will only belatedly come to light in similar circumstances. Compared with this, darting stray dogs on housing estates, cats in quarantine stations, horses on motorways or cattle on railway lines is old hat, but the calls continue to come in as do the requests to rehome many of them. Like most things, there are perceptible trends. At one point in the 1970's, we were inundated with requests from local authorities to dart stray dogs at the height of a rabies scare, most memorably, perhaps, just down the road near Kidderminster. Rabies being, well, rabies(!), it was decided to warn the locals to stay indoors. There was some reluctance from the swimming pool set on that balmy Sunday afternoon until an RSPCA inspector ran out of patience and began brandishing a Colt 45 above his head! The vet and I took one look at each other, slipped through the police cordon and beat a hasty retreat. We reconvened secretly the following day at dawn and I quickly brought the dog to task. He wasn't rabid, merely terrified at having been tipped out of a car to fend for himself in the middle of nowhere some weeks earlier, it transpired. He went on to become a police dog. At the end of the day, however, we are a wildlife park not a rescue service, so the performing dogs, three-legged deer and the five-legged sheep that we've been offered over the years, amongst other things, aren't necessities.

The age-old quest for exotic pets brings problems too. The llama scene only really took off when Michael Jackson began keeping them. Soon, the Americans were over here waving blank cheque books at every keeper of llamas, who duly obliged by putting prices into the stratosphere. Some wanted llamas with straight ears, others with ears curling inwards, curling outwards, long legs, short legs - the permutations were as endless as the colour variations but, invariably, existed purely in the eye of the beholder for what really constituted a llama? They come in all colours, shapes and sizes. A couple of 'Llama societies' came and went. One asked, no demanded, £50 per animal to 'register' the pedigree of our animals. An utter nonsense, of course, for llama, guanacos and alpacas all interbreed, so, in the absence of genetic profiling, who could tell from looks alone? 'Fresh' imports from

Opposite page:
I try my hand at spinning camel fibre. I'm on the right!
(Photo T. Flannigan, Birmingham Post and Mail)

the continent were procured at enormous expense without knowledge of their background. Wiser counsel knew that many had originated from the UK in the first instance! Such is the havoc wreaked by the instant expert. So what beguiling properties did they possess to tempt people into parting with such substantive figures for them? You can eat them, of course (they say hippo tastes nice too!), but at those prices they might stick in the throat. Fleece values were referred to in telephone numbers, but you never met anyone who actually paid them. They are useful for trekking, pulling carts or catching the eye at farm parks and even on the golf course. Because their soft feet make so little impact on the greens, they make excellent caddies. Club selection can be a little erratic, though! Then there is 'llama karma' (in America of course), where there are estimated to be 100,000 camelids kept in North America alone. They are excellent psychotherapists, catalysts for soothing the troubled minds in penal institutions and retreats for burnt-out executives the world over, and intelligent enough to help autistic children. Not content with this, though, after a gap of 30 million years, scientists have recreated the 'cama', a hybrid between a male Old World camel and a female New World llama. Reputedly 'camas' are a more convenient size, produce more wool and have an even better temperament. Psychiatrists beware!

There have been requests for animal fibres, usually from retirees of the local carpet industry who have a passion for weaving and spinning weird and wonderful types of wool. Previously restricted by conventional criteria to domestic sources, this bottomless source of exotic raw material on their doorstep proved irrestistible. Consequently, we frequently find ourselves looking for 'combings' on the scratching posts, dust bowls and fencing. Lion mane, bison, camel, yak - anything, in fact, that will wrap around a spinning wheel is prized material. Two things always struck me about these fibres. Firstly, they are very soft and cause no skin irritation. Secondly, their warmth-retaining properties were exceptional. Often, garments that looked like poorly strung together string vests proved perfectly adaquate in the depth of winter. It does, perhaps, give an insight as to how our ancestors survived. They didn't have central heating in their caves or thermal underwear from 'Damart', just clothing fashioned from raw materials like these.

Vietnamese pot bellied pigs were the next craze, flooding the sanctuaries, wildlife parks and the RSPCA with cast-offs when their potential for sheer destructiveness and escaping became apparent. In one year alone, we were offered two a week on average. After the craze on Rottweilers and Pit Bull Terriers came the hybrid wolf craze with all its problems. Whilst clearly outside the scope of the Dangerous Dogs Act, people offering these animals for sale, frequently for many thousands of pounds per litter, have a problem when challenged to prove what they are. After all, where do the wolf genes come from? Where is their Dangerous Wild Animals Licence? One wonders if Trades Description legislation could put the burden of proof on the vendor. Similarly, local authorities wishing to take the initiative under the Dangerous Wild Animals Act and seize what are potentially very dangerous animals have the same difficulty when the burden of proof falls upon them as accusers. Any hybrid of any animal on the Dangerous Wild Animal Act list is deemed to be within the act's remit if it contains 1% of the forbidden genes. The difficulty with dogs lies in proving it. Scientifically, even with DNA, the wolf hybrid is indistinguishable from dogs, so the courts have to determine between expert evidence which is essentially held purely in the eye of the beholder. We've housed specimens for local authorities that only moult and come into oestrus once a year (like a wolf) whilst possessing a certain panache for silent running, but otherwise much of it hinges around behavioural matters. Personally, I think that if you look hard enough you can see wolf-type behaviour in virtually any dog, if you choose to do so. I am therefore reluctant, even as someone who has hand reared wolves, to become involved in such matters. In Canada, I've seen these hybrids shot on sight. Whatever the rights and wrongs of this, they certainly don't belong in an inner city high-rise block of flats full of unattended children.

Then of course, inevitably, there are the wild cats of Britain. Like most parts of the United Kingdom, we have a constant stream of sightings featuring large wild cats. They come in all colours, shapes and sizes. They follow people home from the pub, hurl dustbins down the street, dance on caravan roofs like manic druids and dig up potatoes - not an item featuring very high in most feline dietary requirements, you'd imagine! The most common sighting, perhaps, is the black one - the puma - invariably, if not exclusively, by people who've never seen a puma in their life! There is no such thing known to science as a black puma. So what is it then, they ask? Well, on one notable day, the sightings passed to us by the police began early morning with a 'monkey' (Siamese cat). Clutching to the end of a bough swaying precariously over a greenhouse, I'd just retrieved the wretched thing when the photographer from the 'Express and Star' popped his head around the garage. Could I hang on? He needed to change film! By mid-afternoon, there was a 'wolf' running down the Bewdley bypass (Husky dog) and by nightfall there was a 'lion' on the golf course (Golden Labrador). Thankfully, by then I was en route to Wales to dart a cow (a real one) so had every excuse to avoid this merry-go-round and delegate the diplomacy to others - until I got there - for it proved a typical call-out. Having involved me in a two hundred mile round trip, not for the first time I was lectured relentlessly on how to do the job. If they were so clever, why then was I there? Fortunately, my friendly neighbourhood windbag ran out of steam and left me to get on with it, for the peril of the mobile 'phone had struck again. There were some deer running loose in the dark on a grouse moor (including the fast road that dissected it) in North Wales. Could I go, asked the police, courtesy of the RSPCA? Why not? I was nearly there anyway and had nothing else to do till 1.30a.m.! They were at least real deer, though - escapees from a farm. At that altitude, in the rolling short-cropped terrain with only the grouse to punctuate the silence, the resemblance to the Namibian desert at night was quite uncanny. After savouring the moment, I darted them all by moonlight thereby removing their daily gauntlet of crossing the main road. It really was one of those days, but at least I didn't see another cat until I got home. One of ours had eaten my supper, another had produced kittens behind the TV.

What, then, are these cats and where do they come from? The theories are as varied as they are frequently absurd. I've been told in complete confidence by total strangers that these cats exist and have been trapped, but that government ministers and chief constables have personally sworn them to secrecy to avoid a panic-stricken rural exodus. Then there are those who insist that their domestic cats and even dogs have been violated under cover

Black Leopard.
(Photo J. Clubb)

The 'Beast of Great Witley', Worcestershire.
(Photo N. Morris)

The 'Beast of Great Witley', Worcestershire.
(Photo N. Morris)

The puma clearly isn't black!
(Photo Author)

of darkness to produce hybrids peculiar to Britain and, like the black puma, hitherto unknown to science. Even the most rational explanation is wearing a bit thin. The introduction of the Dangerous Wild Animals Act in 1976 undoubtedly prompted a clear-out by those unable or unwilling to succumb to the expense and scrutiny involved in keeping exotic pets. But this was a long time ago, far beyond the life span of a wild cat of any species living ferally, unless they are second generation escapees. This cannot be entirely discounted. If cubs were produced at the right time of year, they could undoubtedly survive. Some exotic cats have escaped from travelling circuses and the like, but those involving animal acts are few and far between these days and the escapees invariably only individuals. The answer, if there is one, inevitably takes us back to the Dangerous Wild Animals Act. Like much prohibiting legislation, it forced activity underground. There is a burgeoning black market in many exotic species pandering to the machoism associated with their ownership since time began. If such animals were lost or escaped in transit, for example, and the potential for this is clearly demonstrated in the case of 'our' Motorway Monkeys (see Chapter 12), then the owners could do very little about it without drawing unwelcome attention to themselves. Even if this were to happen, it could never occur with the frequency that the number of sightings even locally would indicate, yet alone nationally. Yet, the feeling persists that, somehow, somewhere out there, there is something that doesn't quite add up. With animals, the more astute say 'usually' or 'invariably' rather than 'always' or 'never'. Certainly, patterns do emerge. An inordinate number of sightings in a locality invariably brings the crowds in like birdwatching 'twitchers', together with the 'expert' trappers and trackers who come out of the woodwork to complicate the equation - living enigmas whose claims to be able to catch anything, anywhere are a contradiction in terms. After all, if they are so adept, why is there anything out there? Because they never catch anything! Once an area is swamped by such attention, the sightings fade, only to begin again thirty to forty miles away a week or so later. The perpetual puzzle to me is that, given the huge increase in camera ownership in general over the last twenty years and latterly the number of video cameras in particular, more pictorial evidence hasn't emerged to support the sightings. Certainly, despite being called out on scores of occasions, often by the police, I've never seen anything definite and only two pictures. One was an unconvincing 'still' and one a piece of video footage. Having lain dormant in an amateur video camera for nearly a year, I was casually asked to take a look. There unfolded before my eyes an astonishing sequence of the legendary large black cat romping in the spring sunshine. As millions of television viewers were subsequently to see, it was black. It could only have been a jaguar or a leopard.

My own specialised experience is very thin on the ground. Very few vets have tranquilliser guns, fewer still the knowledge to use them and, surprisingly enough, the knowledge of the requisite drug that we use in most animals. Many a newly qualified vet has marvelled at a darting operation, for they are no longer even taught the use of these drugs or the strategies for their use. Like everyone else, their knowledge in these matters is gleaned from the fictional nonsense so beloved by film directors. A rugby scrum may appear spectacular at the end of the chase, but the animal beneath won't enjoy it, assuming it survives, any more than the people who invariably get injured in the process. I've seen three people hospitalised just loading a llama into a trailer! Similarly, adopting a course of action because 'that's how it's done in the wild' doesn't qualify it for universal adoption. Losses there invariably go unrecorded - we only see the survivors. Generally, though, much more responsible attitudes now prevail. Rhino losses during translocation, for example, even by helicopter, rarely exceed 1%. Another scenario much adopted by the film industry is the firing of a tranquilliser dart into an animal that, promptly and obligingly, drops in its tracks. Darting is usually the last resort, albeit the only one to effect capture of wild animals, but if ever they did this you'd panic as something would be seriously amiss. It takes several minutes for the drug to take effect at all and, during that time, it is essential to keep the animal in sight. You may lose it altogether if you don't. It may stagger onto roads, slip into holes in the ground, be attacked by other animals who sense a weakness, blunder through buildings or end up in water. All of which, of course, could prove fatal.

I always remember ending up to my waist in icy water one January morning with Ian Ballard when a sedated red stag fell into a large pond in the Lake District. We hung on to him grimly, desperately trying to keep the head above water, both blissfully unaware of what we were floundering in. We later discovered it was called Lake Windermere! Many of these merry capers seem to involve getting wet. I got soaked at dawn one morning in Sussex darting a Roe deer which had had the temerity to encroach upon a Saudi prince's estate and devour his roses. By contrast, I got virtually drowned one Sunday evening on The Duke of Westminster's estate in Cheshire. The remit was to hunt down a prized Fallow buck which had skipped a newly erected cattle grid to roam the estate roads by night. The night was black, the rain torrential and, with much of the land under water, I lay in wait in a lodge garage hoping that the lure of the peanuts on the bird table would tempt him out. After a couple of hours, the night sights filled out - he was there. My knees cracked like pistol shots as I eased into position, a noise drowned fortunately by the rain thundering on the roof. And, still, the anticipated intruder light didn't come on. In desperation, I flicked the car's headlights on. For a fleeting second he stood transfixed, then fled - with a dart in his shoulder. He went down a hundred yards out through the thickest wood on the estate, which was under water. It took three of us to carry him out and return him to the estate, but he was made of pretty stern stuff. We watched him through the night sights for a while until he was fully revived then retired like drowned rats to the keeper's lodge. Here, I was dried out, royally dined on a Sunday roast and sent home at midnight with a bottle of the finest whisky in my pocket. In exchange, I sent some lion dung to be placed beside the offending cattle grid! Return visits have fortunately been in daylight, for the Grosvenor Estate is superbly administered and a delight to behold.

For over twenty years, people have been coming to me to learn the intricacies of the dart weapon. One of the first was a university research team off to work in Africa. Little did I realise that the coals were coming to Newcastle. Within weeks, I had a Tanzanian on a government exchange scheme at Worcester college coming to us on a weekly placement one winter to do the same. It transpired that he was the principal of the college in Tanzania responsible for training the game wardens for their national

Opposite page:
3 legged deer and a 5 legged sheep! (Photos Author)

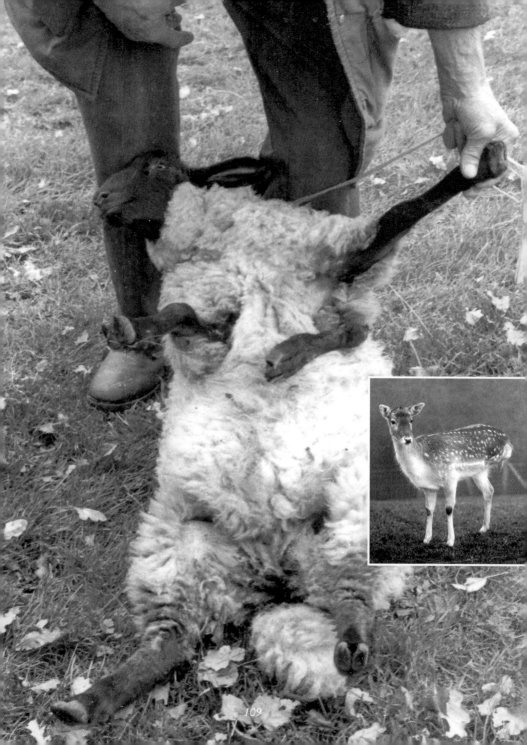

parks. Yet even he, the top man, had never used a tranquilliser gun. It is, perhaps, a trifle unkind to suggest that it doesn't say much for the others, but it did strike me at that time as being a sad indictment of how backwards some of these countries have become when they have to send people over here to discover how to manage what are, after all, essentially their own wild animals. Besides, it would be far better for me to spend the winter months tutoring out there!

This knowledge is utilised far and wide, using prudent precautions, in other zoos, deer parks and deer farms. A frequent annual task here is removing antlers from the deer once they are out of 'velvet', the soft tissue which surrounds the antlers while they grow. As soon as the velvet has gone, the antlers harden and become potentially lethal weapons at any time, not simply during the rut. They will be cast again in the spring but, during the intervening months, they remain capable of damaging fencing, vehicles, each other and, of course, anyone coming into contact with them - as several human mortalities have proved. Removing the antlers makes them considerably safer (but not completely safe), painlessly and without causing harm. The inch or so antler stump remaining will cast again in the spring as if it still had a full 'head'.

Walking along the coast of North Devon one autumn, I'd commented to Sue that from the top of the picturesque summits along the Valley of the Rocks at Lynton you could actually look down on RAF jets flying below you. I'd climbed them many a time, dart rifle over my back, in pursuit of the feral goats that thrive on these peaks, then climbed down with a goat over my shoulder. She was not impressed! The first batch went to the Isle of Wight for the National Trust to use as browsers on a nature reserve. The following autumn, the surplus I extracted went to the Isle of Lundy for much the same purpose. The temptation to accompany them on the steamer to this unique little community and see them released was strong, but I was wary of the fickle weather conditions. I was right. The goats were landed but the weather closed in, stranding all and sundry on the island for a week!

Opposite page:
'Monarch of the Glen' - Red Stag in winter at the West Midland Safari Park.
(Photo Author)

My caution stemmed from earlier experiences further north on Ramsey Island. Once again, all else had failed and Ian Ballard and I had been given the task of removing a hundred red deer from the island, a nature reserve that was being destroyed by uncontrolled overgrazing. (Currently the ecological problem, there is a rat plague with the rats devouring the eggs of nesting seabirds). We herded them into a ready-built corral, darted out the stags with antlers who'd cause damage in a confined space, then drove them all into a handling pen. Here we toiled like slaves, worming, ear tagging and crating every single one of them. In mid-afternoon, one of the hinds reared up, fore legs flailing, and caught Ian just behind the eye. He went down like an ox and stayed there. Years later, I told his young son this story one bedtime. "Really," he said, "Dad's never mentioned this." Dad knew nothing about it! I hauled him out of the way, soaked him in water and kept working to clear the jam of deer in the system in order that we could get out. Even then, though, there was precious little I could do to help him, stuck out there on that breathtaking but desolate place. The Sea King helicopters due to airlift the deer off weren't in the air yet. Fortunately, no lasting harm had occurred but, from that day on, I've never entered a handling system without a hard hat. They were amongst the hardest two days' work of my life but, by nightfall on the second day, we were ecstatic. We'd achieved what all before us had failed to do. The deer were all back on the mainland with, Ian apart, only one heartstopping moment - the sight of a crate plunging seawards from beneath a helicopter. Fortunately, it was the one from the house containing only books! Soon, however, I had to face another trial - getting back. I envied Ian remaining behind on that photographer's paradise for a break. I simply had to return for there was a bank holiday looming. Such peak times are sacrosanct - you do not miss them. Indeed, I've yet to miss a single bank holiday in over twenty seven seasons. But how? The wind had risen abruptly, sweeping the rain in horizontally off the sea. Even the Sea Kings were grounded in that maelstrom. Ramsey Sound is notorious for its currents and its underwater obstacles and, with the waves by now taller than houses, I could appreciate the need for the lifeboat station opposite us somewhere on the mainland.

The inflatable dinghy looked absurdly flimsy in such conditions for a non-swimmer. The zip on the lifeboatman's suit broke as I put it on, but I reckoned the park's ire at my absence would pale the conditions into insignificance so we gave it our best shot. With a local at the helm, we set out. The intricacies of navigation at sea escape me, so how he knew where we were going I'll never know, especially when the engine cut out and we were swept away; first once, then twice as the second outboard failed, too. My helmsman swore furiously over both engines using a spanner from my dart gun kit, while I used the rifle as an oar to keep station and my waxed hat to bail out. The motors took it in turns to function, fitfully at best, as we drifted aimlessly about that watery wilderness for an eternity. Then we hit something. Was it the end? Heart in my landlubber's mouth, I turned to confront my fate only to find myself clutching the ramp of the lifeboat station. We'd made it! We'd left the car keys on the island, I was soaked, stiff in encrusted salt and the dart rifle mechanism had seen better days, but we were safe. The bank holiday weekend was uneventful.

We take animals from other zoos as well, directly and indirectly. I was once called to a caravan park in South Wales to remove a troublesome deer. I was astonished, therefore, to discover myself looking down my dart rifle barrel at a Nilgai bull antelope, a native of India! Its source, Edinburgh Zoo, intrigued me. Many of the establishment zoos in the 70's looked down their noses at these new-fangled upstart safari parks, possibly with good reason. What was hard to reconcile, however, was their refusal to sell us animals when they sold or even gave them away to caravan parks. Similarly, at the same time we were desperately trying to procure wapiti deer for our newly established American reserve. Chester Zoo refused to even discuss a sale with us. What they were prepared to do, however, was to sell them to a two-bit animal dealer, who promptly delivered them to us loose in the back of a Ford transit van, having doubled his money for two hours' work. Over twenty years later, we are one of only two zoological collections in the country able to keep this notoriously difficult species. In fairness to both zoos, much more enlightened views now prevail.

When Guilsborough Grange Zoo, Northants., closed in 1991, the animals had the indignity of being auctioned off on the premises.

The only animals we were interested in were silly money but, come the final lot, the Red Lechwe antelope, the enthusiasm dried up. From £500 each, they dropped to £500 the lot. Guess who took pity on them! The problem was they had to be caught. The day in question dawned black as pitch but there could be no tomorrows. Vacant possession was required with immediate effect. We headed north into torrential rain hoping to feed them into the two shelters and slam the door on them. Some chance! The conditions made vehicular access impossible, the doors disintegrated in our hands and, worse still, the sheds hadn't roofs on them. The rain simply fell in and filled them up. They were unusable. The fence was ramshackle and incapable of withstanding pressure. Indeed, the bull cleared it and disappeared from view in the torrent, never to be seen again. At 11a.m. on that November day, it was almost dark but there was little choice. They had to be darted and we were already drenched. Wrapped in bin liners and armed with a strong beam, I hunted them down in near darkness. Once tranquillised, the ground underfoot was so treacherous that we had to winch them out, keeping their heads and ours(!) above water to prevent them drowning as the stream overflowed, washing away in the process much of our equipment. The head count was as much for the hunters as the hunted, but slowly, inevitably, they succumbed to instinctive marksmanship and were bundled into the luxury of warm, deeply-littered trailers. It was 8p.m. by the time our little convoy had weaved its way through the motorway chaos to reach home. A message from the police control centre awaited us. Their video cameras had picked us up driving through a multiple pile-up. What had we seen of the incident? Absolutely nothing! We saw a lot more of Belle Vue, however.

David Chorley and I had gone there to collect Barbary sheep and American bison when that famous zoo closed in 1977. The sheep, huge fearsome-looking specimens, proved as problematical as the bison were to be later. As the capture team approached, they sensed something untoward and went clean through the one inch thick plated glass used to contain apes, did a lap of the zoo for old times' sake and headed for the Belle Vue shopping centre. Whilst they were hunted down by the Manchester Police's SPG unit (of necessity, in this case, a bunch of burly prop row forwards), I looked at the bison with some foreboding. The bull looked massive. I convinced myself that the impression was enhanced by his wretched surroundings. His world consisted of a thirty foot square concrete yard confined on three sides by a high brick wall and on the fourth by eight foot high wrought-iron railings. He bellowed his anger and indignation as he restlessly paced this prison, goaded by city youths prodding him through the bars of his torture chamber. So much for the home where the bison do roam. Suddenly, I felt rather glad I'd persuaded my 'powers that be' to purchase without telling them I'd already done so! By the time the dented white vans had returned and disgorged (at considerable expense to the ratepayers of Manchester!) the Barbary sheep from beneath a ruck of bruised, sweating policemen - not to mention the torn uniforms, dented helmets and buckled riot shields - the bison were aboard our hired transport.

As the cattle lorry ambled southwards, we paused at Knowsley Safari Park, Liverpool, to renew old acquaintances. It was there that the news caught up with us. The lorry had been involved in an accident 'somewhere in Wolverhampton'. We tore down the motorway in grim silence, every conceivable dire consequence flooding our minds. Fortunately, we found the lorry at the first attempt, at the head of a colossal jam where it straddled a set of traffic lights at a major junction. Neither man nor beast were hurt, but, with the radiator stove in, there was little prospect of the lorry moving again that night. Years later, in a similar predicament with an alligator, we simply called the AA. The animal in question duly arrived at the park a few hours later in an AA van, something their PR people singularly failed to pick up on! By 11p.m. on this occasion, however, all our options were exhausted. The truck couldn't be repaired nor could we find anywhere to leave it. For once, the police were unhelpful. The nearest police station was a converted council house whose only security lay in having plywood sheets nailed over its windows and which was run by an, understandably, highly nervous acting sergeant. The inertia caused by his paranoia over making a mistake that would jeopardise his position becoming permanent was complete. No, he wouldn't take responsibility for having the lorry in his pound (the front garden!). It occurred to me that having bison charging about the town in the early morning rush-hour would add significantly to his responsibilities, but he wouldn't budge.

And so it came about that at midnight on an October evening in pouring rain, in the middle of Wolverhampton, we embarked on the delicate task of transferring the bison to another truck. The relief vehicle reversed up so that, when lowered, both the loading ramps and the side gates met. Despite my weariness, I found myself surprisingly fleet of foot. Playing hide 'n' seek with that monster amongst the flickering shadows, as the dimmed street lighting glinted off the wet pavement, I needed to be. But he was quite comfortable, thank you. He viewed the prospect of the wet street with some disdain. My mind went back to the very early days when we transported giraffe in a converted double-decker bus. It made a strange sight parked outside the driver's council house in Kidderminster complete with occupants and still a source of embarrassment to a then babe-in-arms who now works for me (but has always had to endure the taunts of his classmates). But, at one journey's end, it nearly met its nadir. The giraffe wouldn't budge! The driver was a wily rascal of considerable circus pedigree and the possessor of an uncanny ability to deliver anything anywhere. You could despatch him to the continent to collect a giraffe. Off he'd go, in just the clothes he stood in, without money or papers - nothing, in fact, except his wits and an almost Gaelic gift of the gab - and you'd quickly forget about him. He'd always turn up, invariably out of the blue, with everything in perfect order and a perfectly plausible explanation as to why it had taken two months to get to France and back! The days went by and a lengthy book was opened on whether the giraffe would come out before the road tax and MOT expired or the floor rotted through. I cannot remember the winner, but after two weeks a clap of thunder startled it one night and, finally, the bus was free to resume its journey. At least this was within the security of the park. The middle of Wolverhampton was another matter altogether!

Fortunately, the new day began marginally better than the old one had ended and, again, a little divine intervention helped. An ambulance siren unnerved our recalcitrant hulk and he tumbled meekly out of one lorry into another, blown in by an enormous sigh of relief! We arrived home at 2.30a.m. Upon release the next morning, the bull strolled over to my landrover. Gratitude? Not a bit of it! He went back on his heels, pawed the ground and charged. As the engine mounting came though the dashboard, I was unsure what to do. When he charged again and the radiator ended up on the bonnet, showering me with hot anti-freeze, my mind was made up. I dismounted and fought like a foot soldier; or at least thought about it, briefly, before taking to my heels! Someone else was in full flight about that time, too. In a sun lounge nearby, overlooking a field of my sheep at home, a lady was awakened from her slumber by panic-stricken ewes in full flight. Incensed at the sight of the dog chasing them, she leapt from the sun bed and tore off up the road in pursuit. As the initial flow of adrenalin ebbed two hundred yards up the hill, she began to notice the flashing headlights, then the police car. Suddenly, the realisation dawned on her that, wedding ring and corn plaster apart, she was stark naked! There were other embarrassments, too. I once spent a sweltering weekend in a Kidderminster carpet factory in pursuit of a Barbary sheep which had somehow eluded us and escaped. Finally, late on the Sunday afternoon, the trail went cold and I gave up. Six weeks later, at feeding time one morning, the wretched thing reappeared in the park as bold as brass. How it got out, much less got back, is a secret it took to its grave. But at least it didn't tell the others either! That evening, we went to our local for a bar snack. Suddenly I had the feeling that someone was watching us. I looked around, then down. There at my feet sat a familiar figure on the veranda - our tortoise. He'd disappeared from the garden some weeks earlier. Quite how far he'd travelled (it was at least a mile as the crow flew) or, more to the point, how, through fields of standing ripe corn, we'll never know. That sixth sense was often to stand me in good stead. I was once darting red deer in the grounds of Powys Castle, Welshpool. They'd approached readily enough for their winter morning feed and within ten minutes I'd darted our quota of ten through a peep-hole in the canvas awning of the gamekeeper's landrover. Within another ten minutes, all were safely revived within a trailer but, amidst the back-slapping (they'd budgeted for a day long operation), I was uneasy. Something was wrong, but what? We had ten animals but had retrieved only nine darts. I left the foot soldiers to do a ground search and went for a drive around the

Opposite:
An alligator arrives at the
park, courtesy of the AA!
(Photo Author)

Below Left: The rescued
ostrich in their field of mud
and water.
(Photo J. James, Birmingham
Post and Mail)

Below Right: The double
decker giraffe bus.
(Photo G. Mason)

park, for the instinct told me the answer lay elsewhere. I followed my nose for twenty minutes before stumbling upon the answer to the puzzle I'd set myself. There, atop the hill, lay a fallow deer sound asleep with the tenth dart firmly embedded in her shoulder. Unwitnessed by anybody, the economies of scale had somehow seen me dart eleven deer with ten darts! The following week, when I was actually supposed to be darting fallow deer, a similar thing occurred. A dart deflected off a fallow doe through the ear of a red deer hind with its head down feeding. You'd imagine that the amount of drug absorbed through such minimal contact with a half-expended dart would be miniscule but, having boxed my fallow deer, that twitching feeling returned. Sure enough, a circuit of the park produced a slumbering red deer. The following week when I turned my attention once more to the reds, I tested the theory by reducing their dose by 80%. Although three times the weight of the fallow, they had half the fallow dose - and dropped like flies!

The biggest single rescue package to date was the evacuation of Windsor Safari Park when it closed in 1993. The receivers, Cork Gully, had appointed an Animal Committee to oversee the rehoming process in accordance with the strict guidelines they'd laid down. I knew the principal members well and they, in turn, the park. Windsor's Curator, Paul O'Donahue, Victor Manton, lately of Whipsnade, and the redoubtable David Taylor of the International Zoo Veterinary Group were its principal members, so, when they came up to visit us, we had little difficulty persuading David Farren of Cork Gully that we were eminently suitable recipients for some of the stock. During that winter, a regular shuttle service was run down to Windsor, resulting in the eventual safe relocation of over one hundred and fifty animals. Everything, in fact, from a humble pigmy goat to lions and hippos. At the other end of the spectrum, we had a lady donate her son's pet rabbit to Pets Corner. Overwhelmed by guilt, she regretted it and visited daily in a lurid-coloured sports car to ease her conscience, leaving me gifts which would vary from a pair of socks to a can of lager for putting up with her - and the rabbit!

Other animals, too, joined the inventory equally innocuously. When one of the staff approached me before going on holiday to ask if his son's pet could be left in the park for safekeeping, I agreed without giving it a thought. Busy at the time, I neglected to ask just what form this pet was likely to take but, even so, I was more than a little surprised when Oswald arrived. The creature bearing this unlikeliest of names was, in fact, a thin, scrawny-looking hen that answered to her name and, despite her size, was uninhibitedly bold. By the time her fortnight's holiday was over, Oswald had settled in so well that it was thought a gross unkindness to return her. And so, at the expense no doubt of a small boy's hurt feelings, a minor legend was born. Oswald became a star in her own right. She ignored with complete disdain the advances of the cockerels who came from Pets Corner to visit her and took over completely. Not content with this, she terrorised the tom cat in the food stores, leaving no one in any doubt who ruled the roost. Her ambitions knew no bounds - she appeared anywhere and everywhere at a whim. Her appetite, too, was equally unpredictable. She'd strut through the food stores helping herself from any open bin, even tearing at the meat laid out for the carnivores as if it were layers mash. Her favourite meat? Chicken! At break times, a split second's distraction was sufficient for her beak to be into a sandwich box in a flash and she'd fly away in triumph bearing the fruit of her misdemeanours with her to some predetermined spot out of reach of her pursuers. On one occasion, we thought she'd gone for good when she flew through an open car window to investigate a picnic hamper but, a couple of hours later, she was back. Her nuisance value appeared limitless as she roamed her domain in the endless quest to satisfy the demands of her bottomless stomach. The concrete floors of all the buildings under construction at that time were criss-crossed with her foot patterns. She took a morbid delight in watching the mix painstakingly trowelled to a perfect finish before fluttering down from her perch on cue, systematically strutting all over it whilst contriving to remain those few tantalising inches beyond the reach of the incensed workmen. Like cave drawings, evidence of her handiwork remains to this day. On those occasions, Oswald led a charmed life.

During the summer months, Oswald roosted above my office but, with the onset of winter, took to the sanctuary of the giraffe house. At that time, the elephants, rhino and giraffe all lived beneath the same roof. With the vast amount of body heat generated by these large animals within this carefully insulated building, it remained comfortably warm. As a precaution, however, a thermostatically controlled gas-fired central heating system cut in when the temperature fell below 50°F, thus ensuring a stable environment much to Oswald's satisfaction. Her usual roosting place was on one of the feeders mounted ten feet off the ground. From here, she watched with ill-disguised fascination the activities of the giraffe all around her. As for the giraffe, they would occasionally give her a cursory lick, but otherwise this spy who came in from the cold was left as usual to rule the roost.

CHAPTER 6
Aliens

(To John Robinson who taught me so much)

To most people, British wildlife means the grey squirrel in the local park, the Canada goose on its lake, the pheasant in the hedgerow, the rabbit in the garden or the house mouse in the pantry! Doubtless it will come as a surprise, then, to learn that these everyday species and many more besides hail originally from distant shores. Our crowded islands abound with almost eighty alien species of birds, mammals, reptiles, fish and amphibians. Introduced deliberately or inadvertently by man, they have become established in viable self-perpetuating wild populations or, quite simply, naturalised.

They range from the improbable Mongolian gerbil to the almost bizarre African clawed toad; from the unlikely Tasmanian red-necked or Bennett's wallaby to the common goldfish; the budgerigar and its principal predator, the domestic cat. Whilst their transitions were as diverse as their origins, these exotic introductions have occurred for one or more principal reasons; by accident, or for sporting, aesthetic or economic purposes. Some were imported with an acceptance that they would naturalise but with little or no regard for the consequences. As some were introduced by the wealthy to grace a private collection, stately home or simply as pets, escapes were inevitable. Once loose in sufficient numbers, several factors determine any ability to naturalise; climate, habitat and the food supply within it, absence of predators, fecundity and the effect of these inhibitors on the species' natural instincts. It has, for example, been noticed that

Opposite Page:
Suburban fox 'on safari' in our dustbins.
(Photo Author)

Canada geese in the UK have such a depressed migratory instinct that they are largely residential.

Such introductions are now frowned upon, supported by legislation and a licensing system overseen by English Nature. Although, possibly, a little late in the day with the infinite wisdom afforded by hindsight, it is not hard to see why controls are sought, albeit possibly against the tide of history. After all, since time began, peoples have moved around the world constantly, taking and depositing animals wherever they go. Rats and rabbits cause untold damage to our food chain every year. Mink and Coypu are scarcely less trouble, both from an economic and ecological viewpoint, wherever they appear. Even some goose populations are assuming pest proportions, yet bird problems are not a purely British phenomenon. The traffic has been two-way. The sparrow and the starling, two of the most numerous and damaging avian pests worldwide, have stemmed from our shores. Ironically, perhaps, the former now exists in but a shadow of its former numbers at home for reasons that remain unclear. Likewise, the mallard duck, once the doyen of every lake, pond and water trough, is diminishing in numbers whilst the once widespread common frog is common no more due to habitat loss. All, however, survive in the park.

Since its introduction into Britain in 1876, the grey squirrel has been widely cited as the prime example of the folly of introducing an alien species into an environment ill-equipped to receive it and totally devoid of natural controls. Apart from an undoubted aesthetic charm which enables them to court popularity wherever they exist in proximity to man, they have no redeeming features whatsoever. Utilising the supreme opportunism so typical of pest species and with a catholic diet which encompasses eggs, fledgling birds, bulbs, fruit, cereals, tree bark and virtually anything else remotely edible, these arboreal rats wreak havoc throughout the countryside. Interestingly, their favourite tree for 'barking' throughout our park is the sycamore, itself an introduced species from America, the land of the grey squirrel. Also from America came their crayfish. Introduced for food production, they carried a disease to which our indigenous crayfish have no resistance. When, inevitably, the 'aliens' escaped, the effect was disastrous. There are now none left in our local streams.

Conversely, the Little Owl, widespread throughout the park, is one of the few exceptions to this tide of alien mischief. There was in 1842 (when it was introduced) and remains to this day a niche in the ecology of our countryside for a diurnal owl. It has survived traditional prejudices and persecution to become accepted as a positive addition. Interestingly enough, like the Tawny and Barn Owls that we occasionally see, the Little Owl is classed as a CITES (Convention on International Trade in Endangered Species of Wild Fauna and Flora) Annex A specimen. This means it enjoys the same protected status as the elephants and tigers amongst whom our free-flying specimens live! A more recent acquisition, also kept until recently in the park, has gained acceptance as a British species. Since the escape of the diminutive Chinese water deer from captivity in the 1940's, they have proved their durability, albeit in strictly localised terms, to the point where they now feature in any listing of British deer species. Personal observations have shown that they pose little or no threat to forestry or agricultural interests. For nearly fifty years, the Bennett's wallaby survived in the Peak District, having escaped during the war from a private collection together with a solitary yak, although they now appear to have died out.

Without such additions, any list of purely indigenous species would be meagre, indeed, by most European standards. Historically, this can be traced back to the latter stages of the last glaciation, which extended southwards almost to the Thames valley. Having retreated before it, Northern Europe's wildlife had only partially recolonised the land when Britain became separated from Europe. Since then, the English Channel has proved as effective an ecological barrier as it has against all other newcomers. During subsequent evolution, with its consequential combination of overheating, habitat loss and climatic change, many of our larger mammals have long since disappeared. The European bison, which the park kept until recently, disappeared from these islands possibly up to 14,000 years ago anyway, but the lynx disappeared in the late Stone Age and was followed at intervals by the reindeer (although these were successfully reintroduced into the Cairngorms in 1952), brown bear, beaver, elk, boar and the last of Britain's wolves, slain in the eighteenth century.

A mole emerges (briefly!) into the wolf compound. (Photo Author)

Dormouse feeding near the park. (Photo Author)

Muntjac Deer.
(Photo Author)

Reintroduced; Reindeer in the
Cairngorms. (Photo Author)

Grey Squirrel, the
perpetual pest.
(Photo Author)

Great Crested Grebe on the Park
Lake. (Photo J. Robinson)

Crayfish; extinct locally. (Photo Author)

Not even indigenous species have remained unscathed by introductions. Incredible though it may seem today, vast numbers of foxes were imported in the 18th and 19th centuries to boost the then insignificant native stocks and provide quarry for the huntsmen of England. Think of how the 'anti's' would greet this today! Nowadays, however, the fox, another supreme opportunist, is increasingly an urban dweller to the extent that town centre sightings rarely attract comment. I frequently get called out, too, for the diminutive Chinese or Indian muntjac deer (also now considered a naturalised species) in suburban areas, but leave them well alone. Such is their phenomenal spread that some estimates put their numbers at one and a half *million* and, therefore, comfortably the most numerous deer in Britain. I'm not sure who has counted them, but, belatedly perhaps, English Nature have a moratorium on their licensed movement.

Few species boasting any sporting or commercial value, such as fish and game birds, have escaped restocking attempts. Others, like the badger and the great crested grebe, have historically been severely depleted for what traditionally were regarded as useful by-products i.e. the skins and feathers used principally in military uniforms. Invariably, injections of fresh blood have come from overseas and involved breeds other than our native stock. The resulting confusion of characteristics has, in many cases, resulted in a virtual loss of identity for the native species. A truly wild pheasant, for example, is a rare bird indeed these days. If the passage of occasional migrants or seasonal visitors complicates matters, then the odd scheme to reintroduce extinct species such as the beaver is equally disconcerting. In the case of the much maligned wolf, traditional prejudices make it inconceivable that it could ever work, yet the wolves within the park remain one of our most popular attractions, steeped as they are in the myths and fantasies of folklore. Romantic though such notions are, the implications are rarely thought through. The agents behind the extinction must be clearly understood and only species lost by direct human action and unlikely to recolonise naturally are suitable candidates for such ventures. Suitable natural and isolated habitats to permit and sustain the introduction must then be found. It is a tall order in these congested islands and, for this reason alone, successful rehabilitations have been few and far between. Few vertebrate species have been successfully reintroduced to date - the capercaillie, red kite and white tailed sea eagle being isolated examples. If the loss of a British species is a bitter pill to swallow, small consolation can perhaps be found in the emergence of another - inevitably, though, part of an evolutionary process increasingly dominated by man.

At least the opportunity to see some of these 'lost' species like the wolf is available in captive situations. Some of our exotic species, too, like the Pere David deer, the Formosan Sika deer and the Przewalski's horses have long been extinct in the wild and owe their existence solely to captive situations. We'd all prefer to see them in the wild but, if that means extinction, do we just accept it? It is a sombre fact that when we recently moved on three rhino which had been at the park for twenty five years, it was calculated that their chances of surviving that same term in the wild were no more than 1.5%. It is a fact, too, frequently overlooked by the purists that if some had their way and returned all zoo populations to a utopian wilderness where we all agree they should ideally be, the sheer pressure of the viewing masses would quickly destroy the very habitat that they'd come to see. Restricted public access, introduced as a sheer necessity to some parts of the Peak District and the New Forest at home, are a portent of things to come for our wild places.

Our wallabies then, until recently a naturalised species, live close by the wolves, an extinct species in native terms - their respective habitats freely occupied by rabbits, foxes, pheasants, red legged partridges, the grey squirrel, Canada geese and the Little Owl, all introduced species. Maybe the exotic species amongst whom they also roam aren't in such alien company as many would think. I'm frequently amazed, too, to find that when surrounded by some of the world's most threatened or endangered species, people are content to merely sit and watch the mallard ducks! To an extent, the park, containing nearly thirty acres of SSSI (Site of Special Scientific Interest), is a substantive part of the green belt. It contains an interesting but not spectacular wildlife population. The Little Owls nest in the camel shed, the 'motorway' bird (the kestrel) in the tree-tops above the tigers, the badgers beside the elephant house, the great crested and little grebes on the lake,

A Dunnock (Hedge Sparrow) feeding a fledgling Cuckoo by the Elephant House. The cuckoo is on the left! (Photo Author)

A Little Owl on it's nest in the Camel Shed. Note the voles, wagtails etc. dropped in for the fledglings by the other parent. (Photo Author)

Extinct in Britain - Wolves.
(Photo Author)

Extinct in the wild, but some Pere David Deer have been returned to China.
(Photo Author)

Extinct in Britain - European Bison.
(Photo Author)

John Robinson and friend!
(Photo Author)

Extinct in Britain - Beaver.
(Photo Author)

together with the frogs and newts and an abundance of fish which support the grebes, the herons and the kingfisher. Add the bats in the loft, the woodcock in the woods, the turtle doves by the nilgai shed and the odd cuckoo or so, reared by the hedge sparrow beside the elephant house, along with the visiting ravens that tease the monkeys and you have a unique, albeit local, ecology - but no less fascinating for all that. As I sat in my tractor and watched my lions by day, I pondered such things. By night, I listened for nightjars, read, learnt, inwardly digested..... and photographed them.

CHAPTER 7
Monkey Business
(To Angela who showed such faith)

I'd met Lionel our handyman/carpenter on my first visit to the park for my 'interview'. He was building a rhino house, or so it was said. In keeping with everything else in those days, a few wooden poles and an odd sheet or two of plywood were considered perfectly adequate. The rhino then were so small, however, that it seemed pointless going to so much trouble to contain them when they could simply walk out through the doorway that I'd just entered. But then, I'd never seen a rhino before so what did I know? As honest as a summer's day is long, cheerful, chirpy and with a heart of gold, attributes he retains to this day, Lionel had one calamitous failing. He was notoriously accident prone. I'll take to my grave, for example, the memory of the day Lionel fell off a roof. He slid majestically earthwards until his fall was broken by an old cast-iron gutter bracket which pierced an ear lobe. It held him swinging gently in the breeze, flapping like a marooned bat. As a wartime commando, he'd fought half a war without loosing as much blood or creating as much noise as he did that morning until we freed him and took the pair of them (Lionel and his ear) to hospital to be reunited. Inexplicably, then, we accepted his wartime expertise in building a pontoon bridge to evacuate chimp island prior to the onset of winter, aided and abetted by Boris our elephant keeper. He'd driven army trucks across pontoons so was obviously well qualified to assist in

Opposite Page:
The recapture of 'Wrigglebottom'. (Photo J. James)

their construction! Boris, however, could be an awful malingerer so progress was slow. His wife would invariably ring in with lurid tales of night-long bouts of vomiting, diarrhoea and much else besides which were hard to digest over the breakfast table. Boris would be laughing his head off in the background, a give-away punctuated only by the waves breaking against the beach beside his holiday caravan on the Welsh coast.

Chimp island was a subterranean rat hole. The living quarters were pitch black, below the water table and wringing wet to prove it. There was no light, heating or fresh water and no means of cleaning the place out. I'd love to have interned its designer in it for just one night. As soon as I was in a position to influence matters, I'd resolved to get them off, even if it were only for the winter. If the lake had frozen, they'd have walked off anyway. The consequences of that were unthinkable. At last, though, all was ready, according to Lionel. So, with the chimps duly crated, we set off across the pontoon.

Half way across, bang on cue, the bridge disintegrated throwing eight of us into ten feet of water. Only two intact units remained afloat. One supported the chimps' steel crate which would otherwise have sunk like a stone. Less gratifyingly, the other kept Lionel's feet dry. He leapt ashore and wandered off in search of *the* lifebelt, leaving us floundering in the deep. The two chimps shrieked at us in the water until their eyes ran and their sides ached, for they alone remained dry. Plan B was to row the section still afloat across to the mainland, having first sedated the chimps, taken them from their crate to reduce the weight and bound them hand and foot as a precaution. Muggins, the rookie, was chosen as the on board attendant. Having cleared the lee of the island, the headwind reduced progress to a crawl with a choppy swell breaking uncomfortably over all three of us. By the time we were but half way across, the drenching had served to revive my slumbering companions and they were wide awake. Within minutes, they'd undone Lionel's knots. I was stranded in the middle of a lake with two mature chimps. None of us could swim.

We eyed each other uneasily, acutely aware of the need not to rock the boat, for Lionel had built it. For their part, they appeared unsure whether this chap was the complete ticket or was there a hidden agenda? For me, there was the certain knowledge that they could tear me limb from limb with consummate ease without even pausing for breath, use my arms for paddles, throw me to the fish or retain me as on board cuisine however the whim took them. Mercifully, an icy squall enveloped us, breaking the train of thought. Thankfully, too, it hid our slow, embarrassing drift back to the island where, quite undaunted, Lionel awaited us with another idea. The sleet stopped as abruptly as it had begun but, suddenly, prudently perhaps, Lionel was gone. The chimps, though, were increasingly agitated (which made three of us!) for the water's surface was now being disturbed from within. Had Lionel done the honourable thing? If so, he was on his own, for this ship was not putting about for anyone! Suddenly, in a rush of putrid air, the remnants of our neighbour's pony, which had fallen through the ice the previous winter, surged to the surface 'ad nauseam'. The chimps shrieked in terror and, having capsized it by so doing, broke ship, braving the last few yards of water as they fled the sight and smell of this ghastly apparition of yesteryear. I was saved, or so it seemed, for a few short seconds. Lionel, it quickly transpired, had in fact decided discretion to be the better part of valour and had fled to the mainland, in the dinghy! Now I was simply stranded on the island with two chimps. We all got off in the end (on Lionel's day off!) and the chimps quickly settled into the winter routine. They quickly learnt to smoke, spit at you in the eye at ten paces, break wind assiduously and other unmentionable anti-social behaviour, all of which was firmly attributed to the influence of the visiting circus staff. Once banned, a certain degree of decorum was attained, but most crucially of all, they survived.

At least the chimps didn't escape, although other primates inevitably did. One did so almost incidentally on the roof of a double-decker bus. He seemed quite calm about the whole business, so laid back in fact that I instinctively ordered everyone out of sight to await developments. Sure enough, having first enjoyed a leisurely tour of the park, he climbed off the bus when it reached the car park and caught another, one that was going back in! Another character eluded us by climbing onto the perimeter fence and walking along it out of our reach for half a mile before climbing a signal gantry on the Severn Valley Railway.

He scanned the countryside to assess his options, oblivious to the timetable chaos he'd caused by swinging on the signal. Crossing the bypass via the railway bridge, he followed the footpath for a mile towards the chip shop so beloved by the sea lions of bygone years. Being a Monday, it was closed, so he spent the afternoon in the gardens of the neighbouring estate whose occupants jammed our switchboard with reports of his progress and activity. By tea time he was coming home, but was held up by the rush hour traffic on the bypass as he sought to recross it. By now, the switchboard callers were all from mobile 'phones. As the traffic abated, he crossed onto home soil and walked up the front drive making for the warmth in the roof of Spring Grove House. Doubtless, like any other self-respecting two hundred year old stately home, its walls could tell a tale or two but generally could be relied upon to keep its secrets. For Sue's fortieth birthday, I'd assembled a hundred and twenty people from all over the country - family, friends and acquaintances from way back when - for a dinner party in total secrecy. No one had breathed a word, so Sue hadn't the faintest inkling of what was to unfold when we popped into Spring Grove House one Saturday night with the children, ostensibly to pick up my keys. When I turned on the light, she had the shock of her life!

Surely, though, these passive walls had never witnessed the like of him before - or had they? The doves roosting in the attic blinked impassively at the intruder caught in the beam of my spotlight. For the first time that day, though, I sensed his unease. Agoraphobia? Claustrophobia? In a monkey? Or was it simply unnerved by our ever-present resident ghost? The origin of this lost soul is uncertain. Many years earlier, though, I'd unearthed a possible clue in the park grounds, a tombstone to Fido, a 'truſty' dog at Stanley 'Houſe' in 1795 'poisoned by some foul fiend'. Curiously, the last line disappeared from the inscription shortly after its discovery but, despite years of well-publicised enquiries, I've never found a trace of any such house. Is our lost form searching too? Is it the 'foul fiend' itself? The monkey appeared to think so. Sensing he was about to bolt, I aimed the dart pistol straight down the beam. Too late. Downstairs, a door slammed and the monkey was gone. Someone had ignored the warning to stay clear and was steadily climbing the stairs. Cursing my luck at this untimely intrusion, I swung back through the attic hatch to emerge blinking and sneezing on the landing in a whirlwind of feathers. If I'd expected to find someone standing there with his head under his arm, I was disappointed. There was nobody there at all.

The following morning, in pouring rain, I climbed out of the attic window onto the old stable roof to resume the chase, my dart eventually striking home hard and true. Feeling groggy, the monkey managed to evade us by retreating into the sanctuary of the heater ducting before the drug overwhelmed him. Below him in the restaurant, life carried on as normal, staff continuing to serve customers, all blissfully unaware of the drama unfolding directly above them. I could but pray that he remained continent! Awake again that afternoon and by now hungry, the lure of the vegetable store proved too much for him. The chef slammed the door, I unscrewed the door handle and another dart through the cavity completed the recovery.

Although escapees seldom venture far, having this amazing telepathy to navigate territory hitherto unknown to them and get home, there is always an exception to the rule. One such miscreant, a social outcast and the object of some bullying, simply put his head down one morning, charged a startled gateman and was gone. He didn't look back but simply ran and ran and ran. As I plotted all the sightings on the map, proceeding apace by the hour, I initially thought we had another mass outing on our hands as in 1974, but soon realised that this chap was no ordinary monkey. I was right - he proved very street wise indeed. In six weeks, I travelled over a thousand miles to places I'd never heard of in pursuit of this celebrity. He lived the life of Riley in the halcyon days of high summer along the Worcestershire/ Shropshire border. By day, he lived atop telegraph poles, pylons and telephone boxes, ever alert for the tell-tale zebra-striped jeep in vain pursuit. Every afternoon, the radio station chat shows 'phoned in for an update on his progress. By night, he swam in the river to cool off before coming ashore to be wined and dined in the riverside pubs and caravan sites as his celebrity status dictated. He wasn't the only opportunist afoot, however, and the claims came in his wake. One farmer attributed the disappearance of a

My dogs (Gin and Tonic!) beside the mysterious tombstone.
(Photo Author)

Haunted House? Spring Grove House. (Photo Author)

litter of piglets to the monkey, another a lake full of fish, yet another his tractor keys! When a householder's ceiling collapsed in a deluge, I was presented with the offending tile, which the monkey had dislodged earlier that summer! It couldn't last, though. Such indulgence was undermining his agility and ultimately proved his undoing. Late one sultry Sunday afternoon, after a high speed chase through the suburbs of Bridgnorth, Shropshire, his luck deserted him. He was surrounded on an eighty foot high factory rooftop twenty miles from home by every policeman in town, security staff, the fire brigade and with the police helicopter overhead spotting his every move. I climbed one-handed up a swaying fire escape, dart rifle in the other hand. Falling masonry sent the assembled crowd below scattering, shattered windows and betrayed my presence to 'Wrigglebottom', nicknamed thus by my daughter then and revealed at the risk of embarrassing her now. But there was no wriggling out of this one. Hanging on for grim death in the downthrust of the helicopter, I somehow aimed the rifle one-handed at the monkey, who was preoccupied with the same difficulty, and actually hit it - the monkey, that is, not the helicopter! The downforce of the helicopter now came into its own, being used to good effect to keep the tottering animal away from the edge until it reached full recumbency. Descent was an equally hazardous undertaking, gun in one hand, monkey under my arm, leaving just one hand free for the rusting handrail buckling under our combined weight. An impromptu photo call was followed by a dash for home. It proved a close-run thing. He awoke on the passenger seat beside me as I drove down the drive. After the inevitable blanket press coverage, the following day he was returned to the anonymity of the troop. There was no more bullying, he'd earned the respect of his contemporaries.

The easiest, quickest, yet most unthinkable way of bringing these rascals to heel would be to simply shoot them. Catching them live is infinitely more problematical. After an experiment with wallabies who, it belatedly transpired, could swim rather well, we restocked chimp island eventually with the tougher and hardier Barbary apes because of their alleged, indeed guaranteed, inability to swim. Some chance! They revelled in the water and escaped with complete impunity. They, too, had to go. As they swam ashore, they received a dart up the backside for their pains, in theory at least. One of the last led a charmed life. She fled up a tree one bleak January morning and stayed there. The dart rifle developed an intermittent fault and we spent all day spitting darts ineptly skywards at half power, which the ape caught, dismembered and dropped into the lake. So confident did it become that it soon stopped ducking or taking any form of evasive action when I raised the gun. As dusk enveloped the scene, we were down to our last dart and just time for one final attempt. It worked. With a shriek of indignation, she pulled the dart from her backside and, pausing only to throw it unerringly back at *me*, ran for home. Unfortunately, like many an elderly lady, she slipped on the ice in the dark and broke her arm, but at least she'd already been sedated and ended up beneath the X-ray machine with the minimum delay. She made a complete recovery.

It is uncanny how primates can calculate margins of safety, comfort and discretion. I spent an entire summer's evening helplessly watching one monkey on a Kidderminster rooftop. He sat comfortably in the lee of a chimney stack, a natural catchment area for the delicacies thrown up by housewives. In the sun, out of a chill wind and strategically right in front of an attic window, he knew full well I daren't aim a dart. I relieved the monotony by listening to the radio. He relieved himself regularly, straight down someone's chimney! Ultimately, the impasse was broken when the man of the house returned from work, visibly unimpressed at discovering his supper had been thrown on the roof for a monkey. Initially, I attributed the steam-filled kitchen to his amateurish attempts to replace it. When he burst through the French windows spluttering through the towel over his head, my mind turned briefly to asthma cures, a leaky CS spray in the policeman's holster even? Suddenly, I realised which chimney led where and discreetly beat a sharp exit. Curiously, so too did the monkey. For once, though, I was quickest - he followed hot on *my* heels! Whether he'd caught a whiff of his own stew and consequently become as disorientated as the man of the house I don't know, but this character remained elusive, continually circling the school and the housing estate for days as if lost. One night, as dusk was falling, I put a theory to the test. I let another one out! Sure enough, within twenty four hours they'd paired up by the reservoir, spent the morning chattering in someone's orchard, then the afternoon teasing someone's pony before heading off across the nature reserve with uncanny directness for home at tea time. (This was familiar territory for me, too. A year or so earlier, whilst attending a family funeral in Wales, my pager had gone off. A monkey had escaped and was wreaking havoc in a weekend scout camp. Having returned post haste, I led the search party in a sweep of the same woods, dart rifle in hand, still in my wedding suit!) As dusk fell at ten o'clock that midsummer's night, I sat in the watch tower, reflecting on the memory, as they scrambled back over the fence like naughty schoolboys, together.

Such incidents inevitably trigger memories hereabouts of what initially put us on the map back in 1974, the night the baboons got out. We'd been working late watching a calving antelope and the padlock hasp was through the gate but not fully pressed home. One enterprising baboon undid it and took his friends out for a night on the town, all one hundred and twenty of them! Inexplicably, few of our vehicles proved to have lights, fewer still of their drivers had licences, less still shotgun certificates. However, as this was an emergency, anything went, literally. Everything and anything on wheels was mobilised to pursue the baboons into Kidderminster, to what end I was never entirely sure - landrovers, tractors, our lorry, the coach, the ice cream van. After one circuit of the town centre, I quickly became lost. I'd never driven through the pedestrian precinct in the dark before. Feeling rather conspicuous in a brown and white spotted MkI Landrover without lights, road tax, MOT, insurance, a driver's licence or a shotgun certificate for my shotgun and two blanks, I'd turned into a timber yard to avoid a flashing blue light just in case he had nothing else to do. I lay low for an hour or two hoping for the coast to clear. It didn't. Shots echoed through the darkness, dogs howled and every light glowed. For one night at least, Kidderminster rivalled the Blackpool illuminations, although the latter couldn't begin to match it for sheer entertainment! All it needed, I felt, was for one of our boats to come down the adjoining canal, Old Bill at the helm. Although, with Lionel navigating, he'd probably end up in the North Sea. Eventually, on the stroke of midnight, an ice cream van came into view, as bizarre a sight as you'd ever wish to see. Its speaker jammed on, guns bristled from every window like a World War 1 'Q' boat - 'stop him to buy one' at your peril. But, yes, it was ours, being driven by one of the natives, so I followed it home; past the pub where the nightwatchman was still drinking himself into oblivion, past the crowds on every street corner beneath the dishevelled street signs and the suspiciously vandalised 'phone box. It had been a long night, an even longer day was to follow.

'Baboons Flee Colditz Park', screamed the national headlines even then being printed, though Colditz wasn't renowned for leaving the front door unlocked. Chaos had indeed reigned throughout the hours of darkness as everyone who had a weapon fired at anything that moved. The town's hedgehog population was decimated, traffic lights disabled and stray dogs returned home in droves to avoid annihilation. Miraculously, no one was injured, but dawn brought many wounded egos, shattered greenhouses, petitions to form vigilante groups for the protection of property and sackloads of firearm applications to arm them. Schoolchildren were to be locked in their classrooms, warned the radio stations as local residents assessed their options. Opinion appeared fairly equally divided. Some demanded a rate reduction whilst others thought it better than watching TV! Not so our then MP, Esmond Bulmer, or the leader of the district council whose own garden the baboons had tactlessly trashed. Two years later, he was to recount the evening in detail to the House of Commons during a debate on the Dangerous Wild Animals Act. He mentioned the sea lion run over by the police car, too, and a little matter of an escaped tiger being shot dead. Somehow, he'd got it into his head that the act hadn't gone far enough! He, though, could speak within parliamentry privilege. We couldn't. Indeed, if we did, it was pointed out that we, too, could fall beneath the hammer.

Meanwhile, my future wife and I turned off the electric fence, dumped piles of vegetables in the park hoping that the baboons were still hungry and sat back in the cold, grey light of dawn to await developments. Slowly they appeared out of the morning mist, trooping wearily home like a disgraced rugby side, evoking many a studenthood memory of infamous nights out on the town. They were cold, tired and hungry but as the sun rose, stimulating them into activity, their exuberant chatter drowned out the dawn chorus. They poured back over the fences all around us by the dozen. Soon they'd enriched their natural environment with mementos of a night of infamy. Shoes, garden gnomes, women's underwear, flowers and house names, to mention but a few, all adorned the park. Burdened down with bounty which they wouldn't drop, a handful of miscreants failed to rescale the fences and remained out. We camped out in the woods around the clock for six weeks occupying a network of hastily constructed tree-houses, mopping up and growing rich on overtime we weren't able to spend until it became official. They were all back. For ten years, however, rumours abounded of individuals living in some comfort on waste disposal sites, garden centres and the sugar beet factory, but these were never substantiated - officially!

There was, though, still to come a potential escape that would have done the occupants of Colditz proud. One summer's evening, the howling of the wolves alerted me to the plight of an ailing hot air balloon dragging through the tree-tops. Salvation for the crew appeared heaven-sent when a clearing opened up beneath them and down they came, straight into the monkey enclosure. The pandemonium in the basket had to be seen to be believed as one hundred and fifty baboons converged on it, but it generated sufficient hot air to get the balloon airborne again! They were lucky. For sheer destructiveness, monkeys have few equals. Their ability to dismantle cars is legendary, the object of considerable mirth to those within the sanctuary of a hired or company car, the subject of many a memorable TV commercial and, occasionally, even of some value. Our 'free return' tickets are authenticated by printing the car registration number on them upon issue to validate the return visit. In order to revisit in a larger car, thereby gaining free entry for extra family members, one enterprising schemer fixed his number plate onto another vehicle. However, he hadn't bargained on the monkeys. They ripped the number plate off revealing the original, whereupon the driver of the following car, assuming it to have been stolen, promptly rang the police on his mobile 'phone. He was caught red-handed!

The baboons frequently proved troublesome even when they stayed at home. The cold grey light of dawn one desolate

February morning revealed an eland calf secreted away amongst the gorse bushes beneath a mantle of frozen snow. Closed for the winter and without cars to tear apart, boredom probably accounted for their otherwise inexplicable attacks on the hapless calf. They attacked it remorselessly and without pity. Several times in the following days we were to fight pitched battles using blank rounds and thunderflashes as these ghastly creatures hurled themselves at our defensive cordon. Ultimately, however, we were reduced to defending ourselves, fighting back-to-back in a tense battle of self preservation. Thus distracted, the baboons broke through to inflict fearful wounds on the dazed calf which required stitching. It was by now pitch dark, raw cold, but at least the freshening wind persuaded the baboons to withdraw before the drifting snow. There was little alternative but to extract the calf, preferably with its mother. No easy task this for, despite their size, these huge antelope, Africa's largest, are extremely agile, can leap prodigiously and, by virtue of the huge horns sported by both sexes and unpredictable temperament, are extremely dangerous. Warmth and sanctuary were but two hundred yards away as the flamingo flew, but half a mile or so by foot through deep snow and a reserve full of animals. After the day's trauma, there was no prospect of moving them in tandem so we bore the calf off in a landrover and returned for the mother. It was a desperately dangerous task separating her from the herd in the darkness but, eventually, I lured her away with a food bag through the first gate and set off across the reserve.

It was an eerie and unforgettable experience. Overhead, the sky cleared revealing a full moon and twinkling stars but, at ground level, walking into the teeth of the wind brought the drifting snow directly into my streaming eyes, reducing visibility to near zero. It obscured my vision and muffled the sound of curious activity around us. On we walked, the eland with her nose in the bag, succumbing to my bluff and oblivious, it seemed, to all else. Peculiar shadows danced across the snow as startled camels lurched to their feet and trotted clumsily away. The furious drumming of hooves betrayed the zebras' presence as they pounded excitedly about us, almost drowning the unmistakable but indignant snorts of the wildebeest annoyed at being disturbed. Throughout all this, the majestic bison sat unperturbed as we passed them by. Motionless, their vast bulk encased by snow, they might have escaped notice were it not for the twin geysers of warm air gushing from their nostrils which alone betrayed them. Only once did the eland and I lose contact but, during a lull in the wind, the clicking of her hooves betrayed her whereabouts and we were quickly reunited. The journey couldn't have taken long but it seemed an eternity before the stable block loomed above us from the shadows cast by an avenue of great, snow-laden lime trees. Mother and calf were reunited and, for me, quite the strangest walk of my life was over.

Boldness was to prove the baboons' undoing for they continued to disgrace themselves and us, far outstaying their welcome, and simply had to go. One evening, a huge articulated trailer arrived at the park. It was loaded with fruit and parked in the monkey enclosure. Most of the baboons swallowed the bait, hook, line and sinker and stormed inside, but some kept us on tenterhooks to the very end. The mature males, master strategists, were suspicious of this manna from heaven. They waited outside and stole from the more trusting as they emerged but, eventually, one by one, greed overcame them. When, ultimately, the dominant male appeared at the window making his traditional gesture of goodwill, a 'V' sign (a party trick he'd brought back from Kidderminster!), we knew we were home and dry. The trap door slammed shut and peace once again descended on this sleepy little riverside town in rural Worcestershire.

Another successful recapture from ominous portents came very late in the day. Bedridden, I'd waited in vain for the master keys to be dropped through the letter box at tea time. An hour on, I'd dispatched my wife to search for their temporary holder. Nothing. Dressed by now, I ventured out myself and found the holder's vehicle parked at a crazy angle across the road, doors open and personal effects strewn across the road. Having checked the hospitals, the first policeman on the scene shared my misgivings and called more help - the young lady had to be found.

Found she was, just as darkness fell, with a coachload of cadets en route to supplement the ad hoc search parties already out, with dog handlers converging on the scene from far and wide and a

An Eland 'Family'. (Photo Author)

*'Whiteout' for an American Bison, not in the Mid West but in the West Midlands!
(Photo Author)*

sombre-looking policeman poised at her parents' door. "What on earth are you doing?" asked the relieved policeman of the forlorn figure sitting in the middle of nowhere. She'd seen a monkey out, dropped everything, including her radio, and instinctively followed it, sitting beneath the tree into which it had climbed for the night to prevent it coming back down. "How long were you planning on sitting here?" asked another perplexed questioner, "What did you expect to happen?" "I don't know," came the subdued reply. Earlier that day, she'd brought the tranquilliser kit up to my bedroom for me to assemble the dart that enabled an animal to be treated. She knew, therefore, that I was in bed, scarcely able to move with a debilitating bout of rheumatoid arthritis but, she continued, "I just knew Bob would come and find me." I squirmed uncomfortably in my slippers as the assembled throng stared at me, clad in barely concealed pyjamas, and I at her in utter astonishment. Silhouetted by now against the moonlight, the monkey presented a fairly easy target for the requisite dart. It fell earthwards into a carpet of outstretched arms and we took them both home. And so we recaptured a monkey - and its keeper - by a blind act of faith which, half a lifetime later, is still being repaid.

Monkey Business!

MONKEY BUSINESS

The rhesus monkey decided to take a trip,
So, when the electric fence failed, he simply gave us the slip.
He headed for the woods and merrily swung about -
The sun shone brightly, didn't he just love being out!
Children rushed to him shouting and laughing with glee.
"Why are they so happy?" he chattered, "Is it to do with me?"
The wardens from the safari park tried to ensnare Jim,
But however hard they tried, they couldn't outwit him.
When a cream bun appeared, he consumed it with joy
Ignoring the baited banana, that age old safari ploy.
He laughed at outrunning them having enjoyed the fray.
"Come back when you're fitter," he called, "Try another day!"
Though he enjoyed the freedom and attention,
There came drawbacks no one had mentioned.
By night from the monkey reserve echoed distant chatter galore,
Much ado about cars, aerials, wing mirrors and more.
Was he so wise in his bid to be free?
Surrounded by acre upon acre of empty forestry,
His return was greeted by more than he thought....
They all wanted to know about the freedom he'd sought.
He told of his times abroad and why he'd come back -
Cream buns are very nice but what of the things he'd lacked?
"Remain," Jim advised, "right where you abide,
For despite what they say, it's greener on the INSIDE!"

Poem by Bob Lawrence
Based on an original idea by Rita Hardiman, Kidderminster.

CHAPTER 8
A Day in the Life
(To Christopher and Nicola whose Dad is seldom there)

E ven in the half light, the ewe beneath the hedge looked uncomfortable. She put up little resistance as I caught her and addressed the breach birth. A sturdy enough single lamb ensued and I continued my way to work, my early start some farmer's good fortune. Dawn broke as I drove down the bypass, so, too, did my brakes. Using the gear box to slow down at 60mph., the strain proved the last straw for an ailing half shaft. It snapped and the back axle and nearside rear wheel detached - almost! Regaining control, I carefully nurtured it along the deserted road and limped into the park. The first cattle grid was its nemesis - the wheel fell right off. The slump to a crazy angle caused the front spring to snap for good measure. So far so good, but it was still only 5.15a.m. Like the farmers and gamekeepers in the surrounding hills whose lights were being dimmed by the red smudge in the east, our occupation, too, is more than just a job. It's a way of life, as frenetic and all-consuming as any. There is rarely time to drift down memory lane, time to reflect on what you've done or where you're going. Occasionally, though, something happens to jerk the memory. Once, while we were all tackling something 'en masse', one of the girls mentioned her year of birth. Looking about me, I quickly realised that none of those present were even born when I began working at the park. Sombre reflection indeed! The girl in question had been going out with one of the elephant keepers for some years and seemed set to follow a long tradition in such matters. Over half a dozen or so of the keepers have ended up with partners who'd arrived at the

Opposite Page:
My daughter helps me feed 'Wendy' the giraffe.
(Photo J. James, Birmingham Post and Mail)

park from schools or colleges, ostensibly to do work experience, and been snapped up! With everyone saving to get married to each other, things can get very confused. Having set the precedent, Sue and I certainly have a lot to answer for! Sometimes, Sue and I see parallels of them in us twenty five years ago. We were chatting about this one Sunday lunchtime when, for the first time in years, we managed to grab a pub lunch. Back home, as we sat wallowing in such unaccustomed good fortune, the 'phone rang. It was West Midlands police. A bull had escaped from a farm, swum a canal and was firmly established on a double main railway line in Walsall which had to be closed down. Could I help? Twenty minutes later, their helicopter put down by the house to whisk me away, dart gun and all, before the gaze of a highly impressed daughter. 'Game Warden is Bull Rescue Hero', sang the front page of the 'Express and Star' the next day but, by the time I'd got back home at 9p.m. that night, the time for reflection had long gone.

"Do you work here?" asked the woman of me as I sat in my zebra-striped jeep, "I'm looking for Bob Lawrence." "You're looking at him," I replied. "Where?" Well, to be fair, my name wasn't actually emblazoned all over this, my back-up vehicle, but we had met on three recce briefings before. This was the producer, after all, the one with the brains. "Worked here long?" she added, quite unabashed. "Twenty five years," I replied. "Do you like it?"(!) It was very early in the morning, but it was going to be a long day.

The production company had hired the lion reserve for a film sequence. During the season when we are open, the public come first and, however lucrative such extra-mural side shows are, they have to be accommodated within this criterion, hence the early start. They had until 10a.m. to finish then the lions were coming out into the public domain, come what may! Film work is invariably presumed to be exciting, glamorous even. It isn't. A ninety second sequence can take hours from its inception with the arrival of the prop men, through all the pandering to the army of hangers-on, the countless retakes ('Take 33' on one notorious occasion!) to the clipperboard coming down for the last time. Then there's the problem of dealing with huge egos, invariably with double-barrelled names, who are 'famous' but whom you've never heard of. At least with this particular shower, the pressure was off to the extent that it wasn't for live transmission. That is where the men are sorted out from the boys, a pressure-charged atmosphere with little margin for error - one that I relish for it presents a real challenge - but even earlier starts. One live Channel 4 'Big Breakfast' outside broadcast meant a 4a.m. start after working until 9p.m. the previous evening laying out the set, then a gruelling unremitting schedule until noon. Then they'll disappear as quickly as they came without so much as a thank you or a handshake. Today, however, such an overrun couldn't happen. We were all out on cue at 9.55a.m. sharp, the lions hot on our heels at 10a.m. as required. They were away out my of hair by 11a.m. leaving me to begin my day proper. I'm always being asked to describe a typical day. Typically there is no such thing.

And so to the dentist. Much maligned and on the verge of total inertia, the dental service was under fire from all quarters. Despite its bad press, I'd got my appointment readily enough - excellent service too, for peanuts. Today was crunch day, however, as the legacy of a kick in the face during my last cup final caught up with me. But, with a hemline like hers, my admirable dentist took seven teeth from me quite painlessly and in double-quick time for it was my turn on 'Hippo Watch'.

When Windsor Safari Park closed in 1992, relocation of their four common hippo (a CITES Appendix II species) was high on the list of problems. At a meeting to arrange the transfer of some other animals (we were ultimately to take Bactrian camels, lions - together with their keepers - Barbary sheep, Hog deer and sika deer), my attention became focused firmly on their plight. With this in mind, I'd studied one of our existing two hundred year old lakes of 'Capability Brown' vintage. Measuring 180m by 22m by 1.5m deep when full, one of them had given continual problems with a succession of severe droughts reducing the water table and causing permanent damage to the waterproof membrane. We'd sunk our own borehole nearby with authority to pump five million gallons per annum to maintain water levels. This was intended principally for aesthetic purposes, but the potential for hippos was irresistible. The Windsor liquidators bought my idea lock, stock and barrel and stumped up the cash for it! We built the hippo

Opposite:
The police helicopter
arrives at home, whisking
me away to exotic Walsall!
(Photo Author)

Hippo and new born calf.
(Photo Author)

Mud, mud, glorious mud.
Part of our extended hippo
'family' in typical pose.
(Photo Author)

house, fenced the lake in and one Harvey, Boris, Gertie and Bar-bel duly arrived. It was to prove a far-sighted acquisition. They've proved one of the best and most publicised groups of animals in the park's history. A cynical marketing man would add that they've proved to be worth their huge bulk in gold. He'd be wrong - to us they're priceless.

Mating activity was noted in 1993 and, although the eight month gestation period came and went, I remained convinced that both females were in calf. My concern lay primarily with the possible reaction of Boris who remained strongly attached to his dam Bar-bel. Accordingly, I separated the two cows off for parturition. Unfortunately, they'd demonstrated their intelligence by undoing the gate and going back. Thus forewarned of our intentions, they couldn't be separated again before a birth did in fact occur, under water to Bar-bel. My fears about Boris were justified and a round-the-clock vigil proved necessary to keep him at bay. His intentions were unclear and not necessarily vindictive but, in the absence of any constructive advice from other collections unused to such numbers, I couldn't take the risk.

And so we camped out on the lakeside, a bag of potatoes on our laps, watching for Boris. Every time he came close, he received a potato firmly on the end of his nose to encourage him to keep his head down. Given potato prices at the time, it proved an expensive yet highly effective deterrent in the short term, and an essential one. On the second night, prolonged violent distress from Gertie indicated a further birth. Sure enough, daylight revealed a second calf, her first, and an utterly exhausted mother totally dependent on our protective screen. An ecstatic David Chorley, now Managing Director, had just time to see his first-born hippo before going stateside on holiday. On arrival, he was greeted by a fax from me saying he now had two hippo calves! Keeping them alive, however, was to prove problematical. Day three gave further concern. Bar-bel gave every indication of being in oestrus. It was not what the text books indicated, but it made for deterring an amorous male even more difficult. More so, as the potato trick and the supply were wearing thin. He'd soon learnt that he only had to be a nuisance and he got fed!

On the brink of exhaustion, that night we mounted a final supreme effort. It was all hands to the pumps. Shouting ourselves hoarse, with PA systems and car horns blaring, we finally drove Boris out of this section of lake beneath a barrage of potatoes, turnips, swedes and cabbages. It took the hippo herd the remainder of the night to consume the detritus of this titanic onslaught, but it was worth it. It left both mothers and calves alone in peace and ready for an invasion of visitors, public and media alike. Front pages beckoned, the TV crews drooled. Despite weighing in at over 70lb. each (the weight of one and a half sacks of potatoes!), they were everyone's sweethearts, endearing themselves to one and all. With characteristic intelligence, they sensed this, played to the gallery and thrived on the attention. It came from far and wide. Satisfied that everything was up and running, the following year I entered the hippo complex in the UFAW (Universities Federation for Animal Welfare) national competition for zoo exhibits. We came second. Jersey Wildlife Preservation Trust quite rightly won it with an outstanding 'Home Habitat' for Sumatran Orang-utan but, considering it had cost about £600,000 compared with just £30,000 for our hippo, we ran them close.

In the meantime, however, the children had come down to help me feed Wendy. Although born and bred on the park, we'd outgrown the two-bedroomed house provided on site. With school age approaching, we were looking for the traditional little village school where teaching wasn't a 9-4p.m. chore but rather a dedicated way of life. Some years earlier, we'd bought an overgrown ten acre field a few miles up the road. We'd built a barn, kitted it out with stables for the horses and dug a large fishing pool in the centre to drain the whole site. When the old man in the cottage over the road died and his family put it on the market, it seemed too good an opportunity to miss. One night, then, I found myself at a property auction in a local pub. Without a penny in my pocket, I'd just bid £20,000 for it when the hammer fell. I wrote the cheque for the deposit and went into the bar to think how I could find the money before it was presented! Fortunately, a friend came to the rescue with the deposit until I could find a mortgage. It had dry rot, wood rot, no damp course, every window and door frame needed replacing, as did the chimney, stairs and the roof. There was one cold water tap above a bucket and the loo was in the old pigsty at the bottom of the garden. It was, though, a start - of sorts.

The renovation was the usual nightmare but, at least, unlike many, we weren't living in it or a caravan while we worked. The builder toiled manfully but the 'architect' had made a complete hash of it and soon the budget had gone. It took years of (successful) litigation to resolve but, in the meantime, it was left to us to finish it - inbetween the day job. On completion, the surveyor's figures indicated that we'd completed £40,000 worth of work ourselves. Shortly afterwards, a sceptical bank manager converged on us to query the valuation in person. Reluctantly, he acquiesced, theorising that if we'd built ourselves a house worth £60,000 and still only had a £30,000 mortgage, we hadn't done too badly for ourselves. Come the time, we sold it for £160,000. In the meantime, though, living off site provided just a small margin of detachment from the park when off duty, though it was never far away, physically or mentally, and well within radio range in those pre-mobile 'phone days. So, if Mohammed couldn't go to the mountain, the roles could be reversed and the children could still return to their second home to enjoy the run of a deserted site at night or lend a helping hand. Wendy was quite a handful so the extra pairs of hands often proved invaluable. Every evening when we drove down, we noted a little black rabbit. It sat on the verge waiting to cross the road in exactly the same place at exactly the same time. Soon the superstition arose with the children that, as long he made it, Wendy would survive too. It remains the case to this day.*

Born a few weeks earlier to an apparently uncaring mother who'd stubbornly ignored her first two calves, this calf, too, was faring little better. Hand rearing seemed the only alternative and I the one to do it as she took an instant liking to me. Why not? I had nothing else to do! I decided to do so whilst leaving her with her mother in an attempt to stimulate some parental instincts. I'd been warned that getting her to accept a bottle might take three days. It took three months. In the meantime, it was a stomach tube every six hours, day or night, come dentists, hippo, hell or high water - a labour of love that succeeded in both ensuring the survival of the calf until maturity and of instilling a mothering instinct in the parent which served her well in subsequent deliveries. Wendy, one of our pride and joys, is a giraffe.

It was 3a.m. when I turned for home. The man at the all-night filling station had seen the hippo calves on TV that evening and insisted on telling *me* all about them. The girl in the take-away had seen the giraffe calf in the evening paper and wanted a YTS placement the summer after next. The patrol car on the bypass pulled me over just to ask how the hippo 'twins' were faring - he'd missed the news before coming on duty. There was no escaping who or what I was. In the moonlight 'my' ewe and lamb appeared content as I passed them by, contemplating another run-of-the-mill day at the office. The dentist's aspirin rattled in my pocket, just in case I couldn't sleep! I could, but not for long. Wendy's next feed was at 6a.m. and then it was off to Whipsnade to collect some deer.

Fortunately, when the call came I was only thirty miles away, still ensnared in the congestion that I'd sought to evade by the early start. There'd been a break-in. The keys, the radios, the vehicle keys and a vehicle were missing. The drug and firearm facilities appeared intact but obviously everything was going to need checking in minute detail. I called the police and turned for home. I was back for 8.30. The place was cleared by the police within an hour or so and we began to clear up and start the day's work - then we found the hand grenade. We'd had the bomb scares at the park before, of course, and, in light of contemporary intelligence, had occasionally been warned to check under the car in the morning and not to open suspicious packages. So, the man from special branch was a familiar face. So, too, were most of the local uniforms, CID and dog handlers converging on us from as far afield as North Wales and Stafford. The police helicopter overhead made conversation difficult as we awaited the bomb squad and wondered just how much all this nonsense was costing. At the end of the day, however, there was little else to do but wait.

That area of the park had proved to be a crime hot spot. A year or so earlier, a gang of would-be thieves had been disturbed trying a cunning little scam on the one-arm bandits in the amusement arcade. When challenged, they'd scattered and run. One had scaled the perimeter animal fence and fled across the reserve with me in pursuit. When he began to enter the next reserve without showing any signs of tiring, I thought things were getting a little out of hand and a flying tackle brought him to the ground. As I sat on him awaiting reinforcements, I was astonished to hear him read me my rights! Furthermore, his claims to be a minor were a little hard to countenance for he was over six feet tall. It transpired that he was in fact under age, well known to the police as a streetwise criminal. It was, I was advised, just as well I hadn't hit him when he drew the knife on me! Shortly afterwards, we'd received a tip-off about the intentions of some other gentlemen towards the same place. Forewarned is forearmed, though, and my knowledge of the lie of the land in the small hours was more than sufficient to ensure that they were caught with the jemmy in the safe door and imprisoned. Others fared little better. In one instance, a trail of melting, stolen ice cream led police straight to the culprit's home as soon as dawn broke. Another die-hard criminal dropped his wallet at the scene of his break-in! It didn't contain enough to pay the fine.

And so, accompanied eventually by a 'gentleman from Hereford', I walked into the office area to assess the situation. The grenade appeared genuine enough nestling amongst the petrol cans, so was accorded the respect it demanded. Thankfully, although it was real, it was already disarmed. It was a hoax designed to do just what it inevitably had done - create chaos. It was 3.30p.m., though, before the area was cleared and we started the day (again) and another late finish for everyone. The alleged culprit was engaged on such a crime spree at the time that a trivial little incident like this never even merited a mention on the charge sheet. Such is our current sense of values. Thus ended another day in the life of a Worcestershire whitehunter, or so I thought. That night at home, the sheep started lambing - while we waited for a mare to foal!

*When Wendy came in for the night one Saturday evening in July, 1999, she became extremely ill. She had eaten or had been fed something foreign to her. Despite every effort, she died just three hours later. As I drove home that night, a black rabbit lay dead at that same spot.

CHAPTER 9
Waiting for Lucy
(To the ghosts of things past)

We were waiting for Lucy. It had been a typical, overcast December day, chilly but not unpleasantly so if you remained active. At 4.30, however, as darkness fell, the cloud cover broke to reveal a full moon in a clear sky. Suddenly, it turned very cold indeed. The mist began to rise from our low-lying lakes and the frost pockets within the woodland. The fallen leaf canopy beneath us first stiffened then began to crackle underfoot as the frost hardened - and we waited for Lucy.

All day long, the pride of lions had been unusually active. Lions are lazy creatures at the best of times. Ours are no exception, for well-fed lions in captivity will spend up to 90% of their time sleeping and lying about in the sun, secure in the knowledge that their next meal is guaranteed. Not for them the worries of climate, availability of food supply, predation, illness and disease which are the inhibiting factors determining the longevity of animals in the wild. In colder or wet conditions not conducive to such idleness, younger lionesses and cubs are noticeably more active. And so, all day long they had stalked each other, chased leaves fluttering in the slipstream of passing cars and twigs falling from the trees. They also indulged in another favourite pastime - chasing rabbits.

It's most noticeable that when flushed out and subjected to the terrifying pressure of being pursued by a lion, a rabbit usually bolted uphill. Similarly, they would usually run up the tarmac road deviating neither to left or right, as they will on occasions to shake

Opposite Page:
Burchells Zebra at West Midlands Safari Park. (Photo Author)

off a dog. Perhaps, sensing their predicament, they reckon on a slightly greater turn of speed on the flat; maybe they realise that one stumble on uneven ground will be fatal or, more logically perhaps, they are terrified beyond the bounds of reasoned behaviour, for their survival chances are at best only 50/50. The problem was that at the top of the hill were the exit gates. On several occasions, a startled gateman had seen a rabbit streak between his legs and through the gate. His astonishment quickly gave way to terror as he looked up to see the lion bearing down on him! His frenzied efforts to slam the gate shut were a source of constant amusement to those watching from afar. Whether the lion, intent on his prey, ever even noticed the gateman is perhaps debatable, but no one ever put it to the test. For the rabbit, though, there was little respite or time to draw breath on the other side, for further perils awaited them - deer! Many's the time over the years I've seen deer, our wapiti in particular, eat a rabbit. Clearly the lot of the safari bunny is not a happy one.

Lucy had chased her rabbit up the hill and, although the rabbit had squeezed to safety beneath the gate, she'd been unable to stop as the gate was swung energetically shut and had crashed headlong into it. Shaken and bemused by the disappearance of prey from beneath her very nose, she had wandered back down the hill in the middle of the road. The squeal of a car taking avoiding action finally unnerved her completely and she scrambled up the nearest tree. Initial attempts at dislodgement served only to drive her further up, right into the crown of the tree some fifty feet in the air. We took it in turns to retreat to the office and 'phone wives, mothers and girlfriends with various excuses to delay dinners and dates, for it was obviously going to be a very late homecoming this Sunday night. The looks on the returning faces showed the tale to have been greeted with universal scepticism. There was nothing for it, though, but to retreat a discreet distance and wait, in vain it seemed, for Lucy.

The full moon shone brightly in the cloudless sky heavy with twinkling stars. The mist pockets apart, it picked out the wintry scene in vivid detail. The night was strangely still. One could almost sense the creatures of the night sitting in the sidelines, tense with anticipation and having second thoughts on their sense

Lioness with rabbit. (Photo Author)

Wapiti Hind eating a rabbit. (Photo Author)

of timing for, eerily, it was now as bright as day. The moon shone directly into my cab invading my dog's privacy causing her to shift and whimper uneasily. Suddenly, she stiffened, ears erect. Seconds later, I heard it too. From an inauspicious low-pitched moan across the park, the wolf launched his woeful lament at the full moon. The sound lingered hauntingly yet beautifully on the still night air echoing up the Severn Valley and across the Wyre Forest. It wasn't difficult to imagine superstitious country folk in bygone years checking the door bolts and stoking their fires at such a sound. In my mind's eye I could picture him, a magnificent 130lb. beast astride the hilltop surveying the world at his feet. Doubtless, his refrain stirred a few ghosts, for the Wyre Forest, one of Britain's oldest tracts of woodland, has probably seen the likes of him before. It made little impression on our lion, however, and still we waited for Lucy.

The harsh staccato bark of a baboon broke the resumed silence; a camel moaned softly; in the buildings below us, an elephant trumpeted as someone entered his domain. He would reach out with his trunk for the light switch to see who was there. The beam of light streaming through the skylight startled the tawny owl on the cowling of the building's extractor fan. It swooped unwittingly towards us until it spotted something seriously amiss in the tree ahead. Everything seemed on edge, tense with expectancy, as if the unnatural brightness heralded some truly portentous event or maybe the creatures of the night were, like us, simply waiting for Lucy.

A fox barked in the coppice causing an uneasy stirring amongst the mallard congregating in the centre of the frozen lake. Even the white peafowl roosting some twenty feet up a tall pine screeched in protest at the menace below, likewise the guinea fowl on a lower bough who were always the more vulnerable. Our resident barn owl ghosted silently by, relishing no doubt some easy pickings in such visibility. Then the donkey neighed in the children's zoo. It invariably irritated the park's entire population, man and beast alike. We all knew what was coming. The initial outburst from a solitary individual was quickly taken up by the entire lion pride in unison, bar one of course, and for twenty

Opposite Page:
Waiting for Lucy? (Photo Author)

minutes they strove to outdo each other in a thunderous exhibition of roaring that I knew could be heard for ten miles under such conditions. The echoes reverberated back from the surrounding hills intermingled with the lowing of the Highland cattle whom it had awoken. It triggered a belated roar in reply, too, from the red deer stags. Shorn of velvet, their antlers glistened in the moonlight like the bayonets of an advancing army as they crested the skyline to investigate. Centuries ago, the ranges of deer and lions overlapped. Even today, some subconscious primeval instinct still tells the deer that the smell of a big cat spells trouble. Belatedly, this fact has been 'discovered' by scientists who've recreated the essential odours artificially and now market proprietary lion manure to deter deer from forestry plantations, gardens and the like. You cannot beat the real thing, however, and the demand always exceeds supply. It undoubtedly works, as it does, too, against domestic cats, foxes and even badgers. You only have to tread in it to understand why - certainly no one ever brings it back! The cacophony of echoes faded having excited no reaction, so still we waited for Lucy.

Through the stillness of the night, I could hear my other dog at home yelping for her companion. The response from the zebra was immediate, their shrill, sharp yelps not entirely dissimilar. Of all the equines, zebra are obviously the most distinctive, yet it is often forgotten that the prominent pattern is, in fact, camouflage. Like giraffe patterns and tiger stripes, each animal is unique, the stripes like nature's form of fingerprinting. The Royal Navy, no less, took a leaf from nature's book during two world wars. Warships in the Mediterranean theatre were often daubed in an apparently highly conspicuous pattern of white alternating with various shades of blue and black. Viewed in the right conditions, these break up outlines perfectly as they do on the zebra, blurring the body outline to a prospective predator when it is on the move. In cover, too, the outline is disrupted but, most remarkable even in this country, is the sight of a zebra on a truly hot day. In the shimmering heat caused by atmospheric disturbances and overheating of the earth's surface, zebra can vanish into thin air before one's very eyes. It makes you look twice at night, too, and on several occasions I've had recourse to using the dog to find them at all. Remembering their response to a dog, an unlikely affinity if ever there was one, I've flushed them out and brought them into the yards at night using the dog as a lure. House dog, gun dog, sheep dog, guard dog, my then faithful old spaniel cross had the distinction of being a zebra dog, just for good measure! As a puppy, she'd even slept on my lap during my mis-spent youth as I read Alistair Mclean's novel 'Ice Station Zebra', but nothing could have prepared either of us for this! I couldn't dare, however, risk her as a lion dog so still we waited for Lucy.

Frustrating though it was, there was little else to do - the fire brigade wouldn't have been amused! A lion's claw is well adapted for climbing, but getting down again is another matter. The claws, being inverted, offer little purchase. All the lion can do is to lower itself clumsily down backwards, an embarrassing undertaking for such an athlete and one they clearly don't relish, for it can take them hours to pluck up the courage to attempt it. Sedation is invariably impractical. Even if it proves possible to hit the lion through the canopy of leaves and branches in the failing light (and you're in trouble if you don't for the dart can fall straight back on you!), there still remains the difficulty of getting the lion out of the tree. If, sedated, she falls, the thud of 400lb. hitting the ground from fifty feet is truly awful and capable of causing serious injury. Alternatively, and equally dangerously, a lion can become lodged in a bough. Someone then has to climb up, praying that the lion is as groggy as it appears, rope it and lower it down. I'd been there, done all that and cannot recommend it but, by now, it was pitch dark in the shadow of the trunk. We could but wait.

It was early morning before Lucy stirred. With all the curiosity so typical of the cat family, she finally found the fascination of the ever-whitening frosty world glistening beneath her in the light of the full moon irresistible. As she descended, we deployed rapidly, someone parked beneath every tree. We would look very silly indeed if she climbed another! Within minutes of the bolt sliding shut on the lion house, the entire scene was enveloped in an impenetrable, swirling mass of chilling vapour. So cold was it that we gasped as we stepped from our vehicles with running eyes and it chilled us to the marrow as we trudged belatedly home. Dawn, in fact, came almost imperceptibly that day. An early flight of Canada geese winged in over the house to land on the big lake, as

Highland cow with calf.
(Photo Author)

Red deer stag roaring.
(Photo Author)

Ice station zebra! (Photo Author)

yet not totally iced in. Their landing startled a pair of great crested grebes on an early morning fishing foray into an undignified crash dive. Beneath the surface they lost contact and reappeared out of sight of each other on opposing sides of 'chimp' island. Heads erect, their distinctive 'croaking' recognition call carried far across the still waters as they sought contact, adding a further unusual dimension to the sounds of the night. Closer to hand, the mallard became more vocal out on the ice as they began their daily routine. This invariably, in such conditions, brought them ashore to forage for acorns beneath the thick carpet of oak leaves. Later, when my work force were abroad, they would waddle behind the landrovers plundering anything dropping from them. The milkman's float crawled its way carefully up the frozen track after me. Seconds after he'd left, a magpie appeared and, with quite impertinent aplomb, proceeded to shred the milk tops. Before he could avail himself of the contents, however, there was a great jarring noise from upstairs and he fled. The alarm had gone off before I could get to bed. So began Christmas Eve.

Today, Lucy and the remainder of her pride have long gone, travelling to pastures new on the other side of the world. The tree, an elm, has long since succumbed to its inevitable diseased fate. Not even its stump remains. But for the memories, it is indeed as if the entire incident has been swallowed up in the mists of time.

CHAPTER 10
Time Stood Still
(To Lady Luck who smiled that day)

I t was 6.45a.m. on Friday May 7th, 1976. Like much of the preceding forty eight hours, it remains firmly etched in my memory. My alarm clock/radio awoke me as usual to the voice of a BBC presenter reading 'Today's Papers'. "All the papers carry pictures of Wednesday's horrifying incident at the West Midland Safari Park, Worcestershire," he said. Suddenly, I was wide awake, sat bolt upright in bed. Downstairs the letterbox rattled as our newsagent, a good friend, began pushing every edition of every national paper through the door. 'Grabbed from the Jaws of Death', 'Terror in Safari Park', 'Wife Savaged by Lioness' and 'Fangs for the Memory' from the Sun (yes, they were awful even then!) - screamed just some of the headlines hitting me full in the face with the memories of the last forty eight hours. We were used to publicity in the normal course of events and certainly the regional media had gone to town on the story, but this really was something else !

A local housewife, a Mrs. Carter, had won a 'Grant a Wish' competition with the nearby Halesowen Round Table to meet a lion - all fairly innocuous, routine stuff and someone had agreed to do it. I had Suzi and Suki, two juvenile lions hand reared at home from day-olds and born from a lioness who had herself been hand reared. Brought up with the bottle-fed lambs, the fox cubs, the wolf cubs and our Labrador's puppies, they'd slept

Opposite Page:
Suzi and Suki. (Photo Author)

beside our bed by night and ridden the landrover by day. The only hint of danger had stemmed from their habit of chewing the knob atop the gear stick. Many's the time a sudden gear change was only achieved by a sharp tug of a lion cub's neck! They were familiar with TV studios, press calls, banquets, fêtes, schools and agricultural shows. They had starred in many a cinema foyer as 'Born Free' was showing and been handled by thousands. Still daft as brushes at fifteen months old, they were, however, by now confined to a reserve with a pride of seventeen other hand reared cubs. They seemed the ideal choice, sociable and compliant, but we made the classic mistake of a romp too far. Inevitably, one day they would demonstrate that they weren't playthings but lions. We should all have known better.

The group assembled about 3p.m. that Wednesday afternoon; Mrs. Carter, a representative from the Round Table, and the photographers from the area's two principal regional newspapers, The Birmingham Post and Mail (John James) and The Wolverhampton Express and Star (Frank Rodgers). With the three of them safely shut in their cars, lenses at the ready, I called the cubs up. They came readily, arching their backs about our legs and rolling over to get their tummies tickled. Suddenly, though, Suki, marginally the smaller of the two, sat up on her haunches in a begging posture placing a paw on each of Mrs. Carter's shoulders for balance. She licked her neck once, twice, sniffed the afternoon air, then slowly, deliberately, unbelievably, sank her teeth deep into her victim's throat. I heard a sickening crunch as the skin was pierced and the canine teeth met inside the flesh.

Time stood still. Something had gone dreadfully wrong but we were all rooted to the spot. My life flashed before me, but quickly the stunned silence was punctuated by the clattering of camera shutters as two highly professional photographers swung into action. Subconsciously, the sound must have galvanised me, for someone moved in and tried to support the weight of the pair of them. Suddenly, I realised it was me. Two years earlier, when working on a lion house, I'd heard a shouted warning and turned to see a young lion flying at me in mid-air. Instinctively, I'd flung up my arms, my hands landing on its throat and simply hung on. With the desperation born of necessity, I'd found the strength to hold it at arm's length, its flailing legs out of reach of my body until it went limp. Subconsciously, again, that experience may have saved the day now.

Mrs. Carter had fainted immediately, such was the vice-like grip on the throat. Desperately, I tried to prise open the jaws with one hand whilst maintaining a grip on the lion's neck with the other to prevent any pulling or tearing action, all the time trying to keep the three of us on our feet. Frantic though my efforts were, they were pathetically and hopelessly inadequate against such awesome power. From the corner of one eye, I saw my future wife hopping about on one leg, clutching the other. Such had been her haste to get through the gate and help, she'd wrenched an ankle in the cattle grid. She was not pleased! Eventually, by accident or design, I got one hand in the side of the lion's mouth, grabbed the tongue and hung on. Hung on while she kicked and scratched, hung on when the three of us fell to the ground, hung on when Suzi joined the 'fun'. I lashed out desperately at her with both feet, brutally inflicting any damage I could for the chips were down, the fate of all four of us suddenly and inexorably linked. Stung by such unaccustomed treatment, she at least backed off, yet circled us awaiting another opening.

How long that desperate struggle lasted, no one present ever knew, but as I looked into the victim's glazed eyes I thought it was a forlorn one. She later confessed to thinking she was dead. So did I. Aroused by the noise from their afternoon siesta in the shade of the hedge, I could see the other seventeen lions rising to their haunches and begin to stalk us. We had just seconds to get out. Mercifully, a by now semi-conscious Suki finally let go, freeing my hand and the radio to summon help. Mightily mangled by now and awash in saliva, it spluttered, crackled, then worked. If the static didn't set the spine tingling back at base, my message certainly did. Released now from that savage, unremitting pressure, Mrs. Carter herself stirred. Maybe there was a way out after all, but there was no time to stand on ceremony as I grabbed her and pushed her into the nearest car. We left the scene as if there was no tomorrow - there nearly hadn't been.

Whilst awaiting the ambulance, the then park manager tried to persuade the photographers to part with their film. We didn't, after all, want this sort of publicity, did we? Some chance! Tyres smoked as they raced each other up the drive to fight over the nearest 'phone box, not one wheel remaining on the ground as they crested the hill, neck and neck. It was literally a case of stopping the presses for all the expense it entailed. They'd got the scoop of a lifetime with undoubtedly some of the most dramatic pictures ever taken of a lion attack. That night, I visited Mrs. Carter with her husband as she recovered from an exploratory operation. The teeth had met in her throat, touching the jugular without piercing it. It had been as close as that. At that point, the door was kicked in, there was a flash and a photographer from the Daily Express fled having disgraced himself.

As I contemplated all this spread across the bed before me, the 'phone rang. It was my mother. "It's all very well them going on about this woman escaping with her life," she said, "but not one of the papers says how you are. Are you all right?" Suddenly, I realised I hadn't got a scratch! It was simple, 'I'd told the TV crews. I'd been there, knew what to do and did it. Utter nonsense, of course, but it saved a lot of explanation.

Within days, the letters and cuttings were coming from overseas, too. What on earth would our powers that be 'stateside' say when they opened their New York Times? An anxious wait beside the giant telex machine ensued, but I needn't have worried. 'Upon reflection, it seems clear that Bob Lawrence reacted in a very effective and courageous way during a crisis of considerable magnitude,' our President said from Miami. 'Please convey to him my sincere gratitude and compliments for the way he handled the situation.' Not to be outdone, the Chairman of the Board in New York wasn't slow in coming forward either. He, too, had read the clippings from around the world, he professed. My 'spontaneous heroic actions had undoubtedly saved the life of Mrs. Carter', he wrote. To me, he sent 'his praise and gratitude' until such time as he could do so in person, which he did the following month. The praise was embarrassing and both the photographers and I laid low for a week or so while the fuss subsided. One day, I even found myself parked next to John James in a Bewdley back street, both waiting in tandem for the coast to clear before attempting to shop without attracting attention! It did have one tangible benefit,

Time stands still - the moment of horror. Some of the pictures that flashed around the world. (Photo F. Rogers, Express and Star)

The struggle for survival. (Photo J. James, Birmingham Post and Mail)

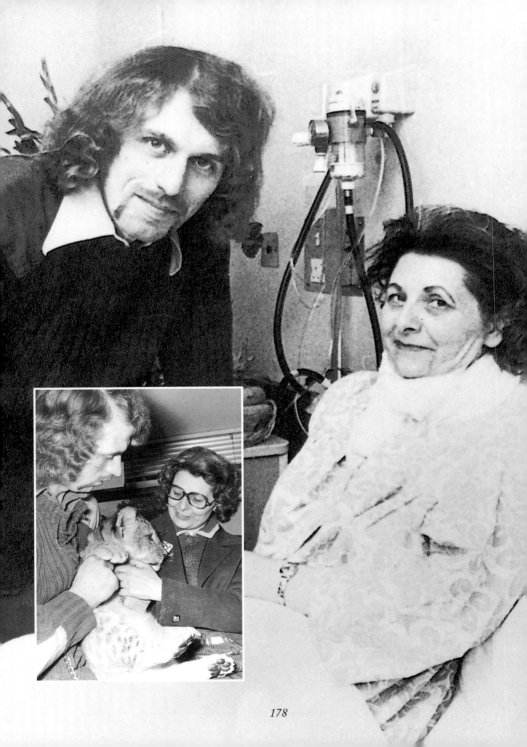

however. The focus on my actions deflected an awful lot of the awkward questions for all of us. From part-villain then to hero, but I could have done without it.

Two weeks later, undaunted and fully recovered, Mrs. Carter returned to try once again to meet a lion. This time, however, it was a very small one indeed, which I never let out of my arms. We never met again.

Opposite Page:
We meet again that same evening - in hospital and
(inset) 2 weeks later with a rather smaller cub.
(Photos Express and Star)

CHAPTER 11
Fire
(To Hereford and Worcestershire Fire Brigade)

L ightning, it is often said, doesn't strike the same place twice. I've often had cause to reflect rather ruefully that the same cannot be said of fire. With the Severn Valley steam railway on one boundary, heathland (often tinder-box dry throughout the year) on another and a park frequently full of overheating vehicles, the capacity for combustion is ever present, indeed almost routine. On one afternoon, there were only three cars in the entire park - two of them caught fire! Occasionally, however, something happens to change the routine, like the evening when the nightwatchman's son set fire to each corner of the haybarn!

By 1975, we'd been lavishly re-equipped, out going the tractors for the patrol drivers. As a hardened veteran of eighteen months, I was one of the first to receive a landrover - ex-MOD, twenty five years old, hand painted in white with brown spots (presumably to resemble something African!) in Dulux household paint and, thankfully, at last equipped with two-way radios. Of such vintage, they were notoriously unreliable but when they did go, they were much quicker than a tractor, a mixed blessing in many respects. To feed the carnivores we had a metal cage which clipped onto the back of a short wheel-based landrover. It was loaded with meat, a keeper climbed inside and it was driven at breakneck speed through the reserves with both driver and passenger praying for reliability, whilst the latter frantically threw the meat out down a

Opposite Page:
The children (bottom) had been born and bred amongst the lions but had never seen a wild lion like this one in the Namibian bush (centre) much less a 'kill' like this in the Etosha Pan. (top)
(Photos Author)

shute at the back. On one occasion, however, the driver hit a rut with such force that the cage was catapulted off, leaving the hapless incumbent in the rear sitting waist deep in a pile of meat and being pursued by thirty lions! Fortunately, the cage landed atop the leading pursuer and caused sufficient distraction for the vehicle to make good its escape. The inquest was unprintable.

It never rains, though, unless it pours (though seldom on a fire!). One morning, a coach full of children was easing its way down a 1:10 incline in the park when its brakes failed. Like an unleashed animal, it surged down the hill, hit an earth mound *between* two deep ponds and literally flew over the oncoming traffic before coming to a halt seventy yards away, still upright. I climbed in through a window into scenes of absolute bedlam. I worked my way down the aisle placating and consoling as best I could for the worst injuries appeared to be in a heap on the back seat. They'd caught the worst of the whiplash and most were eventually stretchered out of the rear emergency door and taken away by ambulance. I was relaxing over coffee awaiting news from the hospital (which turned out to be good) when the radio jerked me into life again. A car had done virtually the same thing on the next bend! It was swaying precariously half over the edge but, fortunately, I'd caught the end of an old movie the night before (Michael Caine's 'Italian Job'), so knew instantly what to do! We were all sitting on the boot, counterbalancing the car while the family got out, when the radio went again. There was another family trapped in their car - in the car park! It transpired that a courting peacock was so enraged at the sight of a 'rival's' reflection in a highly polished car that he was attacking it with such verve that the occupants were too terrified to alight. It simply never occurred to them to drive off!

Meanwhile, my landrover was a revelation. On 'our' first bank holiday Monday, I was to tow out over a hundred broken down cars with it before the congestion became so acute that we abandoned our vehicles and patrolled the traffic queues on foot, jerry cans of water in one hand, shotguns in the other. Over six thousand cars came through that day, an all-time record, before we stopped counting. There simply wasn't time. As bemused as everyone else, the lions just sat it out not moving an inch until after dusk when their instincts got the better of them. In mid-afternoon, however, I did have to sprint for the landrover. Plumes of smoke were pouring from the bear reserve. First on the scene with my new-found mobility, I found the Volvo estate ablaze from bumper to bumper with the bears fascinated onlookers. We didn't carry fire extinguishers in those days but they would have been academic in this situation. All I could do was to take the family of six aboard and beat a hasty retreat, leaving the bears their charred plaything.

The following afternoon I could only stare in horror as a slow motion melodrama unfolded before my eyes. A lion strolling down a queue of cars was attracted to an open rear window. It climbed in, only its rear feet remaining firmly on the ground, and emerged with a child in its mouth. And still my landrover wouldn't start. Fortunately, I was parked on a slope and was able to leap out, push the vehicle, jump back in and bump start before tearing off in pursuit. When pressed, the lion dropped its 'plaything' enabling me to retrieve it. The child was unmarked. Equally astounding, the parents refused all help. I called the police eventually for want of any other way of instilling any sense of reality into them and it was they who took the family away for medical checks. Which occupant they started with is not recorded. An hour later, the cause of my starter motor's indifference revealed its hand. The wiring harness which had been smouldering away beneath the dashboard burst into flames. It was an unenviable predicament. The vehicle ran on LPG (liquefied petroleum gas) or petrol. The gas tank was behind the driver's seat, the petrol tank below it. Both were full and I was surrounded by twenty four lions. By now, the flames had enveloped the radio. Gingerly picking up the baking hot microphone with a gloved hand, I said that if anyone was passing I'd appreciate a lift, then jumped out. There was no reply.

Nothing happened. The lions just sat and looked at this idiot thrust so spectacularly into their midst with nothing more than an empty single-barrelled shotgun (my two blanks had exploded) and a jack handle. Caught between the devil and the deep blue sea, I backed steadily away from this time bomb trying not to excite attention. A couple of lions tensed and rose to their haunches. Running isn't an option in these crises, even assuming there's somewhere to run to and your legs aren't suddenly made of jelly. To do so, however, is as futile as it is hopeless; one is pulled down in seconds and once a lion's prey is down, events assume a certain formality. Conversely, if your nerves hold (and there was no bravado in staying put on this occasion for there was nowhere to seek refuge), the lion, sensing your confidence, invariably stops the length of a cricket pitch away. Nonplussed by their prey's failure to do the instinctive thing by standing their ground, uncertainty is established in the lion's mind to the extent that they will often slink away (it works with gorillas, too!). All more easily said than done and certainly not a course of action to be attempted or recommended if there's an alternative, but what was the choice? I was still staring them out when something came between us. The radio had worked, help had arrived, spectacularly. Blinded by the huge pall of smoke, my first rescuer ploughed into my blazing landrover at 50mph. Soon there were two landrovers burning! I climbed aboard a second rescuer and told him to get us out of it. I'd had quite enough for the time being, but the day still hadn't run its full course. As we cleared the immediate vehicular carnage, I sensed something still amiss - there was still an awful amount of smoke in the air. The staff lodge where I myself had lived until recently was ablaze. With me providing the principal entertainment, no one had seen the flames pouring from the upper windows! But still there was time for yet more drama. Having dealt with this conflagration, the fire brigade were summoned back urgently to the car park where a vehicle had disappeared in a cloud of smoke. The firemen recoiled from it, eyes streaming, clutching their noses and reached for breathing apparatus. Suddenly, I recognised the symptoms. It was the 'muck man'. Every week, he would drive down to the manure pile, reverse up and fork elephant manure into the back of his van until it sank onto its axles in submission. With steam from the freshly-disturbed midden pouring from the vehicle's every orifice, he would tour the local housing estates to sell his foul harvest. This, though, was the final run. The vehicle was corroded by this most putrid of effluents and beyond repair. When a suitably long chain could be found, it was towed away at a respectful distance, still loaded to the gunwales, to some remote downwind scrapyard never to be seen or smelt of again. As his health declined (with chest problems!), his son continued the family business, though he now dispenses the product in plastic bags, as do we, albeit much more hygienically. I first saw 'Zoo Poo' on sale in Montreal Zoo over twenty years ago. Although far too radical a consideration for England then, it is now sold by us, amongst others, once it has been 'sanitised'. In truth, I don't believe the properties claimed of it are much better than any other organic compost, but at least it's a useful way of getting rid of the stuff. It did, however, create quite a stir when we began selling it - on the Internet!

Meanwhile it was still a bank holiday weekend and my vehicle could not be spared. Old Bill the mechanic toiled through the night to rewire it whilst I repainted the brown spots. I was back amongst the lions by opening time the following day, after being ushered in to meet the visiting American company President. I was thanked for saving the child the previous day which had, by then, clean slipped my mind and had an extended and much envied audience. From then on, I was a marked man, clearly destined for greater things. The following year, he wrote to me stressing that I was a key member of the company's management team in Europe. The pay rise that year was £1 per week. I didn't dare ask what the others got!

The incident, however, marked the beginning of a long honeymoon between the landrover and the lion that continues to this day. Nearly twenty five years later, we were tracking lions by landrover one evening in the Namibian bush. We'd heard them roaring by the water-hole before dawn so we knew they weren't far away. Within minutes, we'd picked up tracks, very fresh tracks, and for an hour we'd nosed our way through the dense bush, expectancy rising by the minute to fever pitch. The tracker forsook his exposed game seat on the front bumper for a safer perch on the roof. I clutched the rifle as the guide drove. We were as close as that. Suddenly, I spotted the pair of them just twenty yards away at seven o'clock. We'd almost missed them. We froze, held our breath and admired. The children had been born and bred amongst the lions but never seen a wild one. After a few minutes, we began to inch our way cautiously forward in a half circle to get the sun behind us for the photographs. Suddenly, the bonnet shot skywards. A back wheel had dropped three feet into an aardvark burrow. We were stuck hard and fast like a beached whale on the crest of a perpetual wave.

186

I could see the lodge on the hill two miles away but it may as well have been twenty, for the radio reception on the hand-held was poor and help was miles off. The two lions circled us warily. But I was wary, too - hadn't we been following three sets of tracks? Suddenly, the third lion was there. A very mean, irritable and injured lion, one that had been seen to have been kicked in the face by a zebra ten weeks previously. He pawed the ground and snarled viciously from the dust cloud created as his tail swept the sand. The trap was sprung. We were surrounded by three lions in an open-topped landrover grounded on its back axle. The guide licked his lips, took the rifle and pumped the magazine. There were just two shells in it. A lion rose to its feet, the guide raised the rifle - stalemate. "Have you tried the jack?" crackled the radio. No, it wasn't there. "A spade, anyone?" I asked. No. Ultimately, it came down to logistics. The petrified tracker stayed up top with the rifle (and both shells!), the children and the ice box sat on one side to improve the balance, Sue drove, whilst the guide and I, armed only with a can of coke in each hand, jumped out and somehow managed to lift a long wheel-based twelve-seater landrover from its embarrassment.

We got back to the lodge just as the guinea fowl at the water-hole were becoming nervous. Within minutes 'our' lions were there bold as brass. As a grateful guide plied me with free drinks on the veranda, above which only the previous night he'd shot dead a three metre long Black Mamba (about the deadliest snake on earth), first they lapped at the pool then stretched luxuriously by the water's edge, oblivious to the deprivation they were causing to the hundreds of animals we could see through the night-sight queuing up to drink. As we retired to our chalet after dinner, the lions threw down the gauntlet one last time. They roared and scuffled beneath our very window, choking us in their dust. Short of setting fire to the thatch, there was no way of attracting attention so we sat tight. Fortunately, the children in the adjoining chalet had the sense to follow suit.

In the meantime, a lot of water had flown beneath our bridge. A year after that memorable baptism of fire came the infamous drought of 1976 and a further brush with its hazards. One

Opposite Page:
I launch 'Zoo Poo' on the internet! (Photo Kidderminster Times)

midsummer's morning, the by now familiar pattern of hot, hazy air overhung the little hollows and valleys in the scrubland beyond our boundary fence, obscuring the horizon where it emerged with a cloudless sky. Suddenly, a grey cloud appeared above the trees, then another. Soon, five fires were burning, stoked and encouraged by the same vandals that had lit them. Curiously enough, although the fires quickly merged, the conflagration that one would have expected in such tinder-dry conditions after months without rain didn't immediately develop, stifled almost, it seemed, by its own searing heat. Suddenly, a draft fanned my perspiring brow, the tree-tops swayed and the hazy smoke overhanging the well-contained fire turned ominously black. Within minutes, the fire was out of all control. Fanned by the stiff breeze, flames swept fifty feet at a time across the scrub glades and through the trees. Over the radio, we heard the fire chief evacuating his crews as the fire devoured everything before it. It swept relentlessly forward, the park directly in its path. The area being notorious for scrub fires, I'd long anticipated such an eventuality and had kept two strips of land cultivated as fire-breaks. The first delayed the fire sufficiently to enable us to plunge back into this inferno with a tractor to retrieve a fire engine bogged down in the sand, for the police to evacuate the public from the park and for the fire crews and park staff to regroup behind the second break, which backed immediately onto the animal reserves. It was there, of course, that my main concern lay. I had childhood recollections of 'Tarzan' films in which the animals fled panic-stricken before a fire, oblivious to what they blundered into or where their terror took them. To my surprise, however, even with the heavy smoke smarting our eyes and the crackle of flames clearly audible, there wasn't the slightest sign of alarm, let alone panic. Nevertheless, everything that could conceivably be regarded as dangerous was placed under lock and key with someone in attendance.

The second fire-break, representing our last line of defence, was immediately in front of the monkey fence; a solid twelve foot high structure, lined on the interior with tin to deny the monkeys any purchase should they attempt to climb out. It offered some protection from the forty foot high flames that bore down on us. Behind this protection we waited, two appliances hosing down the fence, six others aiming their hoses over it onto the fire, whilst further back the police and park staff, reinforced by now with a contingent of soldiers, were deployed to beat out secondary fires caused by falling ash and debris. Behind them were the monkeys, quietly chewing away on their favourite fruits, offered to keep them out of harm's way, for it was quite impossible to catch them up at such short notice. The fire raged, the tin glowed red, trees fell about us like the flaming torches of a riotous mob as we toiled like men possessed to hold our ground. Overhead, invisible through the smoke, a helicopter droned, in it the Chief Fire Officer. As the machine swept in to land for a brief consultation, the swirling rotor arms temporarily swept aside the smoke revealing a quite startling sight. There, in a curious half-circle watching the eight fire engines, the police, the soldiers, the helicopter and our own fire parties, sat a hundred and twenty fascinated baboons! To my eternal mortification, the camera film I shot of that remarkable sight was borrowed and lost by the local newspaper, so I've not a single memento of the occasion. By dusk, however, the day had been won. The fire-break had held, the fence was saved and the blaze tamed. It sulked its way along the fire-break during the night, causing further damage to the landscape and keeping us on our toes until 4a.m. but was easily contained. A further five days were spent damping down the ashes of a once beautiful wood but, for the remainder of that summer, we were able to relax in one respect at least. That great charred hinterland itself proved to be the most effective fire-break.

The following year, my luck almost ran out. It had been a glorious record-breaking bank holiday weekend, more than justifying the fundamental rebuilding of the park over the winter, our marketing strategy and everything else. God, alias our American Senior Vice-President back over here for the week, was beside himself with glee and whisky! By mid-afternoon, the rush had abated sufficiently for me to pause to refuel the landrover's LPG tank. Driving away, I'd paused to light one of my very occasional cigars (I'm a ten per year man) in celebration. God was indeed pleased, we were all going out to dinner that night. Somehow, from somewhere, and to this day it is not known precisely from where as little evidence was to survive, gas had leaked from the system. One would have thought that with all the windows open on that sweltering day, any escaping gas would have dispersed. Certainly, there wasn't the slightest whiff of it and I was oblivious to its presence until I struck my lighter. There was a horrendous crash and my vehicle exploded about me in flames. Turning to see its cause, I saw the cab full of flames, an inferno. My face, caught in the rear view mirror, was burning too, flesh dripping from it like a molten candle. Minutes earlier, I'd been dressed in a lightweight short-sleeved nylon safari suit. The change into a heavy duty, cotton boiler suit in anticipation of some manual work probably saved my life. Nevertheless, it was in considerable discomfort that I tumbled out of the vehicle and looked for help. The crowd in the sea lion arena were on their feet in raptures. Applauding wildly, they thought it was a stunt! Later, we were to receive congratulatory letters of fulsome praise for the effect. For the immediate future, however, clearly there was no help to be had there. No sooner had I reached back into the cab through the burning seats and dashboard for the radio microphone to summon assistance (and to retrieve my precious camera!), than I realised the futility of it. The entire park was grid-locked with traffic - such paralysis meant that help would take an eternity to reach me. Notwithstanding the state of my hands, I leapt into one of our newly acquired jeeps in the garage and began battling my way through the car park. Somewhere in my subconscious, I recalled that burns required immediate attention. I hadn't reached the main road, however, before Dave Chorley overtook me. Once again, those robust radios had passed out a vital message 'in extremis'. He was desperately relieved to see me - just six weeks earlier, he'd been the best man at our wedding.

Inexplicably, everyone hearing my call thought I'd been gored by an antelope. In the office, the door had been slammed on the radio room for Sue was working next door. Everyone held their breath and stared at the silent radio. I had no idea I was so popular! Once in Dave's car, I called on the radio again to say where in my vehicle I'd last seen the pass keys and that I wouldn't be long for I was okay. I wasn't. Initially, Dave was calm, reassuring even. We'd be in hospital in no time, after all. I couldn't, of course, see myself which gave me an advantage over Dave, but I was well aware that my face was dripping into my lap. By the latter stages of the journey, the roles were reversed - I was

Back to work after my burns with a beard to hide the scars.
(Photo J. James, Birmingham Post and Mail)

The amorous peacock attacking his own reflection in a car door. (Photo Author)

Playing with fire! The residents of the lion house. Top left: House Sparrow, top right: a brood of Blue Tits. Below: Yellow Necked Woodmouse similar to this one. (Photos Author)

having to reassure Dave. As the casualty doors swung open, I knew why. Jaws sagged, nurses turned away. "Ambulance," snapped a consultant, pausing in mid-stride, "Get me the nearest burns unit." I was still on my feet so they led me away to a private room to begin cutting my clothes away. The ambulance trip to the old Birmingham Accident Hospital was interminable, but our much maligned health service was magnificent. When God visited the following morning, I heard him say (for I couldn't see) that whatever I wanted I could have - just name it. He was appalled at what he saw, I was later told, and suddenly stone cold sober. I resisted the temptation, however, for there was really no more to be done. I was in excellent hands. For want of something better to do, Dave bought me some Lucozade, a whole crate of it, much to the amusement of the entire nursing staff. I felt duty-bound to drink it all but, to this day, the mere sight of it, much less the taste, still makes my stomach heave! I was blind for several days and rather uncomfortable for many more after that, but I could relax in the knowledge that I'd been lucky. Lucky to be alive, lucky to have retained my eyesight, lucky that my bride of just six weeks hadn't been in the vehicle at the time, for I'd been on my way to collect her. One advantage of being in hospital is that there is always someone worse off than you are and there is time to reflect on such things.

A six-week stay in hospital was originally envisaged plus further spells for each piece of plastic surgery. They planned several, but within fourteen days I had willed myself home. In some respects, the burns unit was a ghastly place. Every time I go on hospital radio, I see that ward in my mind's eye - the all-pervading stench of burnt flesh was overwhelming, the sights dreadful. There were no mirrors. The regime was ruthless. On my first morning, I was woken at 5a.m., blind and unable to move, let alone use either hand. "Eat," said a voice as something thudded onto the bedside cabinet. A cleaner took pity eventually. With a proficiency that suggested considerable experience in such matters, she oh, so carefully eased a straw through my charred lips and held a cereal bowl while I sucked up the milk. At about the same time, Sue was experiencing probably our only ever bad moment at the hands of the press. One individual was banging on the front door, demanding an interview and seeking permission for photographs

A lull in the fire fighting gives the firemen a chance to recover sand bogged vehicles on our heathland perimeter. (Photo Author)

at the hospital. As if they could be published! In the event, only a couple of lines would see the light of day on the incident as everyone, including the remainder of the press, closed ranks around me. Goodwill messages poured in from home and abroad (and the press), God kept in personal contact. Grotesquely unrecognisable to my many visitors (even my mother wasn't allowed in until day thirteen for her firstborn was not a pretty sight), I'd lain awake every night practising non-stop the physiotherapy I'd been taught on the mess in the plastic bags that represented my hands. Without due care, the reforming skin grows stiff as a board, extending recovery indefinitely unless it is continually exercised. Some in the same ward had been there months for that reason alone. That was not an option for me. Paradoxically, one of the worst moments was my pre-release clean-up, for I couldn't be allowed out in the state I was in. A sister vented the nasal passages to ease my breathing, then clipped and puckered at my face for a full two hours just to make me marginally presentable. It was agonising, but the tears streaming down my cheeks softened the scar tissue enough eventually for her efforts to become presentable. Equally tense was the consultant's dubious inspection of her handywork. He wasn't convinced by any means. "Can you keep in the house, young man?" Some chance! But he wasn't to know. I lied unashamedly.

And so, on the fourteenth day I came home. I recoiled as the breeze fanned the tender, new flesh about my face and my eyes streamed again. I couldn't shave for months. It would take longer still to regain my strength - even holding a pen would bring blood from my hands, but I was home. Within three days, I found my hands would once more fit around the carefully gloved steering wheel of my refurbished landrover, now minus a gas tank. God had personally instructed every company vehicle grounded until they were removed. I was back in business just in time for a further explosion, this time an infinitely more enjoyable one, a birth explosion. Fifty animals were born in the following month and, despite the months of physiotherapy and the years it would take for the physical scars to disappear, there was never the slightest possibility of my life becoming boring, even in convalescence. The park had taken its pint of blood and its pound of flesh, but spared the rest. Despite this setback, my average time off work through sickness over twenty seven years averages less than half a day per annum.

196

CHAPTER 12
S.O.S.

(To the animals the system failed)

I t was 11.30p.m. The park was quiet and, at home, lambing was complete. I was congratulating myself on getting to bed so early when the phone rang. It set off a chain of events whose ramifications were to continue for over three and a half years. It was West Mercia police. A patrol car on the nearby M5 had pulled over to assist a broken-down van - and found it full of exotic animals. The driver had no transit documents and refused to say where the animals had come from or where they were going. Anxious though they were not to cause a problem with animals in transit, in the absence of any plausible explanation they had no alternative but to hold them. But where? Could we do 'bed and breakfast'? Within the hour, they were at the park. My subsequent statement to the police outlines the situation I was confronted with at 12.30a.m. one April morning:

'At approx. 12.30a.m. on the morning of Thursday 20/4/95, I met Sergeant Fox from West Mercia Police by prior arrangement at the West Midland Safari Park having driven from home 10 miles away. He was escorting a broken-down blue transit van which I understood to have been removed from the M5. We had been asked to provide a safe haven for the van's contents.

On examination, these proved to be 10 South African Vervet monkeys, 2 South American Capuchin monkeys and 1 approx. 5yr. old jungle cat (sub-species uncertain) in a miscellany of 10 assorted

Opposite Page:
(Top): I check over our new arrivals.
(Photo J. James, Birmingham Post and Mail)
(Bottom): Sue, Chris and Nicky with Molly Badham and friends at Twycross Zoo.
(Photo Author)

boxes. There were also 2 other empty wire mesh containers of very approx.18" by 12" by 8" whose purpose was unclear. They had straw bedding in them. There were six wooden boxes containing a single vervet each, 2 wooded boxes containing 2 vervets each in individual compartments, one flimsy wire mesh container holding 2 capuchins together with one plastic box containing the cat. None of the boxes except the cat one were purpose-built. All were crudely fashioned and/or adapted from previous use (3 appeared to have been rabbit hutches, for example). The doors were loose-fitting with wide gaps around them and secured with (bathroom) cabinet latches, two of which had come undone. Some of the staples holding the mesh grills in place were half out, having been nailed into the grain of the plywood and therefore easily removed. Five of the boxes (one of the doubles containing 2 vervets, 2 containing a single vervet, the one containing 2 capuchins and the cat box) had no bedding of any description. Others only had sparse amounts of wood shavings. None had anything with warmth-retaining properties i.e. straw, for example. There was none on the lorry.

The cat crate was of the type commonly used to transport domestic cats. It was totally and wholly unsuitable for a wild feline like a jungle cat. When the driver, Mr. Drummond, came to collect his cat on the 21/4/95, I asked him to bring a better box. He did not do so. None of the crates contained food, none was carried on the lorry. None of the crates contained water or provision for it - there were no utensils, for example. Likewise, the lorry carried no water. The capuchin 'crate' was wholly inadequate. It was 32" by 22" by 22", constructed of lightweight, white plastic-coated mesh which offered no protection whatsoever, with a lightweight unlittered tray. It is more suited to the carriage of domestic cats. The handles were unsuitable in that, when in use, they folded up, thereby exposing one's hands to the cage's occupants. In their distressed state, the monkeys were scratching and biting. Such injuries are not therapeutic - given their alleged laboratory background, this is even less so. The box was locked, the driver did not have the key.

The capuchins (one elderly 10yrs. plus, one 3/4yrs. old) were soiled and wet in their own excreta and were particularly wet, cold and distressed. The elderly specimen had most of the hair missing from 50% of its body. There was a fairly recent abrasion about 6" by 2" on its middle spine area. The poor condition was explained by Mr.

Drummond as down to laboratory conditions from where it had just been rescued. Such an unknown, undocumented background was a major concern. None of the boxes was marked in any way i.e. which way up they were to be stacked, details of the occupants such as age, sex, diet etc.

The vehicle was not heated, ventilated and had no internal light. It is pertinent to point out that the national forecast since at least Friday 14/4/95 had warned daily of cold weather during the latter half of the week and in particular of severe overnight temperatures. The temperature was well below freezing. These monkeys require heated accommodation of 60/65°F. The boxes were not secured. They were free to slide about the bed of the van at each turn. The cat box in particular, by virtue of its weight, narrow floor base and its hexagonal shape, could easily roll loosely about in an upturned state. From the debris in the animal's coat, I find it inconceivable that it had not done so. In any event, it could easily have broken open in uncontrolled movement.

The vehicle too was not secure. The hasp on the rear roller blind-type tailboard was not padlocked. It was secured by loose wire. Not only, therefore, were the occupants at risk when inevitably the driver had to leave the vehicle, but, had the wire broken or dislodged, the occupants would have spilt out causing death, injury or at very least escape, not to mention the consequential road hazard. The monkeys were fed, given fruit for their thirst through the mesh which was eagerly taken and left in a warm room overnight. The cat could not be fed as there was no meat thawed out at that time of night and, of course, it was impossible to provide it with water.

There can be no doubt whatsoever in my view that these animals, particularly the capuchins, were caused considerable, preventable and therefore unnecessary suffering as a result of this ill-conceived exercise.' Statement ends.

We did all this in conditions of near-perfect visibility - the frost was hard, the night clear.

The following day, the case hit the fan. The media swamped us, national TV and all, as the plight of the 'Motorway Monkeys' caught everyone's imagination. Amidst all this came another rescue. A bus driver walked in with a piglet he'd found wandering down the Worcester Road! The police investigation continued though critically, as it later transpired, neither MAFF nor Trading Standards officers put in an appearance either on the night or the following day. It was a tactical error with profound implications. Not for the first time, I pondered the case for some sort of single Wildlife Agency in this country. It could incorporate the functions, legislative animal enforcement and welfare roles currently overseen by the police, local authorities, trading standards, MAFF and the DETR, amongst others, beneath a single umbrella. It transpired that none of the animals had been rescued from a laboratory at all, but from two zoos in the West Country. Both members of The National Federation of Zoological Gardens of Great Britain and Ireland, they had ignored the self-regulatory guidelines on the disposal of surplus animals laid down by their own organisation. At the time these stated:

'It is vitally important that members make sure that when animals are being sent to another location, the recipient has accommodation of a suitable standard together with the financial and physical resources to maintain the individual animals. It is equally important that all the correct papers have been processed and are available, and that suitable transport and containers have been arranged. Please remember to pass on animal records, including veterinary records........'

This advice was out of date for it should have said, as it later did (I believe as a direct result of this matter), *'and to use the Animal Transport Certificate'* (as required by law under Article 8 of the Welfare of Animals during Transport Order 1994).

Notwithstanding this, both zoos had quite clearly and irresponsibly failed to carry out any checks at all. They had simply handed the hapless animals over to a middle man without any thought for the consequences. The Federation carried out an investigation then closed ranks. They certainly weren't prepared to discuss the matter - after all, we were only the people who'd had the problem thrust upon us in the middle of the night. No one would get animals from us, for example, without at least sight of a Dangerous Wild Animals Licence or Zoo Licence, then a visit. Clearly, neither had been done (although the vet from one zoo claimed to have checked the travel arrangements and found them satisfactory!). And, long-since tired of such duplicity on the Federation's part, we're no longer even in the Federation. The annual subscription of £7,000 didn't appear to provide us with anything that wasn't available elsewhere. I did, however, apply as a private individual to become an Associate Member of the Federation to keep in touch. I was seconded by several zoo directors and the Membership and Licensing Committee approved the application and advised me accordingly. Five days later, however, the matter was brought to the attention of the Federation Council and rescinded. If the park wasn't a member, then no one who worked for it could be. It was nothing personal, said the Chairman, Grenville Llewellyn Lucas OBE, B.Sc., F.L.S, F.R.G.S., writing to inform me two weeks later. It was just the way it was. I have since given them the opportunity they suggested to reconsider but was told 'not to waste my stamp'.

With the exception of the jungle cat, the animals were destined for a 'Wildlife and Bird of Prey Sanctuary' based in a garden centre in Staffordshire. Years ago, it was caravan parks which caused problems by having exotic animals on site to 'entertain' their clients. Nowadays, garden centres and such like have them. As these centres become all-embracing, congregating more and more concessionaires under one roof or on one site to 'hold' people longer, they too can cause considerable problems for the animals' welfare when kept in situations entirely out of context. The owner, with what little credit he was to emerge from the mess with, had smelt a rat over the conflicting and contradictory stories he'd been given about the animals' origin and travel arrangements and had tipped off his local police who were in waiting. The target, however, had already fallen foul of another police force! Once ownership was established thirty six hours later, his local police vouched for the credentials of the 'rescue centre' and off they went. I was a trifle surprised, though, to be asked upon collection what the monkeys ate but, having provided some specialist primate diet, thought little more of it for Mr. Drummond was there, too, to collect his jungle cat - and be cautioned and charged by the police. He left without a word of thanks or offering to make a donation for the inordinate amount of time, trouble and effort expended in digging him out of the mess he'd created. It wasn't as if he couldn't afford it. I was to discover that the sanctuary had paid him many hundreds of pounds of 'expenses' to effect this 'rescue'. That, though, I thought was the end of that. However, letting those animals leave the park proved, in retrospect, to be an appalling mistake. We'd been dreadfully ill advised.

Having driven the tortuous eighty or so miles home with the jungle cat in its inadequate box perched on his daughter's lap, Drummond was back in Staffordshire by 10.30 p.m. He wanted the capuchins back. He was still citing the never-to-be-substantiated threat (and one he must have known to be false, having collected them from a wildlife park) that they came from a research centre and may pose an immediate danger to the health and well-being of the owner's family. Escorted from the town by the police, he was back on the 'phone to the proprietor in the small hours, intimidating him to such an extent that he had them returned to Drummond's own dubiously-named 'Rescue Centre' near Bala, North Wales, the next day. Whereupon, Drummond professed himself at a loss to have anywhere to put them! Throughout all the time they were in his possession, most of these animals were in excess of those permitted under the terms of his Dangerous Wild Animal Licence. But that was a frequent occurrence. The local authority had previously decided it was 'not in the public interest' (following the escape of an unauthorised animal subsequently shot by a farmer) to bring a prosecution. Likewise, they ignored the sign at the entrance welcoming visitors, thus bringing the establishment within the jurisdiction of the Zoo Licensing Act. The temperatures were sub zero, it was a Saturday night and the monkeys were still in a crate in the back of a car, I was told. At 11p.m., I spoke to a chief inspector in the North Wales police, urging action. They, too, were aware of Drummond's activities. He promised to galvanise the local RCPCA. There was nothing else I could do.

Returned, therefore, under the pretext of requiring urgent veterinary checks because of their laboratory background, the RSPCA were never able to establish what, if any, veterinary checks were carried out on these wretched animals, much less by whom - or how. Before they'd left the park, we'd transferred them into a stronger and marginally more suitable box for the anticipated forty five minute journey to what we'd thought to be their final destination. When they finally arrived back in Staffordshire from Wales some five days later, they were still in the same box, the centre's owner even commenting that the seal we'd placed on the door was still intact.

Things were, however, to get even worse. Having been assured of the rescue centre's credentials, within days I was to become alarmed at newspaper articles claiming the monkeys had been rescued by the centre from the motorway and appealing for public donations of £5,000 with which to build accommodation - and for greengrocers to donate food! This, of course, neatly overlooked the fact that the animals wouldn't have been on the motorway if they hadn't acquired them in the first place and that we'd been assured that facilities were already in place. Where, then, were they being kept? A check revealed an appalling sight. The accommodation had been designed to Drummond's specification, we were told, and was lamentably inept. Alarming reports began to trickle back. Both myself and my assistant visited at intervals. The RSPCA and I both made urgent and near identical recommendations to the local authority, Stafford Borough Council. Things still didn't improve, so Molly Badham, director of Twycross Zoo, and I paid a visit. She, too, had heard of this 'haven' within a garden centre. Like other zoos (including other Federation ones but excepting Twycross), some of whom had also placed animals into his possession, Molly had been duped by Drummond's gift of the gab for he was a class act.

'The conditions were appalling,' we told the local authority in writing, *'the very epitome of everything a 'zoo' shouldn't be.'* It took us both back twenty years to an era when such things were commonplace, the very thing the Zoo Licensing Act (which we'd helped to draft) was introduced for and had been largely successful in preventing again - we thought. It was by no means clear whether the premises were even licensed for these additions - certainly there was no licence on display as required by law. There had already been an escape involving one of the monkeys, but the real concern remained for the living conditions of both the primates and the collection's other incumbents. We knew of no

other authority who would permit such conditions. And Molly was a zoo inspector. We continued, *'What possessed (the proprietor) to get involved in animals that he and his staff know nothing about, cannot feed, house or provide the most rudimentary care for, is beyond rational comprehension at least, woeful and inept misjudgement at worst.'* Of the 109 standard questions on a zoo inspector's report form, we could tick less than ten in the affirmative. Free-standing paraffin stoves stood in straw litter, the 'pens' were constructed of larch lap panels, inches deep in mud, excrement and rotten food, there were no 'stand off' barriers, as required by law, to prevent visitors reaching the occupants or vice versa. One could go on and on. It was appalling.

In the meantime, we'd had a zoo inspection at the safari park. After pontificating from 9a.m. until 9.30p.m., all the king's horses and all the king's men, leading lights in the zoological world and, as such, appointed on the secretary of state's list of zoo inspectors, solemnly declared that we needed a longer hose-pipe in the lion house within two months, or else. We're still dining out on that one! Such contradictions rendered me speechless. The Zoo Licensing Act was intended to introduce a degree of uniformity into zoo standards when it was drafted. To a considerable degree, it has failed in that particular regard although, in retrospect, given the huge divergence in zoological collections, each of which is unique, it may have been an elusive goal anyway, albeit a necessary one. The problems have always been two-fold. Firstly, from the onset there's been an enormous variance in the inspectors' interpretations of the standards. Secondly, the willingness of local authorities to use their powers with regard to wild animals (principally under the Dangerous Wild Animal and Zoo Licensing legislation) has been at best patchy. Something, though, had to be done. Drafted loosely on the old Zoological Federation inspection for prospective members, which in itself had presented too formidable a criterion for many zoos to comply with at the time (hence the short-lived rival National Zoological Association), it is, however, all we've got. Prospective uniform European zoo legislation, though, uses our act as its blueprint. For all its faults, the fact is that if our zoo licensing legislation were in force throughout the EEC now, the horror stories that we are frequently subjected to in connection with some European zoos could not happen. But, when my thoughts drifted not across the water but those few miles up the road, I really did wonder.

It took two months for the local authority to reply. With collectively over sixty years top-flight animal management between us, Molly and I were wrong. So, too, was the zoo inspector with a further thirty years experience. Objecting to the manner and tone of my continual involvement, they wrote to my directors in an attempt to silence me. They didn't. Two months later, I visited again. Little had changed except a new monkey house had risen from an area previously condemned as unfit for pigs. I was able to walk straight into the building, into the animal quarters and out again unchallenged, then out of the centre through a rear entrance. The only crumb of comfort to be derived from the visit was that only two other visitors were in the place - the ticket office was unmanned anyway. Perhaps, after all, people were voting with their feet. Once again, the local authority were advised. They noted my comments - and put them on file for future reference. Later that winter, the new house burnt down, all the capuchins dying within it. Whether the council looked back in their files I don't know, but I doubt it.

Meantime, legal proceedings had been instigated against Drummond. Listening to a transcript of a preliminary hearing being read to me over the 'phone by a media friend, I again realised something had gone terribly wrong. Up to forty charges had been contemplated at one point, now a mere handful remained. Consternation reigned when I queried this with the arresting officer. There had been a complete cock-up within the Crown Prosecution Service, it was discovered. The six-month statute had nearly elapsed, however, and although the RSPCA took up the cudgel at the eleventh hour, there wasn't time to prepare more than a handful of the original charges.

Ten months after I'd been roused from my bed by that SOS, the case came up. It was here that the failure of both MAFF and Trading Standards to be available on the night and the morning after presented a crucial problem. No one had summoned a vet who could verify my findings. The police officer could, but wasn't called. As far as the RSPCA were concerned, I was an expert witness. I was all they had. It was a farce. The prosecution was as inept as any I've ever encountered. One of the cages was produced in court to support my evidence. It was fine, the defendant said, after all, he'd used it to move pumas in! Briefly, I thought he was asking for further offences to be taken into consideration but, no, this was his defence - and the bench believed him! And so, the perpetuator of this untold catalogue of distress and suffering, the source of so much bungling ineptitude (in a system which had permitted everything that could never happen, everything that should never have happened, to take place) was fined just £100 for failing to label the boxes - and given time to pay. Surely, there could scarcely be a more classic example of well-meaning but misguided people dabbling in things they know nothing about, with resources they don't have, with more disastrous consequences for those that they would presume to have 'rescued'. Doubtless, if the source zoos had destroyed the animals, they would have been castigated, but the animals would have suffered less.

It highlighted the perpetual dilemma with surplus animals. In days of old, zoos were invariably net consumers of animals. Losses were simply replaced with fresh captures from the wild. Contemporary collections, of which the West Midland Safari Park is typical, are net producers. Ninety five per cent of our animals aren't just captive-bred - they were actually born in Bewdley. Breeding is invariably assumed to be a sign of a contented, well-husbanded collection. Yet, when the surplus produced involves numbers or sex ratios (the latter being something you have no control over) that cannot be placed, you're criticised for producing it or for allowing an artificial situation to arise. However, the same purists who support that view often make the same observation if animals are prevented from breeding, something we're advised to do by the Taxon advisory groups from time to time. The consequences of getting the equation wrong are frequently dire, as Woburn Safari Park were to discover to their cost in the spring of 1999. Two male lions, surplus to requirements, were to be shot - so ran the lurid reports leaked to the national press. If Woburn had circulated a surplus list, we'd never received it, so the matter only came to my attention when the Kidderminster Times asked for my reaction to the tabloid front pages. As it happened, there was a niche in the hierarchy of

Rescued! Wild Boar in Lancashire.
(Photo Author)

Capybara (the world's largest rodent) in
Worcestershire. (Photo Author)

Roe Deer in Wiltshire..............
(Photo Author)

and a different sort of jungle! 9p.m. on a
February night in Smethwick. A stray Pit Bull
Terrier I'd just darted. (Photo Author)

our lion pride at the time. Assimilating complete strangers within it was fraught with problems, but I gave it a try. Within days, they were in Bewdley under the watchful eye of three TV crews broadcasting live and assorted photographers. There were no guarantees that they would mix, I stressed. The only guarantee I could give was that no effort would be spared in the attempt to adopt them. In the event, Woburn got off the hook - we managed it. The tabloids vied with each other to claim credit for rescuing them but, in all truth, the Kidderminster Times and I had outdone them all! The 'anti's' were disappointed. One got the impression that it would have suited them far better if the animals couldn't have been relocated. Sulkily, they dismissed our rescue package as a cheap publicity stunt. It cut little ice with me. There was no mileage in that for us - we were closed for the winter at the time! However, with our 'motorway monkeys', I'd done all I could in another situation not of our making, but you always feel you could have done more.

One further sting remained in the tail. Although Mr. Drummond's 'rescue centre' was no more, following an item on this incident broadcast on ITV's poorly-researched 'The Big Story' in October 1997 which utilised contemporary news footage, he complained to both the Independent Television Commission and the Broadcasting Standards Commission about the way the programme portrayed him in connection with this matter. The programme, incidentally, showed undercover footage of Zoo Federation members again breaking every rule in the book by selling animals to complete strangers for cash. Curious double standards, really. Perhaps my own ineligibility was a blessing in disguise. The thrust of the programme's argument wasn't helped by the inadvertent placing of animals by its commissioned animal consultant in the very Staffordshire garden centre attracting so much criticism! Much of the 'evidence' Drummond cited in connection with my involvement was a tissue of untruths and utter nonsense. Indeed, much of the blame for the animals' state was attached to me! Everyone, including the police, had lied about the incident, he inferred - on national TV, too, for the original story had gone out not just on Central TV and BBC Midlands Today, both regional networks, but on John Craven's Newsround and GMTV. My statement was 'ludicrous', my status little more than that of a discredited witness. The truth was, in fact, transparently and undeniably crystal clear. The ITC rejected the complaint outright. The BSC, though, held a hearing in London, which I attended together with the programme's producer, its director and accompanied by a solicitor from Carlton TV. I wasn't prepared to have the park's good name dragged into such nonsense. The complaint was partially upheld, but that part involving the park and myself was not. Justice of sorts - at last.

CHAPTER 13
Sticks and Stones
(To the stalwarts of the Vale Veterinary Group)

I n any cocktail of people, vehicles and animals, there is always the potential for an explosive accident. Although surprisingly rare, the consequences can be spectacular. One of the principal reasons why 'drive through' tiger reserves are so few and far between is the tigers' fascination for tyres, lots of them. On one notable occasion in the 1970's, a pair of luxury continental coaches, complete with bars and loos (the latter substantially oversubscribed in the event!), had to drive out on their wheel rims without an intact tyre left between them - all spectacularly removed by the tigers! Lions are equally adventurous. Two of the lions we rescued from the receivers of Windsor Safari Park upon its closure had the procedure down to a fine art. One would lie in the middle of the road to stop a car and be admired whilst the other approached from behind to take out the back tyres. I remember, too, a massive, five hundred pound tiger climbing onto a car. Under its weight, the roof popped in, all four windows popped out but, fortunately, its occupants couldn't follow suit. The tiger's weight pinned all four of them tightly in their seats far better than any seat belt ever could! A giraffe, too, once fell on a car, writing it off without harming its occupants or itself, but prompting lurid speculation in the tabloids as to what it was about!

Another infinitely more famous mounting of a vehicle was to follow, albeit over twenty five years later, when a rhino climbed onto a car, a Volvo estate. The scene was captured on film and the

Opposite Page:
Angela with 'Wobbily' the infant wallaby. (Photo Author)

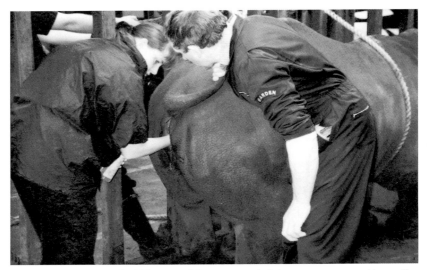

Sunday morning in paradise! The vet and I prepare to administer an enema to a rhino - all four gallons of it! The rope holds the sedated rhino upright for ease of access! (Photo A. Potter)

The famous rhino/Volvo incident. (Photo courtesy of the Webb family)

pictures attracted some contemporary attention in the media. For some extraordinary reason, eight months later they did the rounds again - this time with full half-page colour spreads in many national papers, without, of course, a mention of when the incident actually occurred. 'It's a jungle out there' ran the subsequent full page Volvo advert in The Daily Telegraph the next day. Again, another important fact was omitted. The car may have survived its tussle with the rhino with relatively minor damage (£1,500) but, in the meantime, it had been written off in a collision with a humble Renault! Rhinos' short-sightedness is legendary, but it didn't seem to prevent them reading the papers - incredibly, on the very day this fresh publicity re-emerged after eight months, the same rhino promptly sat on another car! There was, alas, for the tabloids at least, no injury to the car's occupants or the rhino on either occasion. People's reaction in such adversity is always interesting. If a rhino thunders towards a car, the alacrity with which the windows are wound up is astonishing. It is hard, however, to imagine a bigger exercise in futility!

Injuries can occur, however. One lady managed to run over a deer. Unsure what she'd done, she reversed up to see what had happened - and ran over it again. Aghast at what she saw, she panicked and tore off, running it over for a third time. She subsequently complained bitterly when I destroyed it on the spot. Cassidy was more fortunate. We never discovered the precise circumstances, but a letter to the park a week later expressing the hope that the deer they'd run over was all right gave us a clue. Quite how they expected it to be after a week with a broken leg is difficult to imagine, but I'd found him long before that, huddled forlornly amongst the foxgloves. Instinctively, I'd sensed something wrong and fired a dart into my hapless target before he could stumble off. In its distressed and weakened state, it succumbed within two minutes, barely time, in fact, for me to ring the surgery to establish whether one of the partners was in. Lady Luck smiled and within twenty minutes our vet Stan Kilby and I had him beneath the X-ray machine. Like so many people, Stan's connection with us had come about purely by chance. One of the first arrivals at the park had been an ostrich requiring veterinary attention. The yellow pages had been opened on 'Vet' and the pin had landed on 'Vale and Partners'. Over twenty five years on,

Stan, now in the autumn of his career, still winces at the thought almost as if the pin had landed in him! In the interim, the park had contributed fully to a life of immense enrichment and was about to do so again. Normally, when confronted with a wild animal in such distress, the only option is to destroy it as quickly and humanely as possible but, in an almost perverse sense, it was fortunate that it appeared to have been hit extremely hard. The femur was broken cleanly mid-way along its length, with no unsightly fractures or bone splinters protruding through the flesh. For an older animal, to give even such a clean repair any chance of healing under field conditions would have involved a totally unrealistic and unkind length of restrictive convalescence. On the other hand, there was a strong argument in favour of this otherwise healthy young calf. Some 18lb. at birth and now growing at a good pound a day, there was, we felt, a good chance of effecting a repair once the bones were fused. Accordingly, the limb was encased in plaster, wrapped in polythene to protect it from the elements and, within two hours, he was back home.

For a week he scarcely stirred, being content to lie in the shade of the long grass browsing from anything within reach. He would rise briefly to hop (hence the nickname 'Cassidy'!) beneath his ever-attendant hind to suckle before relapsing back into the grass. Week two saw weight placed on the foot but, by its end, the plaster was clearly restrictive so off I bore him to the surgery once more under sedation. To this day, I instinctively hold my breath as plaster is removed, fearful of all the complications that it can hide, but there were no problems and I returned him resplendent in fresh plaster to the park, his nursery paddock and an anxious hind. His last trip to the surgery came a month later with similar results, although his homecoming, now minus his plaster, proved harrowing. The flabby muscles in his withered leg proved incapable of supporting his weight and continual nose-dives into the ground caused us to wonder more than once whether the leg had, indeed, gone again. Day five, however, saw this plucky character once more hobbling behind his mother as she made for the shade. Flies buzzed in the sultry heat of that oppressive summer's afternoon, several of them landing on Cassidy's ear. With an involuntary shudder, he shook off his tormentors, raised his 'broken' leg and gave his ear a vigorous scratch. He never

An Albino Bennett's Wallaby.
(Photo Author)

White Fallow buck.
(Photo Author)

White Pheasant nesting in
a Shropshire Hedgerow.
(Photo Author)

215

looked back and lived on to a ripe old age on a deer farm. Every year, I would visit in the autumn to 'de-antler' him prior to the rut, essential protocol for most farmed deer stags to protect the fencing, other deer and the work-force from injury. Our duty of care thus fulfilled in what, in those days, was a fairly pioneering fashion, we'd gained an enormous amount of invaluable experience that would hold us in good stead in the years to come. Of course, it was 'only' a red deer, of no great value in financial or conservation terms, but we owed it that care and, of course, next time the knowledge might be utilised on something infinitely more valuable or quite simply irreplaceable. Foot care, of course, is an alien science when caring for free-ranging animals and is a problem seen almost exclusively in captive stocks. In the wild, damaged feet form part of the chain of natural selection. Defective feet mean you lag behind and the predators get you.

The next visit to the surgery was uneventful..... until we got home. We'd performed an entropian on a Bengal tiger, an operation to relieve an ingrowing eyelid. By removing a sliver of skin from above the eyelash and stitching the resulting wound up, the eyelid is directed out of the eye thereby relieving the irritation. We invariably do this sort of thing outside surgery hours to avoid alarming clients, their pets and the neighbours, who might become a little restless at the sight of 500lb. tigers being bundled in the back door. It was dark, therefore, before we got home, carried the sedated tiger inside its house and busied ourselves with bedding the pen down. Suddenly, I had that uncomfortable feeling you get when you're being watched. The intuition was uncanny. Turning around, I saw our tiger, sat up, fully awake and watching my every move with studied concentration. If ever there was a sharp exit to grace a lager advert, that was it!

I soon learnt the intricacies of many of our species and evolved husbandry and management strategies to suit, often by ignoring conventional, contemporary or fashionable advice. A 1982 edition of the New Scientist, for example, suggested that eland and other antelope didn't like damp, soft English safari park grass (presumably zoo grass is different!). The result, apparently, was infected and overgrown feet. This hadn't and never has been a problem for me - I've never treated an eland for foot problems.

Girl Power! The girls help 'deantler' a sedated wapiti stag. (Photo Author)

Nor has the predicted plague of the British strain of Cowpox virus, a danger to animals and staff alike, which had broken out in Moscow Zoo killing several carnivores which had been fed laboratory bred rats (white ones!) who'd caught the virus from a wild gerbil! Accordingly, the article concluded that safari parks faced an uncertain future. With advice like that, I suppose they did. We would, in fact, be more concerned with BSE, the very real risk of things like the tick-borne Lyme Disease (a recognised occupational zoonosis) and the risk, real or imagined, of Salmonella and E-coli poisoning from animals we handle every day without actually ever managing to contract it. The advice is frequently as confusing today as it was then. The National Farmers Union guidelines on farm visits, for example, suggest the avoidance of both animals and their feedstuffs. When people feed an animal, they are, of course, doing both. The reality, though, is that there is an infinitely greater risk of children contracting the sight-threatening Toxocara eggs from dog faeces on the lawn at home, of pregnant women coming into contact with the abortion-threatening and congenitally deforming Toxoplasmosis, or even of having a traffic accident on the way to a wildlife park, than there ever is of coming to harm within it. It didn't, however, prevent one mother claiming her child had contracted Foot and Mouth disease at the park! What she actually meant was *Hand,* Foot and Mouth disease which, it transpired, was a long-standing condition in the child. There is, too, a very real and frequently overlooked risk of disease being transmitted the other way, passed on by humans to animals, to which primates are particularly vulnerable. Domestic pets, too, can transmit various unpleasantnesses. Cats can transmit the Toxoplasmosis-causing agent *(Toxoplasma gondii)* in their faeces which can cause abortion in virtually any species. With this in mind, the traditional rural ideal of the cats living in the barn, soiling everything within it, will make the stockman recoil in horror.

I soon realised that the gestation of a camel varied between eleven and thirteen months. Naturally enough, unless you are a camel, this makes it difficult to ascertain what or if there are complications, much less when to intervene. There is on record the birth of camel twins - two weeks apart! Once born, conventional wisdom has it that calves must be up and about quickly to avoid predation. I've seen camels born and not stand, much less move, for a month. One presumes that they utilise the long neck to suckle from the mother when she stands over them. However, they are as tough as an old boot and take a long time to die, so, if there's something amiss, it can often only become apparent at the eleventh hour and requires precipitous action. Such matters, then, are a matter of knife-edge judgement. One calf, I decided, wasn't suckling or standing. Orthopaedic bandages were placed around the knees which, upon examination, were clearly a problem. We began bottle feeding to sustain the calf whilst leaving it with its mother to maintain the maternal link. By the time it could stand, fourteen days later, the mother's udder had dried up. Again, conventional wisdom dictated that was that until the next lactation but, wary by now of the species' non-conformity, I injected a milk-releasing hormone and tipped a trailer of grass into the stable. Unfortunately, I forgot all about it until the following morning when a young lady came flying out over the stable door to land at my feet. The camel now had an udder like a football and flew at her in a rage at the sight of the bottle for her calf. Either when calving or opening them up for surgery, the inner odours of a camel are such that you marvel that anything so foul is alive and thriving, but it is and they are. Again, diagnosis if they're not thriving is difficult. 'Normal' body temperature varies according to age!

It's well worth having these little pearls of wisdom at your fingertips because things will only go wrong on days off, at weekends or in the middle of the night - ask any vet. Invariably, too, it will involve considerable ingenuity to resolve unavailability of utensils at such ungodly hours. We once ran into difficulty operating on a camel calf for an angular deformity which, in common parlance, means it was becoming increasingly 'knock-kneed'. A growth plate had closed prematurely on one side of the knee, whilst the other had continued growing. It was drilled out, pinned and wired to stop the growth, thus allowing the other side to catch up and the leg to straighten. Suddenly, the realisation dawned on us that we had nothing remotely capable of supporting the repair. Eyes raised in search of inspiration, they alighted on the four inch guttering around the eaves of the office roof. Off it came in double-quick time. It fitted admirably - surely the original

gutter splint. The story caught the imagination of the press and 'Biggles' the camel became quite a high flyer for the duration of his convalescence. So, too, did 'Five', one of our African elephants. The cause of her discomfort was never really accurately diagnosed. She may have slipped in her box during her six thousand mile journey from Africa and simply twisted her ankle or, by virtue of being hand reared, may have suffered a deficiency during her upbringing (probably calcium) - or both. However, a suitably supplemented diet and the ankle support hand-made for her not only worked admirably, but put her into the national headlines.

Similar inspiration was sought one Saturday night when a wolf broke a leg and required instant surgery. That was the easiest bit. Stopping the revived wolf chewing the plaster off was the problem. 'Elizabethan collars' weren't common in those days, at least not ones big or strong enough for wolves! Going outside for a breath of fresh air to ponder the dilemma, I spotted a bucket on someone's doorstep containing ashes. With the vet keeping a wary eye open, I pinched it and we retreated inside to convert it. We cut a hole in the bottom, slid it over the head and attached it to a dog collar. A vertical slit in the side, adjusted with one of my bootlaces, gave us the flexibility for the animal to eat, drink and see without being able to chew her plaster. It didn't, of course, stop her cubs doing so! It took liberal doses of mustard smeared over it to hold them at bay for three weeks until we took the plaster off. Like camels, wolves are as tough as old boots. The shattered bone had healed so remarkably that, for an instant, we thought we'd X-rayed the wrong leg! Unfortunately, my case wasn't so clear-cut - the vet couldn't provide a good alibi. The theft of the bucket had been witnessed, resulting in an irate 'phone call, but I was only too pleased to forward the £1.50 for a new one! The litter of cubs didn't fare so well. Parvo virus was to strike down many of that year's cubs. Blood tests showed that the adults' immunity wasn't sufficient to safeguard the cubs until the conventional vaccination age of twelve weeks. To the consternation of many a veterinary pundit, I quickly discovered that if they weren't vaccinated within three weeks, their survival rate was minimal.

Opposite Page:
I size up the 'gutter' splint on our bandy legged camel. (Photo Shropshire Star, inset Author)

Other casualties occur, too, from outside factors beyond our control, barbiturate poisoning being but one. Over a period of time, it became clear that either a vet or an errant farmer was destroying farm animals with barbiturates without applying the requisite labelling to the carcasses. Unseen and undetectable, therefore, the carcasses would go through the usual processing at the abattoir, culminating in delivery to us if they were unfit for human consumption. The first sign of trouble would be about eight hours after feeding, with the barbiturates by then fully absorbed into the bloodstream. Invariably, in these races against time the odds are heavily stacked against the exotic animal and highlight the perpetual dilemma in dealing with them. If a tiger, for example, is so incapacitated that it can be handled and therefore treated, the chances are that it's too late, as it occasionally has been, but you still try. Curiously, the cases to date remain individual ones. Logically, one would suppose that if an animal was euthanised with barbiturates, then the entire carcass might be affected and, with the animal dissected into the requisite number of 15lb. pieces, each could be potentially fatal. Illogically, the only rational explanation appears to be that only the chunk containing the actual injection site contains sufficient fatal toxicity. Nevertheless, having treated an unsuspecting cat, it's meant many an anxious night camped out in the carnivore houses keeping it warm, topped up with fluids and keeping a weather eye open less further cases develop. A wait not helped, of course, by the prospect of having to dig out up to three tons of deep-frozen meat from the cold room the next day for disposal, as no one can tell what hidden terrors the remainder of the consignment holds. Then, of course, there's the three tons of replacement meat to unload! It takes the County Analyst time to confirm our suspicions with an accurate diagnosis - time we don't have. Meanwhile, we make intelligent guesses and keep a cool head. Sometimes, if the symptoms aren't classic ones, I've used the 'Immobilon' drugs antagonist 'Revivon' on lethargic cats with success, on the assumption that this, too, has entered their food chain via an unmarked carcass. 'Starve' days are a common feature in the management of captive carnivores. In a natural

Opposite Page:
'Five' and her famous boot.
(Photo J. James, Birmingham Post and Mail)

environment, they don't, of course, eat every day or even every week, sometimes not properly even for weeks. A healthy wolf can survive a month without eating, so, to simulate these conditions, we 'starve' them two days a week. This gives their appetite an edge and keeps them lean, mean and agile like any athlete should be. On occasion, we still use the feed cage concept, too, though it's no longer tied onto the back of the landrover! Instead, a caged trailer is filled with the day's ration, a keeper and often the odd cameraman or two and towed through the big cats for whom it does, in a sense, represent the thrill of the chase and is, perhaps, the ultimate 'meals on wheels'.

We quickly found that African animals weren't as predictable in their birth cycles as their European counterparts who invariably have specific breeding seasons. Therefore, at a time of year when we are closed and it is popularly assumed that we're all in hibernation, we're usually at full stretch. You can have giraffe for Christmas, a gnu for New Year, lion cubs on Valentine's Day or a hippo for Easter. There's always something born on Mothering Sunday, too. You cannot let a photographic opportunity like that slip by! Meanwhile, the ostrich and emu can be laying by January, by which time we're keeping a weather eye open for the first wallabies in the pouch. Asian species are similar, with tiger cubs, Bactrian camel and Yak calves no strangers to our deep mid-winters. Prize of place here would undoubtedly go to a yak calf born at 2.30a.m., in temperatures of -19°F, which survived with consummate ease. Probably the worst winter to date came in 1980/1 and gave my first Suzuki jeep a real baptism of fire. For days on end, it was the only thing that moved within the entire park. It snowed non-stop for three days and nights, then froze hard for seven weeks. We hired industrial blowers to thaw out the meat, then filed off through the snow drifts to the carnivore houses like Smithfield porters, with a joint of meat on each shoulder. More than once, we found on arrival that the meat had frozen to our jackets and gloves, so we had to return and begin the tortuous process all over again. We thawed out the taps and the locks but fed the animals in near darkness, for we could do nothing about the penetrating cold that sapped the power from

Opposite Page:
Moving a sedated lion. The bevy of blondes is a complete coincidence! (Photo Author)

224

the cables buried beneath the ground. Not a single animal died, although we came close to losing one or two. We'd brought many of the deer and cattle down to the buildings by the lakeside for ease of care, only to find that with the ice six inches deep and thickening by the day, they were wandering off across the ice to the other side. With drugs freezing in the darts, bringing them to heel proved difficult. Ultimately, though, the only inventory changes reflected births, but the first daffodil was a welcome sight that spring.

The inability of the veterinary work to respect terms of time or consideration is unending. Where were you when Ian Botham stopped the Stock Exchange with his test match heroics? Feeding lions. When David Beckham was sent off against Argentina? With the elephants. During the eclipse? With our white tigers. Then there was the monsoon-like Christmas Day which flooded us out and the Boxing Day hurricane that blew many a fence down. I've darted deer (a Pere David) with Stan by moonlight at 2a.m. to facilitate a calving, firing the dart straight down the beam of a headlamp. As a 'green' teenager, my sister-in-law will never forget the Sunday morning after the night before she spent with me in the vet's surgery unravelling a lion cub's intestines to find the blockage. But then, she knew she'd drunk too much! The unsociable hours bring other problems, too. Who draws the short straw for the late shifts and the weekends? The rookie vet, of course! One Sunday morning, one poor girl spent two hours with me (on *my* day off!) administering an enema to a constipated rhino - all four gallons of it! She'd scarcely seen a rhino before, much less worked on one. Soon afterwards, she decided on a career in a small animal practice! A Sunday evening was once the scene of a post mortem. I wasn't keen on the way that Stan was wielding the knife but the warning was only half out of my mouth when the inevitable happened..... it slipped and plunged deep into his wrist. He turned as white as his gown and dropped like an ox. I wrapped him up and half dragged, half carried him to his car, 'phoned his wife and rushed him to hospital. He'd never have made it alone. White in fact is a distinctly unlucky colour in the animal world. Being born white (whether albino or not) is one of the cruelest hands that mother nature can deal. Conspicuous from afar, (see page 215,) to man and beast alike and invariably a prized specimen to the former, survival into old age is seldom achieved. And it's not just insects and reptiles that can be as dangerous dead as alive. A two-ton hippo once fell on my mobile 'phone. Unfortunately, it was in my pocket at the time! The animal had died and we were retrieving it from the water late one Saturday night. The rest of the herd were displaying very keen close-quarters interest, so the only way in was on the crane jib which lowered me precariously over the fence to attach the hoist. As it took the strain, the hippo was hauled from the deep, leaving me on the bank. Suddenly, the noose slipped on the wet flesh and this great hulk fell straight back on top of me. Flat on my back, pinned by both feet and sliding inexorably back into the water under its weight, by rolling my eyes I could see the other hippo closing in over the top of my head. Fortunately, we came to a halt in the nick of time with just my head and shoulders out of the water. Consternation reigned up on the bank for they couldn't see me beneath the carcass, but, eventually, they were persuaded that I was still alive, if not kicking! Once extracted, I returned, bruised black and blue and stinking to high heaven, and got it right second time around. I was not popular in the Chinese takeaway on the way home!

The advance of science, or the veterinary application of it, was never more vividly illustrated than in the case of 'Sammy', a Bennett's wallaby found naked and cold in the pouch of its dead mother by her keeper. Angela had come to the park to spend a day working in Pets Corner with her lifelong friend, my sister-in-law, and simply never went home. At agricultural college, she'd passed out with distinction only to find that farmers weren't interested in employing girls. That industry's loss proved to be our gain, practically and academically, for when Angela and I decided that she'd be the first of our keepers to attempt the City and Guilds Zoo Management Correspondence Course (she as the student, I the tutor), she did it again. This time, however, it was a double distinction - the only one of her year. Totally dedicated and a slave to her animals' every need, there can be no better role model for any aspiring guardian of animals. She represents everything that is decent and honest in this life and it rubs off on everything and everyone she comes into contact with. A woollen hat made an ideal artificial pouch. In it, Sammy, weighing a mere

6oz., travelled everywhere with Angela in order to get his hourly feed of tinned Carnation milk. Our children invariably looked forward to us going out because Sammy came to babysit! Like many others, they couldn't get their tongues around 'wallaby', it always came out as 'wobbily'(!), as indeed it would one day from Angela's own daughter. For two months, all went well and Sammy lived happily with the cats, dogs and everything else in Angela's menagerie of orphans. One morning, disaster struck. The minute I saw Angela, I knew something was wrong. As the little waif peered from his pouch, I saw the white milky cataract which had appeared overnight first in one eye, then the following day in the other. After all the blood, sweat and tears expended in rearing him, he was totally and permanently blind - by conventional criteria.

One evening, whilst the staff were distracted, I spirited Sammy away. In these situations, staff require handling with as much tact and acumen as the animals themselves. People who profess to being animal lovers can be a nightmare. Once sentiment and human emotion intervene, sweet logic and reason go by the board, at the very time when objectivity must be paramount in assessing options and quality of life thereafter. Our vets, the long suffering and newly renamed Vale Veterinary Group, had heard of a specialist ophthalmic vet and got me a referral. So, off I set for 'our' appointment. It was surprisingly easy to find - a little village outside Leominster, Herefordshire, called Eye! It transpired that the cataracts had developed due to a peculiarity of the nutrition within wallaby lenses. An enzyme responsible for lactose breakdown was missing, almost certainly because of the mother's poor and aged condition. The build-up of osmolarity within his lenses as the sugar levels increased, a drawing in of extra water and an overhydration of the lens fibres all contributed to the resulting milky whiteness. As the surgeon, Paul Evans, explained all this to me in layman's terms, I felt vindicated in leaving Angela behind, as much in the dark as Sammy was. There was no need for her to be there when he was euthanised. Then, I heard him say that all this was really no problem given the machine before me, the same thing using the same intraocular surgery techniques that are used on human eyes. The only difficulty was the anaesthesia. That was easy. I'd done that much many times! So, a date was set for Sammy's return, with Angela. One eye was tackled first, restoring 70% vision and when recuperation was complete the other, all filmed and photographed through the same Zeiss operating microscope used to do the operation. Like the DNA testing, the birth control implants, the micro-chipping, the laser optics on the dart rifle and the electro-magnet in the dart flight that enables us to track the location of the animal (or the dart itself if it becomes detached), we'd moved on light years since the first operation Stan and I had performed on an exotic animal - extracting a tooth from a lioness laid out on the bonnet of the manager's car, in full view of twenty other lions, whilst the public looked on. Sammy became a celebrity, but after an appearance at the British Small Animals Veterinary Association Congress at Birmingham's International Conference Centre's inaugural muster, he retired from public life into 'anonymity' - beneath the annual gaze of 450,000 summer visitors - as just another wallaby. For all the space-age, state-of-the-art veterinary progress, however, there's still a place for the age-old tried and trusted methods. The next veterinary problem was a case of laminitis in a pony from Pets Corner. The cure? The traditional one of standing the patient in the pond to cool the feet down.

Sammy, however, was lucky in that he had a defined future and was readily absorbed back into the wallaby group. This is not always the case with hand reared animals, felines in particular. I've reared lions, tigers, leopards and pumas, but the minute they're removed from the mother, however laudable the reason, a question mark hangs over them. I've reared wolves, too, and reintroduced them to the pack, but it's much more difficult with cats, who instinctively turn on a 'stranger' thrust back into their midst a few months on. Once, one of the girls and I had to rear thirty six lion cubs together! This inadvertently solved the problem because we'd simply created an entire pride! On another occasion, we removed a tiger cub suffering from a vitamin B12 deficiency from one of two litters born almost simultaneously. Ian, one of my deputies, painstakingly reared her for three months, then the problems began. The cub had been fine at home, but was becoming more agitated by the day at the park. Then Ian stumbled upon the answer. He lived in Shropshire and, at home, the cub had become accustomed to Radio Shropshire. Here, the cub was listening to Radio Hereford and Worcester and didn't like it one little bit! Retuning the radio had the desired effect. It may sound far-fetched until one considers the latest theory as to how the giraffe communicates. Hitherto considered mute in the conventional sense of the word, scientists now believe they use infrasonic sound to 'speak' to each other, a sound normally inaudible to the human ear. I've only heard this startling, high-pitched squeak a couple of times in high stress situations, which may indicate the tone has broken down in the heat of the moment. However, in America (where else!), this 'language' has apparently been broken down into regional dialects, with South Carolina giraffes developing a distinct infrasonic regional drawl! But what, meanwhile, of our tiger cub? Although more settled, she couldn't rock along to Radio Shropshire for ever, so we took a chance. The two mothers and their respective litters were released outside for the first time on the same day and mixed. With so much to preoccupy them, no one noticed the extra cub back in their midst! Another factor which cannot be ignored is that hand reared animals often develop behavioural trends totally out of character with the rest of their kind, giving people totally the wrong impression of the species. If you were, for instance, to release a hand reared deer, it would become a menace. Fearless of man, it would destroy crops, gardens and even attack people (if it were a male), quite apart from probably being a road hazard with no fear of vehicles either. We once had a hand reared eland on the inventory with which you could do anything and take anywhere. If an uninitiated observer were to try this with just any eland, the results would be catastrophic.

Perhaps the most important veterinary lesson of all, though, is to know when to leave well alone. Fools rush in. The biggest single cause of illness and disease in exotic animals is that vague, indefinable thing called stress. Stress can manifest itself in many ways, perhaps the most common cause in captive situations being excessive numbers. Once a population has passed a certain level,

Opposite Page:
Left: The first operation that Stan Kilby and I performed, removing a lions tooth on a car bonnet. (Photo P. Smith)
Right: By comparison modern laser surgery on the wallaby's eye.
(Photo P. Evans, Eye Veterinary Clinic)

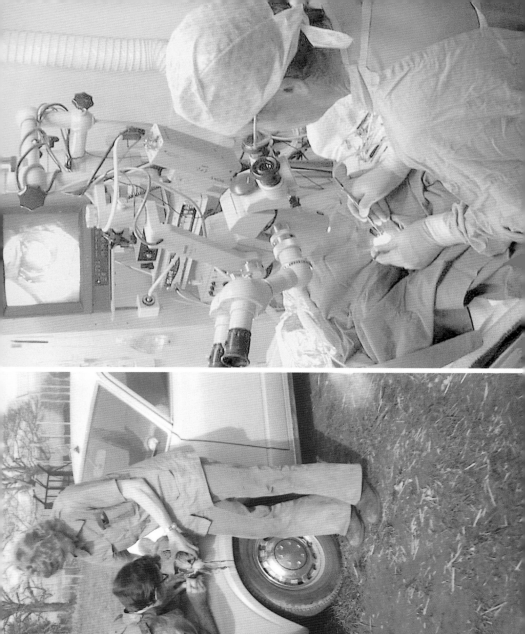

nature decides 'enough is enough' and all manner of problems will emerge. Often, it transpires that the condition has been carried for years to no ill effect until the stress threshold is breached, as it does in us. So often, too, the trauma associated with treatment compounds the original problem beyond all justification. The wiser hand will often leave well alone or apply but the most subtle of touches. Sometimes, for example, when a problem suggests that vaccinations are the answer, traditionally two inoculations a few weeks apart are required before cover is established. The second shot is frequently impractical, with the exotic animal not readily to hand, but the first is often sufficient. Given this nudge in the right direction, the animals will adjust and cope. Curiously, too, if you are looking after animals properly and applying the 'prevention is better than cure' philosophy, you get little or no experience in many of the more common maladies. You simply don't encounter them. Frequently, though, we are forced to treat animals and/or take them from the public domain knowing full well that they are best left to Mother Nature. An animal left amongst his own kind will invariably fare better than the one isolated 'off limits' because of a condition which might offend public sensitivities. Try explaining it, though, to the lady who complains bitterly of the 'bad taste' when animals mate before the public, the 'obscenity' of them giving birth during opening hours or eating raw meat in front of her children. Why, then, if these scenes of unparalleled debauchery are so offensive, didn't she simply drive on? She was busy videoing the scenes, of course - lock, stock and barrel! Similarly, one occasionally receives letters expressing concern about something witnessed during a visit, often weeks previously. Given the inordinate delay in expressing the concern, one must question its validity.

Calving time invariably results in veterinary work. I've calved most of our species at various times, including ten deer species, camels, bison, zebra and, during our honeymoon, a giraffe, to mention but a few. Like domestic farm stock, if there's going to be a problem it's invariably with a first calver - but not always. We once spent an inordinate amount of time deliberating over a perceived problem with one of the Highland cattle, only to conclude that she was shaping up for milk fever. We were wrong. The next morning we arrived at work to discover that, at the age of twenty, she'd suddenly produced twins during the night unaided, and went on to rear them. If this is highly unusual in this breed, then we were to be further dumbfounded when another cow repeated the feat. So, too, did a bison, a zebra, red and fallow deer all in the same year, something that had never happened before or since. Was it something in the water?! If there are problems and if mother and calf are alive when we begin, in 95% of cases I can save both. You quickly learn the tricks of the trade when calving animals that have to be sedated to make them approachable. One common mistake is failing to appreciate that if the mother is tranquillised, so too is the calf within her and it will need the reviving agent on withdrawal. Most important is the need to retain mother and progeny on recovery. Once revived, a mother rarely relates to the wet bundle thrust under her nose on awakening and invariably disappears without it. Confinement as tightly as possible in a stall or trailer for a day or so, until a bond is formed, will ensure that the calf will be reared upon release - though great care is needed to avoid separation during the release procedure. Sometimes, after lengthy labour, an animal will simply give up and not care what you do as long as you relieve them of their burden, sentiments expressed no doubt, at times, by many women! Outside, their menfolk fret and pace the corridor, a behavioural trait which, when seen in captive animals, is attributed to that most cardinal of sins - stereotyped behaviour. Sensing this acquiescence, I've calved animals up to camel size on many occasions without sedation at all.

Often forgotten, too, is the potentially huge difference in recommended dose rates when tranquillising animals, depending on seasonal variations in behaviour, the condition of the animal and extremes of temperature. If action cannot be avoided during the latter, a half dose is often sufficient. If an animal is ill, again a fraction of the suggested dose will invariably put it down for treatment. It's common sense if one thinks about it. After all, if you are suffering with flu, you're pretty drowsy and need little encouragement to fall asleep. When called out with the dart rifle to assist in an emergency, I've had many a disagreement with a vet intent on blindly following manufacturers' instructions on the label. Recognising the potential for disaster, in some cases I've refused to help unless they've backed down. So much per live hundredweight becomes meaningless after, say, the half-ton mark, when you can halve the dose to achieve the end result - a point vividly illustrated one afternoon when I was called onto a farm to dart a bull. The farmer, a stubborn old character who persisted in carrying on despite being confined to a walking frame, hadn't cleaned his bull pen out for years. As the bedding accumulated, he merely employed a builder to add a further layer of blocks to the wall. By now, the bull was stranded 8ft. in the air with chronically overgrown feet which needed trimming before the hapless creature could be packed off to market. The vet calculated a dose comprising an entire bottle of the dreaded drug 'Immobilon'. The price of my co-operation was half that dose and, duly subdued, the bull was soon lowered to ground level for the first time in years. Seconds later, the vet and I were startled out of our skins by a thunderous roar behind us. Still on crutches, the farmer had started a chain saw and was waving it wildly about out his head (and ours!) as he slashed one-handed at the overgrown feet of the recumbent bull. Another sharp exit! Conversely, with a sedative, once an animal is stressed or excited (after an escape, for example), you can administer it by the pint to no obvious effect other than to ultimately kill it. Much, too, depends on what you're attempting to do with the animal. Operating requires one dose, calving another, whilst simply walking it into a transport box is another matter altogether. An animal's temperament is crucial, too. A hand reared animal can often be brought to earth with little more than a wet needle, an agitated one at the height of the rut will invariably need higher than the standard dose for an animal of its weight. No operation, though, is without its perils. I was once called to another county to bring a deer to task for an operation. Having darted it and done my bit, I returned the gun to the safety of the car and set the alarm. On my return, though, it was immediately obvious that all was not well. I coughed, spluttered and dropped veiled hints in veterinary parlance that I hoped the watching owner wouldn't understand, all to no avail. Eventually, I managed to distract him by discreetly ringing the 'phone number in the house from my mobile 'phone. This gave me the opportunity to point out to the two vets and their nurse that they were castrating a dead deer!

There is, too, much variation between species as to their susceptibility to a given drug. It fascinates many to discover that with one, the oft-mentioned 'Immobilon', an Etorphine-based drug a hundred times more powerful than morphine, the dose needed to drop a wolf is the same required for a three year old rhino, yet it would have to be increased fivefold at least to catch the average fallow deer doe or a six year old African elephant. To catch an adult ostrich, however, you'd have to triple the dose again, knowing full well that the contents of the syringe *needle* could kill a person. In the early days, a Home Office licence was required under the Misuse of Drugs Act 1971 to both possess and use it. Curiously, it was belatedly discovered that the licensing system couldn't be legally upheld, and it was promptly abandoned. With the risk of Home Office inspectors descending upon you at dawn like VAT men now gone, the responsibility fell squarely on the shoulders of any vet who chose to dispense it to a client. If there were a disaster, the vet gets it in the neck - such is the trust that Stan and his partners have always shown in me, for it is not done lightly. Indeed, members of their own profession have succumbed to its accidental misuse. It is, though, perhaps the ultimate form of 'jungle juice'. Cheap, safe and highly effective across a wide range of species in relatively small doses (which is important when it is being administered via a dart) and readily reversible, it revolutionised the capture and care of exotic animals - both in the wild and in captivity. It's just that it's potentially deadly in the homo sapien!

Fortunately, such products aren't required when dealing with venomous reptiles, for there is danger enough in the reptile house as it is. Luckily, since the inception of the reptile house, my contemporary in this field has been the redoubtable Mark O'Shea or, to give him his full title, Mark O'Shea, B.Sc, FRGS, Curator of Reptiles and star of many a documentary on his speciality, in which he is undoubtedly amongst the world's finest. Under his watchful eyes, I have, on occasion, been seen stomach-tubing the odd alligator 'in extremis' with black treacle and sugar to redress low blood sugar levels and feeding the occasional cobra. In extremis, too, I found that the resuscitation methods learnt in the lambing sheds work equally well on sea lions and my search and rescue techniques on snakes. One Sunday afternoon, I drew the

*Mark O'Shea loads up an alligator.
I concentrate on taking the photos!
(Photo Author)*

*Ian Dean Netscher, his tiger cub and radio
Shropshire!
(Photo Author)*

*The lion feeding cage and occupants. On this occasion a Central TV camera crew doing a
live broadcast! (Photo Author)*

short straw and answered a call to investigate an adder in a detached house ten miles away. After an hour or two tearing up skirting and floorboards, I felt the need to remind the owner that I wasn't a joiner. Someone would have to restore the property. United in their dread of snakes, the couple urged me on for another hour. It was, of course, only a grass snake!

Once many of the early absurdities were ironed out of our system, enabling me to evolve coherent management strategies, assiduous record keeping began to reveal many genuine husbandry problems. Crucial even then, obligatory now under the Zoo Licensing Act, the value of records is inestimable. Each animal will have an individual record like we all have at our doctor's - if they can find them! The value of what you're recording may not become apparent for years, decades even, but one day something will trigger, like the lifting of a shroud from your eyes, to reveal startling conclusions as many hitherto unfathomable matters slip neatly into place. Much illness and disease runs in patterns or specific cycles. Record keeping highlights these, enabling pre-emptive measures to be instigated. In animals that aren't readily handlable, prevention is even more important than cure. In a broader context, of course, if an animal population is in such dire straights that conservation efforts are required, then nothing can be achieved without first knowing what remains and where. Without the records, of course, the dire straights may well pass unnoticed or simply be dismissed as one of the 'fashionable' trends in keeping animals. Many of our species appear, too, in the national, European or even international stud books for their kind as we become ever more accountable.

Even the most simplistic form of records, like ear-tagging for identification, can provide a fascinating insight into animal behaviour. Seeing a mother with two or three calves at foot, suckling them even, most people invariably assume twins or triplets, yet none may be her own progeny. By tagging calves born to dams which are themselves tagged, one establishes a clear datum level. If a calf dies, you sometimes see its mother steal another. Similarly, an orphaned calf may begin running with another dam. To the consternation, no doubt, of many a farmer who's spent hours trying to persuade a ewe to adopt a lamb, most species of deer and antelope seem to 'multiple suckle' naturally. I've got the photo's to prove it! By the same token, unless you are fortunate enough to actually witness twins born, you can never assume that they are twins. You may have a stockman's intuition or have strong suspicions, but with a record system you can state categorically that something has, indeed, happened and draw the appropriate conclusions.

Our soil is poor and chronically deficient in copper, which can manifest itself within the animals in many ways. Physically, scouring, discoloration of the pelage (to the point where 'red' deer turn white), loss of condition and ricket-like appearance are all attributed to this, as, too, is loss of fertility. Part of the remedy used to be to double the copper content of the ration which typically, twenty years ago, was only eighteen parts per million. Nowadays, it is such a universally accepted problem that thirty eight parts per million is virtually standard in all cattle rations. It is even appearing now in horse rations. No wonder people query what we eat. Sometimes, even this isn't sufficient, so copper injections have long become part of our veterinary armoury. The variety of ailments in all species that I've corrected with that little blue syringe is quite astounding. Invariably, if correctly diagnosed, the transformation can be spectacular - occurring literally overnight. Whilst I've never seen a bovine species suffer from a copper overdose, sheep, especially continental and exotic breeds, have no tolerance to copper whatsoever, which is why its maximum legal limit in sheep rations is thirteen parts per million. Not that any is added - this is simply to allow for the copper that exists within the constituent ingredients, like the grass. Conversely, pig rations are so steeped in copper that if the manure is spread on the ground, copper toxicity levels sufficient to kill entire flocks of sheep have occurred. Once in the system, there is no removing it. It remains a complex problem, often varying from paddock to paddock, species to species. I've encountered animals with no detectable copper in their system at all, but in a perfect state of health, yet, when moved elsewhere, they fall apart as their metabolism seems unable to adapt to the change.

The dilemma is complicated for us by the presence of the 'yellow peril', ragwort - the tall, yellow flowering plant often seen swaying in the breeze on motorway embankments. An acute biological toxin, it is invariably fatal when eaten and it becomes highly palatable when dry, in hay or even when ensiled, when the level of toxicity will percolate the entire clamp. On our dry, shallow, free-draining sandy soil, it takes but ten days without rain in the summer for it to wilt and become palatable. Once eaten, animals frequently develop a craving for it and the time-scale for action is short - just seven pounds of the green plant is sufficient to kill an animal the size of an adult cow. There has been much discusion in country magazines over the last couple of summers on dealing with ragwort. One piece of advice invariably missing is to wear gloves when handling it. It can be absorbed through the skin. We've long since instilled a control programme of spraying and digging it up, a thankless but essential undertaking. There is a theory that ragwort is rich in copper. Quite why, then, it proliferates on our copper-deficient soil and why one of the commonly advocated methods of control is grazing with sheep (the one species relatively immune to the plant), who have no tolerance to copper at all, is obscure!

On such things, one learnt to make knife-edge decisions which had to be right. Again, one of them was keeping calm. In the early days, amongst the proliferation of comings and goings, came the appointment of a company veterinary supremo over our European parks. The CV showed him to be a real whiz-kid. Despite his tender years, he'd been everywhere and done everything, except stay put anywhere for more than five minutes. My experience of people of this ilk casts them as a disruptive menace. Going in both feet first, like the proverbial bull in the china shop, they turn an institution upside down and inside out like a whirlwind. They then depart as abruptly as they came, leaving others to clean up the mess. So it proved. Unfortunately, his arrival coincided with the decimation of both the wolf pack and one of our deer herds. Despite all efforts, no prognosis was forthcoming. Special vaccines were prepared for the wolf cubs, containing antibodies against everything the laboratory could think off, all to no avail. Stan and I were put through the mill repeatedly. For several months, there was dark talk of ineptitude, poor diets, negligence even, on the part of all concerned - strong words, indeed, in professional parlance. The solutions suggested

were as absurd as they were impractical but, ominously, amongst them was to come - 'maybe it was time for fresh faces'. Then, one day, whilst taking some soil samples, I found a plant I'd never seen before. At that time, it was extremely rare locally: it was ragwort. Had the lab checked the liver samples for ragwort? The silence spoke volumes, but they soon confirmed it. But what, then, of the wolves? The inspiration came in the early hours, so I had to wait to ring Stan and he, in turn, the lab, albeit a different one this time. We were in luck. Baffled by the extent of the damage to the liver tissue, the like of which they'd never seen before in canines, they'd preserved the livers and were able to re-examine them nearly a year on. I was right. The cubs had played with those tall stems swaying in the wind, had chewed them, tugged at them and, it seemed, ingested enough of the toxin to kill them. The findings were unique enough to be written up in an odd journal or two, but our veterinary overlord wasn't there to read them. He'd never heard of ragwort. We never heard of him again, either.

One of our finest veterinary hours undoubtedly came as a result of a panic-stricken call to me one bleak December afternoon whilst I was at Longleat safari park. One of our giraffe bulls had caught his mouth in a fence and smashed his lower jaw. He was a complete mess. With a weekend looming, the omens were not auspicious. I charged home through the winter evening but, at 8p.m. on a Friday evening, Stan Kilby and I concluded there was little to be done except keep him isolated, warm and quiet. In a drama, a cool head is priceless and we had long since become dab hands at it. On Saturday morning, Stan and I pored over ancient text books and an old giraffe skull, which my hapless assistant, Ian, had unearthed from a dusty cupboard. These things only ever happen to him when I'm away! It was all the reference material available. We talked to other vets, dispatched staff to hospitals around the Midlands to collect orthopaedic attachments and instruments that might just conceivably be needed, for nothing like this had ever been contemplated before. Sunday saw a further conference, this time with Dr. John Lewis of the International Zoo Veterinary Group (David Taylor and all) who had driven up

Opposite Page:
A donkey grazes a field full of ragwort and (inset) biological control:- Cinnabar Moth caterpillars feeding on the plants.
(Photos Author)

from London. My first recollection of this notable trio (Andrew Greenwood being the third) was in 1974 when, like so many establishments, we undertook a disastrous project to keep dolphins. Even in the dizzy naivety of those distant days, it should have been readily apparent to all that our facility wasn't, and never could be, suitable for these graceful and intelligent creatures of the deep for whom it had, nevertheless, been purpose-built. They 'performed' fitfully and unenthusiastically for a few months (before audiences more enamoured by the low-cut cleavage of the trainer's undersize swimwear) before falling prey, one by one, to a succession of ailments. Night after summer night, we would pump out the 30,000 gallons of water from the pool and spend hours placing tubes up and down various bodily orifices to diagnose and treat ulcers and other stress-related conditions. All the time, the plaintive squealing and calling was pitiful to behold. Finally, after a year without a 'show', they went. In the early 70's, there were about twenty five dolphin pools in the country. Thankfully, modern zoo criteria for keeping these enthralling creatures is so stringent that, with Windsor Safari Park's closure twenty years later, there wasn't a single facility suitable for them in the entire country. I hope it remains so.

We pondered on these matters over many mugs of tea, debating the pros and cons of the current situation. It was worth a try. I rang both the Managing Director, David Chorley, and the Director of Operations, Ivan Knezovich, at their respective homes that Sunday lunchtime. Like Vales, both had always shown total faith in me and I could have gone ahead regardless and spent the estimated £4,500 on an animal only worth £1,000, but it was only fair to at least advise them. Neither even knew we had a giraffe with a broken jaw. Once I explained the problem, both, to their eternal credit and quite independently of each other, said the same thing, 'Forget the money - we can stand it. If you think you can do it, go ahead.' Preparations were already well advanced! I'd administered the pre-operation dose of antibiotics and gone home for a breather. Monday was going to be a long day.

I loathe tranquillising giraffe. All legs and neck, there's an enormous risk of something breaking when they hit the ground, for they do so with an enormous crash. Once down, the immediate worry is the regurgitation of the stomach contents within that long windpipe. In days of old, they were routinely denied anything by mouth for up to seventy two hours before a planned operation, to reduce this risk. The drawback, though, was that they were frequently too weak to get up again afterwards. On one horrendous morning, I'd once seen four giraffe perish in this manner and determined that there must be a better way. The risks are high, though much reduced with experience and careful forward planning. It's not always possible, of course. Once, a giraffe put his head clean through a door and went careering around the park with it stuck firmly over its neck. I dropped it quickly, revived it even faster and prayed while I rehung the retrieved door - a welcome distraction this, for the lack of preparation was scarcely ideal. It survived.

On this occasion, the staff had toiled to line the pen walls and, by Monday morning, the entire pen was padded to a height of ten feet with straw bales and the floor deep-littered. An adjoining pen was converted into a temporary ante-room, with all the equipment piled into it just in case it were needed. With the door tightly closed and the central heating on full blast, Stan Kilby and Chris Carter (one of Stan's partners), together with Messrs. Greenwood and Lewis and myself, went through it all one last time and fired the first dart. Once sedated, a controlled fall under rigged lines left the staff little to do except watch from the 'balcony', the feeding platform ten feet up the wall, as the vets went to work. Carpenters, mechanics, secretaries and gardeners entered the hushed auditorium as the first 'hands-on' diagnosis was made. How bad was it? Was there any point in going further? The prognosis wasn't good but, once started, their was no stopping us. We went for it.

It 'only' took two hours to drill, pin and unite the jaw. I fussed around administering as directed, as the vets well and truly earnt their corn. Then came the difficult bit. Many elaborate operations are possible on exotic species, as with any other. We've done caesareans, for example, on lions and camels, others have done them on elephants, but the difficulty is the aftercare with animals that aren't readily handlable. A giraffe lurches forward as a prelude to rising and one could see all the hard work literally

*The giraffe we calved on honeymoon!
(Photo J. James, Birmingham Post and Mail)*

*The broken jaw.
(Photo A. Potter)*

244

disintegrating before our eyes as, temporarily disorientated, his chin hit the floor. But, blindfolded and held down for as long as possible to ensure maximum recovery from anaesthesia, we avoided this pitfall and he lurched upright to tower above us. Then, the going really got tough. For days, he couldn't eat or drink. Slowly, he learnt to sip warm water and lectate and suck up the mashed banana, grapes and diced soft lettuce that Angela administered around the clock as a labour of love. The sheer imperativeness of maintaining antibiotic cover soon became apparent. If we stopped cover, he deteriorated within twelve hours to the point where he wouldn't eat. Throughout Christmas and the New Year, I gave him this life-saving succour twice a day to stave off the malingering infection. The dart equipment was performing indifferently, but salvation wouldn't be at hand until after the holiday period that normal people have. At 11p.m.on New Year's Eve, a dart exploded on impact, the metal tail flight coming back past my ear clean through the wall and out into the darkness. But we weren't to be denied, we'd come too far. Slowly but surely, Angela's painstaking efforts at nutrition paid off as we kept him in his centrally heated individual pen all winter, weaning him once again onto solids. Luck, as ever, played a part. I was dreading the prospect of a repeat performance to remove the pins, but slowly they worked themselves loose of their own accord and, ultimately, simply fell out. By Easter, he was united once more with the others, indistinguishable from them as he once more roamed the park where he remains to this day - as unique a giraffe as ever there was, a world first and a living tribute to all who assisted in his darkest hours. 'Sticks and stones shall break my bones but you will never break me',' he may think. And so say all of us.

CHAPTER 14
PR Man

(To Wendy Jackson, my silent partner in PR)

I nitially, like everything else, public relations were a disaster. Everyone could talk to anyone about anything and frequently did so. Many a calamity (and there were plenty of them) was to be compounded beyond all measure by subsequent mishandling of the consequences. Bad publicity is made worse when the media perceive it incorrectly. Naturally suspicious, inherently cynical, the moment they smell 'cover-up', you've got problems. The difficulty was recognised by the appointment of a public relations officer, a Mr. Blott, fairly early on. With no ground rules or background on which to draw, the nickname of 'Blott the Clott', although apt, was perhaps unfair. Subsequent internal appointments fared little better, so the net was cast wider. Agencies in Birmingham and even London were expected to control day-to-day handling of the media. The problem was always the same, yet naively overlooked - 99% of the PR emanating from a wildlife park evolves around animals, believe it or not! If you knew anything about animals, you could spot a story and/or a picture a mile off. If you couldn't tell a wallaby's pouch from a camel's backside, then such opportunities slipped by. If everything had to go through a PR person, he couldn't move without me at his elbow. Seeing or sensing this, a questioner would inevitably begin to address me directly, thereby making the publicity man redundant in most situations. Any live interviews couldn't, of course, come across like that so, again, the man involved, or the man with the background, came to the fore.

Opposite Page:
Beauty and the bird! A classical Easter shot from J. James, Birmingham Post and Mail.
(Emu chick on the left, Ostrich on the right.)

Preparing a press release was equally perilous. Little clangers about going to Africa to see the tigers didn't endear much credibility. Similarly, giving Vietnamese boat people a free day out was fine, but photographing them in rowing boats on the lake?! Then there was the little matter of the 'tame' wolf that went off to star in 'The Legend of the Werewolf' being filmed at Pinewood Studios in Buckinghamshire. It didn't live up to its billing, escaped and was shot dead near the M4 the following day. Essentially, the facts and the judgements had to involve people at the cutting edge. A media agency trying to do the same thing from the remoteness of a distant city office was even worse. Any newsworthy event, like a birth or, heaven forbid, an accident, requires instant answers in the swift-moving high-tech world of modern media work. Waiting for the agency to turn up is rarely appropriate, although, on occasion, it can allow sufficient breathing space to get your act together! Once again, though, the press release a week later scarcely sufficed. In addition, a further problem frequently arose. These guys in their high-rise city centre office blocks worked office hours and had holidays. Our needs rarely coincided with such a lifestyle. The institutional reaction in extremis must be quick and accurate. This will determine how the media interprets information and how they play you and the story, both currently and in the future. The instant you waver, control of the situation is lost.

Public relations and/or justifying keeping animals in captivity can prove problematical. Purists point out that the animals belong in the wild and I certainly wouldn't disagree, but that assumes that there is a 'wild' left. For many species there isn't. Then consider what has happened to some in the wild which have been reduced to near or total extinction. It isn't even as if the lessons have always been heeded, for in Mozambique white rhino have been exterminated twice this century. By contrast, without the restraints imposed by the climate, availability of food supply, predation, disease and, above all, poaching to contend with, the park's original rhino imports in 1973 are all now over thirty and still in good heart. Some species, like our Pere David deer or the Przewalski's horses, owe their existence today solely to captive breeding. Were it not for this, we'd read about them in the history books rather than zoo guide books. Similarly, if the purists had their way and closed all zoos, where then the debate? With ever-enlightened methods of keeping animals in captivity coming to the fore, this call is decreasing. But, putting aside for a moment the uncertain fate of the world's captive populations, if this scenario ever unfolded, how could one, for instance, stimulate debate on rhino or tiger poaching to people who'd never seen one. Seeing the subject matter in the flesh gives an immediate sense of perspective. Conversely, if the only place where they could be viewed were in the wild, then the exodus to do so would undoubtably contribute in no small measure to the destruction of the very habitat and eco-structure they need in order to survive. Any species that survives on this planet, with the exception of man (the root cause of the problem), will inevitably do so in infinitely fewer numbers than ever before. This makes the margin for error in an error shrewn, man manipulated ecology even less. Even animals like the lion, synonymous with the public's popular perception of the African continent, is struggling to hold its own in the 'wild' as distinct from game reserves and parks. Ever fewer species can be said to exist totally independent of man and, therefore, held to be truly wild. Even a European success story, that of the saving of the European bison by captive breeding and subsequent reintroduction into the last vestige of its former range in the Bialowieza forest along the Russian-Polish border, is man-manipulated by virtue of bull exchanges and winter feeding.

In all honesty, the much vaunted reintroduction programmes from captive breeding are few and far between in terms of sheer practicality in this day and age, but captive populations nevertheless can make immense practical contributions to conserving gene pools and our understanding of the species, often in overlooked ways. Keeping a species in captivity in collections scattered around the world, for example, ensures, albeit perhaps incidently, that it is extremely unlikely that any single, natural or man-made disaster like an outbreak of war or disease could decimate a population that is concentrated in a single known habitat and, therefore, highly vulnerable. The margin for error is forever decreasing. Seeing is undoubtedly not just believing but educating too. It isn't, for instance, until people see even a humble deer in the flesh, hitherto vague darting shadows in car headlights at night, that they can really appreciate them - and where else are they likely to see them? We once gave an elderly gentleman from a nearby village a privileged glimpse behind the scenes. Why? He'd lived all his life in the same village without ever leaving it. Incredible though it may seem today, this was commonplace in rural areas until the early part of this century. His face was a picture as he stared open-mouthed at a rhino, then an elephant. Then a giraffe leant over him. Whatever was going through his mind, he kept to himself, he was speechless. Once home, however, he talked of nothing else till his dying day. There still remain, however, perpetual contradictions. Twenty five years ago, breeding tigers was perhaps the ultimate ambition of many a zoo. As we refine our management techniques, the animals mature earlier, live longer in better condition and with a greatly enhanced breeding span. Now, some tiger species (like Przewalski's horses amongst others) are so oversubscribed in captivity due to successful breeding that, notwithstanding their perilous state in the wild, we are asked by the stud book keepers to stop breeding them. The dilemma is no less when it comes to defining standards of husbandry. A camel, for instance, is popularly assumed to have the ability to travel long distances or survive long periods without water. It's nothing to do with the fact that the hump contains water (because it doesn't!) but the welfare codes insist that, in captivity, they must have access to water twenty four hours a day. Similarly, an animal that can survive the rigours of a desert environment hardly needs the shelter that the same codes dictate we must provide permanent access to. We remain, though, as living laboratories, where many management and husbandry techniques that will ultimately be used in the wild are tried, tested and perfected under controlled conditions.

As each attempt to find the glaringly obvious solution failed, the PR mantle fell back into my lap - and eventually stuck there. It was a niche that appeared tailor-made for me. I'd begun dabbling with a camera soon after my arrival at the park by borrowing my mother's ancient 12/6d Kodak Brownie Vecta (which I've still got). Essentially, it was just a plastic box through which you wound 127mm. film and somehow got a photograph, often a pretty good one. Looking at the curling negatives even today, I recognise my own hallmark - the attempts at animal pictures without the roads, fences and buildings to clutter up the background. Soon, though, I'd graduated to a Zenith at a cost of three months' wages. Self taught in this, as in so many other things, I made all the usual mistakes. The most common was buying ever longer lenses to try and get better and better pictures by being 'closer'. It seldom works that way and, although I have had good results with modern mirror lenses, they are largely redundant these days from my repertoire of lenses. Most of Princess Di's wedding photos in a certain Midlands newspaper, however, appeared courtesy of my 500mm. single mirror lens when a photographer borrowed it at the last minute. Soon, I developed a certain panache with my camera which rapidly developed along the Nikon range, the sturdy reliable old FM's proving ideal in an outdoor environment. I had six in no time. In 1981, I entered the British Deer Society's annual photographic competition for the first time, sweeping the board with the three first prizes. It ruffled the feathers of some of the old school, especially when I had similar success the following year! Subsequent portfolio entries comprising the best deer photographs I've ever taken, ones that were to sell around the world and ones which the BDS could have had for nothing, were rejected. It opened my eyes to the opportunities, however, and any spare time I had prior to the children's arrival was spent on photography crusades. I scoured the countryside for wildlife and photogenic aspects of our rural heritage, always looking for new subjects and different perspectives on them. Looking about one from a canal barge, a train or even on horseback gives one a completely different view from the stereotyped perspectives that we are accustomed to from more familiar angles in a car or on foot; from the inside looking out, as it were, a lesson remembered from an earlier life. One of my years out from college was spent on an inaccessible island. Horseback was the only means of covering much of the ground and in summer, amidst the tall, waist high, wavy marsh grass, the only platform from which you would see the cattle you were tending or direct the sheep dogs. Dry stone walling, hedge-laying, thatching, hurdle-making, travelling tinkers and country sports, for example, were all fair photographic game. Middle-page spreads in Amateur Photographer ensued, front pages in 'The Field' and the Royal Show edition of 'Country Life' were further encouragement. The latter was no more than a hay cart parked in a barn door. It taught me that more often than not it was the simplest of pictures that sold, even if it were for no other reason than no one else thought to photograph them!

I soon met John Robinson, English Nature's warden in the region, who lived in an idyllic setting amidst the Wyre Forest. Unselfishly, he taught me much, opening up my eyes to the new horizons of bird, small mammal, studio and flash photography. Additionally, he is a quite outstanding naturalist and I learnt much here too. Many's the night we spent chewing sandwiches, browsing through books, whilst ever alert for the sound of dormice or nightjars picked up on microphones we'd located in woodland rides. On the night my daughter was born, I had first to place him in a photographic hide overlooking a fox earth beneath the dodgem cars in the fairground before dashing off to Sue in hospital! We utilised the old birdwatchers' 'trick'. Two approach and one leaves the scene, leaving the other in the hide so the wildlife think that the coast is clear. With very sensitive subjects, the reverse is done to extract the photographer and avoid the subject becoming suspicious of the hide. I've used the same trick, too, in hides when darting animals. I learnt fast, too. One day, I recall ringing John up to say I'd rattled off half a dozen rolls of film on a moorhen nesting beside one of the park lakes. Did he want to have a go before I moved the hide? He laughed like a drain in disbelief. I didn't know that moorhens were a difficult subject matter. He was over in a 'flash' - no pun intended!

Putting pen to paper to describe what I'd seen and done came naturally, too. Invariably illustrated by my own pictures, editors seemed to like such ready-made packages and everything I threw together was used, usually in national outlets. Again, all invaluable experience for the PR fray, contributions to scientific journals and even preparing guide books! It couldn't last, however. With a young family by now and an occupation which was an all-demanding way of life as much as a job, there wasn't time to sustain such interests; sufficient for me, however, to know that I could do it and confine my vast library of negatives to a leading natural history agency for them to do the leg work - and then pay me! To lay another myth - working amongst wildlife doesn't necessarily make photography 'easy'. True, you have a greater chance of being in the right place at the right time, but one has to remember, as the animals do, that whenever one of them needs catching or treating, mine is the vehicle from which little tranquilliser darts spit! For either purpose, then, I frequently have to borrow another vehicle. Frustratingly, too, when many things are happening I'm either the one doing them so I cannot take photographs or there's no one else present with a camera to provide me with a memento of the occasion. There is also, of course, the fact that one is supposed to be working not taking pictures! Usually, these days, they are photographs for a future guide book and/or our own press releases, which we always handle 'in house'. I take the photograph, Wendy Jackson, our lovely PR lady, and I write the caption, before Wendy pops it in the post to over a hundred media outlets. This gives us total control over what we say and do and, even if the photo's issued aren't good enough or don't match a publication's own requirements or format, once alerted to the subject matter a publisher can always send out their own photographer without causing offence. Either way, the result is the same - we've alerted them to the story. The stories are often as bizarre as they are diverse. One day, I noticed a painter working on the sea lion pool, using Ronseal. Incredibly, too, his name was Ron! There's a 'Lion Street' in Kidderminster which provides much scope for photographic licence. Then there was the expedition tracking Hannibal's route over the Himalayas with elephants. They used our elephants to test the harness and the instruments for monitoring the ESG. Similar equipment was developed, too, to monitor the performance of racing camels in Saudi Arabia. Then there was the fluorescent harness designed to make domestic camels more visible on desert highways at night, albeit of dubious value, I thought. The sight of a camel suddenly appearing in your headlights illuminated like a Christmas tree was as likely to cause an accident, I thought, as to prevent one! The sea lion holding the hose-pipe (preferably somewhere near a young lady's cleavage!) is ever a favourite come hot spells, as is my hand reared giraffe who appears to enjoy wearing a hat. As ever, the simplest ideas invariably worked best. To persuade a bear to do a passable impression of pushing my landrover out of the mud simply required smearing the tailboard with fish or filling the back up with apples. The initial attempt produced a full double middle-page spread in The Daily Mirror. Over twenty years later, the picture appeared in my children's weekend supplement in The Daily Telegraph and the picture is still selling around the world for the photographer and generating PR for the park. Similarly, reversing through the lions with a rope tied to the front bumper quickly arouses the interest of an inquisitive cat. Within seconds, one of them would have it in its mouth. It gives a highly passable impression of giving the vehicle a tow. Such pictures are a caption writer's dream. Flexibility is important, too, in media work. One visiting camera crew threw away their script upon seeing a blackbird nesting beneath the seat of the tractor which took the lion meat out every day. The girls used it, too, when cleaning out the lions. They never bat an eyelid at the presence of a 400lb. lion six inches away through the mesh panel but, when a mouse pops out of the cavity wall, your camera crew will get flattened in the stampede to escape! It's curious, too, to see people's sense of perspective on occasions. They can sit in their cars surrounded by some of the rarest animals on earth and what do they do? Feed the mallard ducks! It makes an off-beat story, though.

Whilst my first ever television appearance was over forty years ago on Anglia TV, rotating golden knight and all, as a musician (in addition to singing as a choir boy in Peterborough cathedral!), one of the first TV shows I was involved with for the park was the then ATV's Saturday morning 'Tizwas', live with Chris Tarrant - as hazardous an undertaking then as is today! The 'Animal Magic' style stunts required of us were sufficiently far-fetched to go frequently wrong, as of course it was always hoped they would. I remember once a requirement for two penguins to sit either side of Chris Tarrant on each arm of a chair. They wouldn't and soon disappeared behind stage curtains. Moments later, live on national networked children's television came a great shout and appalling profanities from the stage-hand sent to fetch them back. He burst back through the canopy clutching a hand substantially minus two fingers! He'd tried to pick them up and the razor-sharp beaks had done the rest. The ITV producer always has a priceless advantage over his BBC counterpart on such occasions and on shows like that had frequent recourse to it. A flick of a switch sent him straight into the next commercial package! Chris Tarrant and I were to do many other items before he moved on, most of them memorable! Another programme of particular note involved broadcasting from a pen containing the thirty six lion cubs that one of the girls and I had hand reared. Both clad in old clothes, in

One way of feeding the giraffe! (Photo Author)

Ready Steady Tow! (Photo J. Drysdale)

'Ready Teddy Go', a famous picture from J. Drysdale as a Brown Bear helps push a stranded vehicle. I'm on the left!

A study in concentration (and nerve!) 25 years after it was taken I find this photo on the internet, captioned in Russian! (Photo J. James, Birmingham Post and Mail)

expectation of a thorough going over, we were not disappointed. If we didn't look like scarecrows going into the lions' den, we certainly did when we emerged, but it was the radio mikes trailing from our back pockets that proved the real problem. The cubs chewed off so many that replacements had to be sought from Birmingham before the item could be completed. It's when they missed, however, that the real damage was done and those razor-sharp teeth and claws sink right into your backside. Once, too, when filming with Michaela Strachan, a cub missed the radio mike and gave a passable impression of half removing one of my fingers. But, when you're with Michaela Strachan, you tend not to notice such things! She's great fun, a 'natural', who makes life easy for man and beast alike on the many 'Owl TV' and 'Really Wild Shows' we've recorded both at home and on the road. We've had regular input too, in many other established programmes ('Stop, Look and Listen', 'Top Gear', 'Countryfile' and 'Real Rooms' to name but a few) and endless fun making them. Invariably, there's a familiar face or two in every film unit.

Also appearing on the scene at that time was an innocuous-looking photographer from the Birmingham Post and Mail, John James. The photographic requirements of the Mail were, from the onset, demanding, of the standard expected virtually of a national. In John, they found and still have one of their principal providers and in him, I a kindred spirit. Being a photographer, I knew what he wanted. Knowing the animals, I knew the possibilities and John maximised them. He's never left the park without a usable picture, invariably of the highest front-page quality for both the Mail and its sister, the Birmingham Post. Justifiably, he's won many an award for his work. I don't believe he's ever submitted a portfolio without a picture of the park in it on merit. Whenever there's a photo call, I can sense his presence and instinctively know whither to turn to find his lens. We've been firm friends for over twenty five years. In the early days, I'd drop his used film off for him at the Kidderminster office for the delivery vans to pick up or even put them on the Birmingham bus for collection by the office boy at the other end. Today, however, the photos are taken on a digital i.e. filmless camera, scanned in and scrutinised on a laptop computer then sent down a telephone line, a mobile line at that if necessary, straight into the office. They can be in the paper

LION STREET

258

before John gets back to Birmingham. Such is the appliance of science! Whilst all this is going on, the man from the Express and Star is taking his film down to Boots the chemists! When the crunch comes, though, nothing serves you better than knowing the people behind the camera or the word processor with whom you can speak frankly. You'll know what they want, when and how. It's highly effective communication.

Most of the other photographers, too, from the Express and Star, the Kidderminster Times and the Worcester Evening News amongst others, have been ever present for many years, as have many of the cameramen and reporters from Central TV, its forebears and those of Midlands Today. Many of them, like Chris Tarrant, I've known for over twenty years. John Swallow, Tony Maycock and Michelle Newman, to name but a few, are or were well known to us in their time - as are the faces behind the camera itself. The same can be said of John Yates, Hugh Owens, Tony Butler and Mike Kilbane, all regulars from the 'other side'. It applies also to Radio Hereford and Worcester's stalwarts since the station's inception and virtually all the burgeoning number of radio stations we've seen burst upon the scene in recent years. Life is so much easier when we all know each other.

Openness has always been our policy. Allowing the media behind the scenes at will, without prior notice, gives them confidence in us and giving them straight answers to straight questions makes for incisive reporting. It always works - they trust us, place great store in our integrity and, consequently, never fail to give us a fair say and incalculable amounts of free publicity in the process. Furthermore, the plethora of publicity (our cuttings agency says our output far exceeds our contemporaries') invariably generated every year is positive publicity. The old adage that there's no such thing as bad publicity still holds true. I'm constantly amazed by the amount of publicity coming our way simply because other institutions aren't interested or cannot be bothered, even when prime time television is involved. Interestingly, too, when filming recently, I heard mutterings from some bystanders who'd

Opposite Page:
'Lion Street' Kidderminster provides obvious photographic opportunities for this lion cub.
(Photo J. James, Birmingham Post and Mail)
So does Wendy Jackson (inset) and friend. (Photo Author)

misinterpreted both the situation and my actions. I was agreeably surprised to hear the photographers and film crews, with their behind-the-scenes knowledge of us, put the dissenting voices very firmly in their place. No, the much maligned press has been very good to us. Frequently vilified, their reports rubbished, it is one of life's more curious paradoxes that when we watch a thriller, what does our detective hero do when he wants to discover what really happened all those years ago? He turns up news archives, of course, and suddenly they are gospel!

Working in the full glare of the media brings its own peculiar pressures. The most obvious, of course, being that any cock-up can be broadcast to the world lock, stock and barrel. Once, when filming a squirrel, it almost happened. Its drey had been discovered a hundred feet in the air atop a multi-million pound white-knuckle roller-coaster ride. The mother went up and down the service ladder all day to feed her young, oblivious to the bedlam about her. It was a good story but, on checking her presence, the amusement area manager startled the squirrel - and it fell. Horror-stricken, we could only stare in disbelief as the poor thing plummeted earthwards - on TV! Incredibly, however, it gathered its wits quickly, instinctively spread-eagling itself and floating down like a sky-diver to land apparently unharmed in thick, lush grass. Within twenty minutes, normal service was resumed and it continued its ascent once more to check its young, quite unperturbed as the passenger cars full of screaming teenagers hurtled by. This panache for the dizzy heights had unexpected side effects for some. During the winter months, all our administrators retreat from the ticket offices into Spring Grove House. One day, an adventurous squirrel decided he wanted to be administered. He climbed two flights of stairs, circumnavigated the maze of corridors and kept going, right up Wendy's legs as she sat typing!

Media space does, however, give you an unparalleled opportunity to put a message across, but it must be done incisively, particularly in a crisis. The instinctive reaction of most people to media interest sees them on the defensive. Invariably perceived as intrusive, particularly during difficult times or on sensitive issues, the press are nevertheless simply doing their job, often grappling with a subject about which they know little or nothing. The institutional reaction to a problem must be quick and accurate. Decide your version of events, adhere to them, supply the same information to everyone, but never, ever lie. Summarise, by all means, but never lie, for the truth will out in the end. Lying to cover up previous lies comes next as you sink into an ever-escalating morass of confusion, which itself spawns further investigation. "Once you've got them by the balls, their hearts and minds soon follow," said President Nixon of the people. The people's press turned the tables. All this is easier said than done, of course, but if you fail, you loose credibility and with it control of the situation and escalating difficulties. The public's perception of events within your institution is largely shaped by how the media interprets the story. There are three factors to be borne in mind with the rapid response. Firstly, avoid the knee-jerk reaction. Secondly, it's not what a solicitor would necessarily advocate! Thirdly, it is not always easy in a swift-moving media world requiring instant answers. We've all seen the instant analysis of the crash cause (whilst the wreckage is still warm) by a bevy of hitherto unheard-of 'experts' who crawl from the woodwork to proffer their services to the highest bidder. The rewards for getting it right, however, are immense and mutually beneficial, for the media are getting exactly what they want and they are getting it direct from us - good off-beat stories, good pictures with human and local interest. Such items, too, are invariably more memorable in the public's mind than an advertisement which, of course, costs you money - lots of it. It works both ways, too, and I've learnt to look after my friends. It doesn't pay for them to feel that you're only interested in them when you want them - that is not what friends are for. If they're stuck for a story in mid-winter when there's little happening or they want a nice Christmas picture, you find them one, regardless of the fact that the park is closed and any publicity resulting from it is purely incidental. Within months, we may need a picture - that way I get it.

Sometimes, though, you get it whether you like it or not. On arriving for work one June morning, the first thing I saw was a new-born hippo with its mother, Bar-bel. Immediately, I sensed a problem. Hippos are normally born in or under water, shallow

The colour, shapes, patterns and pelage of exotic animals give endless scope for photographic license.
(Photo Author)

water. Overnight, half the entire month's average rainfall had fallen, swelling the lake to two feet above its normal level. The pair of them had retreated as the waters had risen and were on a ledge. Unfortunately, the calf was, I felt, slightly premature because the mother had no milk and, as it blundered along its mother's flank seeking her udder, it couldn't see the submerged perimeter of the ledge they were on. Three times it fell off the invisible edge and three times the mother dived in, bringing it to the surface on her nose. It was exhausted and had ingested water. Clearly, something had to be done and fast. The outlet sluice was blocked by bottles and other debris thoughtfully deposited by our visitors. I hired a pump in an effort to speed the emptying process, but soon realised the futility of it. The fire brigade were the only answer.

Experience had shown that the media quickly latched onto such calls and generally arrived before the appliance! Talk about ambulance-chasing. Years earlier, shortly after Victor, Marwell Zoo's famous giraffe, had done the splits in full view of the public, we too had sought help from the fire brigade when an elephant collapsed and it was clearly beyond our resources to raise her. The then new-fangled air bags seemed the only chance. After an epic morning's struggle, we finally raised her in the full glare of the media. Fortunately, everyone was outside back slapping when the day ended in heroic failure. The strain had all been too much for some damaged lung tissue and the poor old lady died quite abruptly. This case was no exception and the day's drama was played out before a full house, never less than six camera lenses and two television crews plus the associated reporters and the incessant enquiries for progress over the 'phone. Thank goodness I could count them all as friends! If we needed a bit of muscle, they helped. We pumped at least 25,000 gallons an hour out of the lake, but it was late afternoon before the levels had dropped sufficiently for the calf to tread shallow water. It continued to struggle despite its mother's close attention - but it was fading. I effected a long-handled syringe from broom handles to administer a quick acting antibiotic and a respiratory stimulant, waited a short while for them to work, then we went for the calf. Mum was not best pleased but there was no choice.

Most people are familiar with the classic hippo picture, mouth open 'yawning' five, six feet wide perhaps, with those awesome pieces of ivory revealed. Not lightly are they regarded as the most dangerous animal in Africa, killing more people even than lions. Six times, though, I'd been within a metre of this to clear the drain. "Can't he actually get in with it?" asked a voice deep within the satellite van. "We need the human interest!" Maybe, but it wasn't going to be mine! With a net now attached to the same broom handles, we pulled the calf in close then hooked it with the crook at the end of a fire ladder and pulled her up and over the fence. I gathered her, all 80lbs. of her, and fled out of the mother's sight.

The firemen were magnificent. They revived her with oxygen so well that I was already thinking of the next step. The heat box was prepared. "Did I want the stretcher?", came a voice over the radio. Not likely - there wasn't the time nor the room. The boys could finally get their human interest. I picked the 80lb. calf up again, saw John James from the corner of my eye, turned and staggered the hundred and twenty yards through the media scrum to our treatment room, knowing full well that these were tomorrow morning's pictures - the icing on the cake for the picture editors. The revival continued, the calf sat up and further oxygen was summoned urgently. The vet checked her over as we thought further ahead again. We threw together an effective incubator fashioned from the box normally used to hatch emu eggs. Heat came from an adapted hair dryer blowing warm air through a pipe removed from one of the Suzuki jeeps. The oxygen continued to flow through another similar device.

The day had finally run its course, everyone had gone. After the nine hour media melee, the perpetual roar of the pumps, the incessant shrill from the batteries of mobile 'phones, the silence was golden. A sandwich appeared under my nose as I slumped to the floor. I'd been soaked through all day. Suddenly, I was too tired to move. Wendy rang from home to ask if there was any more she could do to help but, suddenly, the hippo proved beyond all help. We'd removed a lot of water from its lungs but it wasn't enough, the calf died before my eyes. We'd given it our best shot but it hadn't been enough. If, heaven forbid, the same thing were

Hippo rescue - I carry the revived calf away to the treatment room.
(Photo D. Clapp, Express and Star)

Six times I ventured within a metre of this to unblock the drains.
(Photo J. James. Birmingham Post and Mail)

to happen again tomorrow, how much more could we do and how much better could we do it? Very little, I thought, even with the infinite wisdom afforded by hindsight.

Animal deaths, particularly high profile ones in the public domain, have traditionally been taboo topics and probably present zoo PR personnel with their biggest challenge when emotions run high. Unfortunately, being rare, endangered or beautiful doesn't render animals immortal and die they inevitably will, albeit usually at the end of a significantly longer span than their wild counterparts. Occasionally, there are slight compensations. When one of our old giraffe died at the age of thirty, she'd already been immortalised in porcelain with one of her calves at foot by Border Fine Arts, so there was much to remember her by. It supplemented a complete range featuring our wolf pack. Here, though, was a young life snuffed out in the full glare of the media. As the animal man's battery discharged, the PR man's brain swung into gear again. The time! My goodness, the time! The evening editions had been printed and the TV news broadcast on both channels, full of heroic hippo rescues. Still more items were in irreversible preparation. Some could be stopped, but what a shambles - 80% of the media running top-of-the-programme and front-page rescue stories, the remainder obituaries and negative ones at that. How on earth could a hippo drown? You could hear it already. Better, I decided, to tell no one at this point and let the story run. Let media power show the nation the herculean effort that had gone into the rescue. It would soften the blow when, inevitably, I had to release the news. The calls continued throughout a sleepless night. I stressed caution. The chances on this mission-near-impossible had never been good, after all. By breakfast time, I felt the let-down was sufficient to announce the death but, incredibly, the media interest merely intensified. Three TV crews greeted my arrival at work. ITN carried it at midday, Central TV carried it live at lunch time and again live the same evening. Even the sleepy old Beeb had caught up by then and wanted to carry it live too - at precisely the same time as Central! Central had asked first, so 'Midlands Today' had to back begrudgingly down. They sat in their satellite van watching me on Central on their monitor having timed how long it would take for me to get between the two of them and cued me in from that! I arrived in a cloud of dust, exchanged microphones and interviewers and simply carried on talking. For those watching with their feet up at home, it worked rather well! Any breathlessness was attributed to the undoubted charm of the truly delectable presenter. In the following days, I received calls from several zoo directors. The unanimous view was that the situation, in general, had been handled superbly and, in particular, the press coverage of the calamity had been admirably and positively presented.

This was an animal story under relative control, however. Others burst upon you quite bizarrely without warning. One morning, a keeper cutting open a bale of hay felt a sharp pin prick, far removed from the usual scratch you expect from thistles or nettles harvested in the hay. I felt it, too, when investigating another bale. As we poked them gingerly open with a pitchfork, we were horrified to see they contained vast swathes of medical waste. Poor John. Painfully shy and retiring, he'd come to me on work experience from a special needs school ten years earlier. He'd enjoyed his first contact with the outside world so much that he surprised everyone by jumping out of his shell and actually asking to come back. To the school's surprise, I agreed and gave him a weekend job. When they decided that he'd come as far academically as they could take him, they released him early so he could start full-time work amongst his friends. I stipulated one condition; he must go to college on day release. Petrified at the mere thought of it, he was dragged kicking and screaming under personal escort into another strange, new world where someone had arranged one-to-one tuition in the three 'R's. He'd passed out with his certificates, a credit to himself and his family, relishing the opportunity chance had presented him. Now, at the height of an Aids scare, I found myself staring at him nursing a cut caused by this mess. Crushed 'sharps' containers, thousands of syringe needles, scalpel blades, partially used drug bottles, loaded syringes and soiled dressings spilled out onto the yard before us. The park ground to a standstill as we assessed our dilemma. The load had been distributed throughout the park, yet we dare not touch a thing. John was dispatched to hospital whilst the Environmental Health department descended on us in force, together with the police, the butcher, the baker, the candlestick maker and hordes of pressmen, whose reports were still being transmitted live from the park at 7p.m. that evening. It was only then that I could get off for my own check-up. The story ran for weeks, the insurance saga for years, as the tortuous process of collecting up all the affected batch of hay commenced using the necessary precautions. The floor of the barn was excavated, its spoil buried and relaid with fresh stone whilst the investigation continued. It quickly emerged that medical waste had been 'fly-tipped' in a field and gone through the baler when the hay was harvested. Despite the proliferation of batch numbers on many of the discarded items and a prolonged investigation lasting over a year, the source was never traced. This always struck me as odd because I'd imagined that this was precisely what batch numbers were for.

But, meanwhile, poor Bar-bel - how desolate, how despairing. Who could say animals had no feelings as she lay forlornly where her calf had been plucked from her for day after day. But I was watching her companion, Gertie. Like Bar-bel, she wasn't over-large and had little milk, but I wondered and waited. For five weeks I left the sluice open, ignoring the stagnating low water levels and the comments it attracted, then she calved. Her yearling calf, a female, ignored her sister but the previous calf, a three year old male, proved a despot. His inquisitiveness (or was it vindictiveness?) knew few bounds. Time and again, he bore in. Twice, he actually picked up the calf in his mouth drawing a fusillade of blank rounds from the twenty four hour guard. The 'hippo watch' had never been issued with guns before but, forty eight hours on, we were still fending him off by the skin of our teeth when a live round, fired accidentally like the blanks into the ground, frightened the life out of him and he fled to the other lake. Like Gertie, we could breathe again - and get some sleep!

But still, we kept our new arrival under wraps. After Bar-bel's experience, we had, for once, attracted a small degree of criticism from the anti-everything brigade. How cruel. Hippos shouldn't be kept in captivity etc. Something they'd never thought of before. Maybe, maybe not, but the reality was that they were and they had

to be cared for. Maybe, too, in due course, these pie-in-the-sky merchants could repatriate some to Mozambique, where government helicopter gunships have been known to slaughter 3,000 hippos a day. If you are actually doing something for wildlife, as distinct from just talking about it, these are the realities you have to contend with. But that was for the future. Now was for caring. Let us be sure first of a good start to life.

And so, then, at ten days of age, the calf came into the world as a sprightly two day old! We risked, of course, breaking the age-old adage that you never, ever, lie to the press, ever. If anyone noticed or even cared, they certainly didn't ask. It was the happy ending that fairy tales are made of. That morning, I walked over to see her with an old friend. Gertie turned (surely she didn't recognise us both?), 'yawned' and posed. The living lens of John James was there. Once, twice, three times the camera shutters fell. "Coffee, John?" He fell about himself laughing. It was as easy as that. And so, Gertie and her calf went straight onto the front page of the Birmingham Evening Mail in colour one Friday and onto full pages in colour in the nationals on the Saturday. A fitting sequel to the tragedy of the previous month. The other regional papers scarcely held back either with their own full-page spreads, nor did the TV, all triggered by sublime and quite priceless PR from two old pros.

There is, though, a potential down side to all the cuddly little baby animal pictures and the perceived glamour of TV work. It can give aspiring animal keepers a totally false impression of what they wish to embark on. The green, green grass of home isn't particularly pleasant when it's been through a camel or a zebra. Indeed, when voyaged through an elephant or a rhino, it is particularly pungent with an all-pervading stench that is hard to dispel. Yet, it has to be removed every day (or night) come hell or high water, be it your birthday, a bank holiday or Christmas Day and regardless of the weather or anything else. Those who are going to make the grade readily admit that it is far harder work than they'd ever imagined - and grit it out. The rest fall by the wayside. Ironically, perhaps, the law of the jungle sorts outs the chiff from the chaff. If you cannot or won't fit into a team structure, you'll not survive either.

Curiously, even within the park, the closeness of the animal keepers as a tightly-knit bunch is often criticised (or envied?) by the other departments within it. It is crucial in a crisis. More than once only this team work has prevented a calamity. I'm constantly asked if the animals are 'real', really dangerous or if they'd really kill. The answer is simple really - yes! Even a pretty little 'bambi' deer can rear up and beat you senseless with flailing fore legs. One morning, though, I found myself staring down in horror at a limp bundle lying at my feet. A bull elephant had tusked it right above the heart, sending it flying through the air for me to half catch, half hold. I didn't see an elephant keeper but the babe-in-arms I'd first seen in the arms of its father in another elephant house over twenty years earlier - the same house that a vet had been in when he'd collapsed with a heart condition in the bull pen. I was the only one in attendance, apart from its three-ton occupant. At least on this occasion, though, I was not alone as the eyes glazed over and the convulsions subsided. My stomach churned. As I positioned myself to impede the girlfriend's view of the unthinkable, our eyes met across the building through the mayhem. The tears were there, of course, but those brown eyes were ablaze with a fierce determination. The long, blonde hair streamed in the wind as she hung on grimly to a restraining rope attatched to the elephant. Her man was down and almost out. It had been a hell of a year and an appalling winter of unprecedented attrition in which we'd achieved more than anyone had any right to expect, but which had exhausted everyone in the process. I'd had to reorganise the entire structure of the park, bringing back some old blood to boost and supplement our resources. But we'd stuck together. We'd sweat blood together, we'd lived and worked together, wined and dined together and now we were in desperate trouble, together. The noise precluded radio use and the 'phone was ringing twenty yards away to add to the bedlam but we all had our hands full. No one dared let go, least of all me, holding my rope and the baby.

We wear green overalls and are often mistaken for paramedics, which we're not, but you learn the tricks of the trade. Avoiding the point of impact, I massaged the chest. As the lungs reflated, the breathing returned and the eyelids flickered. At last, the first rope was tied off. There was a free pair of hands, that of the *trained* first aider. Our eyes met, too. 'Ambulance,' we mouthed in unison as she ran for the 'phone. Brown-eyes still hadn't given up. Three years earlier, she'd rung up from agricultural college to ask if she could come on a work experience placement. The call was put through to 'a grumpy old man'. He gave her the placement and, subsequently, weekend jobs during the summer holidays. Then she kicked her heels in Dorothy Perkins department store for a winter. But the grumpy old man hadn't forgotten. When the call came the next summer, she took the opportunity with both hands, so well, in fact, that the grumpy old man asked her to join the staff, stay on for the winter and tutor her through the City and Guilds Zoo Animal Management Course. Unknown to her, on this particular day I'd already nominated her (successfully) as the company's 'employee of the month'. It was a far cry from Dorothy Perkins but, although her twenty first birthday was still weeks away, she came of age before my very eyes. There were no hysterics, no running away, no running *in* to compound the problem and the danger. Just an unshakable conviction that somehow everything would be alright as long as she hung on and followed orders. At last, she had a single free hand to flick a radio button onto a spare channel and send the message I dictated. After the initial pause of disbelief, the message sank in and was acknowledged - relief was at hand. The airwaves fell silent. Someone would be waiting to escort the ambulance in, others moving to clear gateways, a hundred others, perhaps, simply holding their breath and staring at a radio. Then her rope, too, was finally lashed down to restrict the elephant's potential radius of destruction. And still the discipline held her back. She'd earned my undying admiration. Now, though, with a nod of my head, she was free at last to join me in the arena and comfort her fella. He was a very lucky chap *and* he was going to be OK. As the pair of them were borne away, my reassurance raised a smile and I knew the day was won. He wouldn't be detained long in hospital, I promised confidently. Having been rolled along the floor of the elephant house, he simply stank to high heaven! With the twenty first birthday approaching, I remembered their shared ambitions. She to fly in a hot air balloon, another helicopter trip, his to go behind the scenes in the elephant facility at Walt Disney's new 'Animal World' in Florida. The 'grumpy old man' would ensure that all were realised. When we next ate Chinese, he'd also buy him a spare rib! Of such crises are lifelong bonds forged.

With a consultant's entreaty to take a complete break ringing in my ears, I'd managed a short ten hour day on Monday. At 3a.m. on Tuesday, I'd left for Sweden (arriving just in time to see myself on the 'National Geographic' channel in the hotel!), arriving back at 11p.m. on Wednesday. It was still only 11a.m. on Thursday. If I was reeling then, by 11p.m. when I arrived home I was positively rocking, but we were all at home in our own beds in one piece. We'd pulled through, together. I'd clean forgotten that it was my birthday.

The demarcation line between being a boss and a friend is, of course, perilously thin, but knowing the subject matter pays dividends. Once, when on a tutors' training course, I was asked to define the first steps in a procedure. Reading the instructions seemed a good bet, but I was overruled! There are still many people, though, who cannot read (although that wasn't the reason given for my rebuttal) or are dyslexic, which can have the most unfortunate consequences if the presumption is that they can. There are, too, the most unfathomable allergies. If you've been eating a peanut-based product, it's no good attempting to give the kiss of life to someone with a peanut allergy - you'll kill them. Similarly, if your antidote or anti-venom is colour-coded, it's no good relying on someone in a crisis who is colour blind. I've had it happen. The results can be disastrous.

Zoo keepers in general and, perhaps, what I'd call the 'specialist' ones in particular i.e. elephant and reptile keepers, for example, often come cast in the traditional mould of the great British eccentric; absolutely brilliant at what they do, yet totally unconventional in their approach to it. Often the greatest challenge in handling them lies in imbuing them with the realities of the modern work environment of COSH, risk assessment etc. (Even my wellington boots these days come complete with a bilingual 'Owners Manual' in *eleven* languages!) whilst retaining the individualism that makes them such a powerhouse of knowledge and experience. Such dedication makes, however, for a very insular personality. The conversation overheard some years ago at the funeral of a colleague was quite revealing: "What's the dose for eland these days?" echoed tactlessly through the church. "Wormed your zebra yet?" came from the choir stalls and "How many emu you hatched this year?" at the reception. I rest my case!

There remain, though, very few keeper vacancies to satisfy the demand for them. The average length of service for my staff has always far exceeded that of any other department. Even the ones we know aren't likely to stop for more than a year or two (if they are pursuing further education, for example), will have the time of their lives for a precious summer or two before moving on with memories they will cherish for ever - and they stay in touch. One favour, for example, in the early seventies, was so appreciated that a little tin of delicious, home-made mince pies appeared on the doorstep on Christmas Eve shortly afterwards, as it has done every year since. Others graduate from work experience (from their school) to weekend and/or holiday jobs to seasonal work, possibly returning for a second summer before, perhaps, becoming full time i.e. year-round staff. If in further education, they may arrive on day release before converting to full time, but with day release back to college stipulated by me to continue their education. Others come from further afield. Just as this sleepy little market town in Worcestershire has exported animals around the world (lions to Japan, zebra to Germany, gnu to France, eland to Dubia, wallabies to Canada etc.), we've imported staff on work experience from far and wide - Holland, Canada, Tanzania, France and, memorably, a diminutive but quite delightful pair of mischievously identical Russian twin sisters training to become veterinary nurses. Upon leaving us, they utilised a partisan recipe to cook us a herb pie. I got the bit with the stinging nettles in it! Like everything else, though, successful recruiting does produce problems. Like farmers' sons who are born and bred on the farm and who stay at home to work the family business, often without even going off to college first, many of the keepers have been at Bewdley since their schooldays or even earlier and have never worked anywhere else. So they, too, go off to other zoos for short spells to see how the other half lives - cultural exchanges I call them! Invariably, though, they are glad to return for they remain at large a close-knit group, both in and out of working hours. A summer evening's entertainment, for instance, might include a barbecue or clay pigeon shoot. After one such evening, we were in the bar after the guns were put away and I was asking what they'd like next on the agenda. A hot air balloon was mentioned, then the word 'helicopter'. A quick straw poll revealed that none of them had ever been in one. Accordingly, one summer's evening, a helicopter duly materialised and all the keepers had a few circuits of the park to see their world from an entirely new perspective. Meanwhile, behind the scenes, there is a small army of mechanics, gardeners, maintenance men, office staff, ride operators, retail and catering staff - right down to the humblest litter pickers and loo cleaners; all of whom play a key function, often in direct support of the animal staff, who invariably operate more in the public domain, but whom they will outnumber by up to ten to one.

It's always interesting, too, to see how other institutions handle PR. Some years ago, the local paper, the Kidderminster Times, and our then Conservative MP, Anthony Coombs, organised a schools essay competition. The subject, 'What Parliament Does', attracted eighty entries and Christopher won his class. The prize? A day trip to The House of Commons to include lunch, Question Time and, somewhat improbably everyone thought, a meeting with the Prime Minister. And so, nine year old Christopher went off to London for the first time with his dad, had the time of his life and did indeed meet the Prime Minister, John Major, in his private office at the House of Commons. It was an intriguing display of humility deserving, perhaps, of a far greater audience. He took immense interest in the winning essay, autographed it, engaged an awestruck youngster in a long conversation and happily posed for photographs. If the nation could see the man I saw that day, he'd still be in Downing Street today.

It is, then, dealing with people not the animals that taxes you to the limit. Early one morning, someone brought a plastic sack into the park which he'd seen run over by a lorry on the road outside. It contained kittens, or what was left of them, for there was only one badly-injured survivor. After much investigation, our vets decided to destroy it. The vitriol directed against us for allowing this, by a letter writer in the local paper, was quite astounding. One might have thought it better directed at the person who'd consigned the kittens to the sealed bag and thrown it into the road. One bank holiday, a gentleman stormed into the office to

10 DOWNING STREET
LONDON SW1A 2AA

THE PRIME MINISTER   13 January 1994

Dear Mr. Lawrence,

I was so pleased to receive your letter and to learn how much you and your son enjoyed your visit to the House of Commons in December.

I can only say it was a real pleasure to meet you and Christopher and I welcomed the opportunity of encouraging a young man who had shown a great deal of interest in Parliament.

May I wish you and your family a very happy New Year.

Yours sincerely,

John Major

R P Lawrence Esq

My letter from the Rt. Honourable John Major M.P.

The P.M.'s right hand man! Christopher is at the front. (Photo Kate Forbes)

berate me over the theft of his car. It was a full ten minutes before I could get a word in, but it didn't matter. The place was jam-packed, pedestrians could scarcely move, much less a car. There was as much chance of the police attention he was demanding as there was of the car leaving the premises for hours, but he remained adamant - his car had been stolen and, besides, came the punchline, his wife was in it! On viewing the photographic evidence, it seemed an unlikely scenario, wishful thinking even, but at least her photograph soon enabled me to find the car - right where he'd left it.

Meanwhile, back in Nottingham, some elderly care residents had returned home from their day at the park, been given supper and tucked up in bed. But there was an empty bed. After the 'phone call, we searched high and low before, eventually, at 10.30p.m., finding a forlorn elderly lady stuck on a loo suffering from exposure and packing her off to hospital. On another occasion, whilst turning a sharp corner within the park, an elderly coach passenger simply fell out of the seat. A post mortem revealed death had occurred hours beforehand. Someone had even paid the entrance fee. As far as I'm aware, no action resulted from either incident. If we'd neglected animals in such a manner, we'd have been pilloried.

Shortly afterwards, an off-duty keeper waved at me through the fence from the staff accommodation. Could I pop round sometime when I had a moment? Knowing that I'd be tied up all

day, by the grace of God, I went straight away. "Could I have a look at her?" I turned to look, not at some animal, but at the girlfriend. What did I think? I thought she was as white as the sheets that enveloped her, unconscious, her lips were blue and the empty bottles still clasped in each clenched fist didn't appear to present an entirely therapeutic picture. What did I think? I thought I needed a 'phone, quickly. The medical centre told me how to hold the fort until the cavalry arrived. She survived. That evening, as I contemplated the appalling consequences had I not paid a visit until after work, there was a knock on the door. "We're camped down the road," the traveller said, "but Jossie hasn't got enough milk to feed the kid." Had I anything to give her? "Tie her up on fresh grass," I advised. Alas, Jossie wasn't the goat - she was his wife!

Opposite Page:
Sunny signorina! A heatwave picture.
(Photo Mike Manning, Shropshire Star)

CHAPTER 15
Epilogue
(To Ivan and Sonya Knezovich who showed us Africa)

1998 was a momentous year. It began with the reintroduction of elephants to the park and all the work that it entailed. Ten years on, the old elephant building had long since been converted to other use so we had to construct a new house, an entire new infrastructure and all on an entirely new site at that. Everything, from the building itself, supporting hay barns and day accommodation to water, power supply, roads and even the telephone, had to be built in from scratch. Initially a pre-Christmas 1997 deadline was the timetable. To that end, we'd begun work on site within a week of the park's traditional winter closing in early November. We'd toiled beneath the stars and the full moon amidst the snow flurries and the ever-hardening frosts late into the November nights, seven days a week, welding the huge steel infrastructure into place. The remainder of the house was built around it. It was big enough to hangar an aircraft, as the accountant never tired of reminding me, but out of little elephants do big elephants grow. Few who weren't actually present would ever subsequently believe it but, incredibly, the building was completed in six weeks. It was a magnificent feat which pushed everyone to the very limits of their endurance after a long, hard summer season - but a futile one. In the event, the elephants arrived two months late and, even then, only four of the envisaged six materialised. When I'd first told David Chorley that

Opposite Page:
The sand dunes at Sossusvlei in the Namib Naukluft Park. (Photo Author)

I'd obtained CITES import permits for elephants from Africa itself, he'd stared at me in disbelief. They were like gold dust at the time and still are. We'd crossed our fingers, held our breath and waited.

When they did arrive at 10.30 one Sunday evening in February, the work load escalated beyond all measure. I knew from the onset that staffing would present us with our biggest problem. Elephant keeping, above all, is a particular speciality known to but a dedicated few. There were only two of us old-stagers, Angela and myself, with any previous experience of elephants at all. One of our keepers, Andy Plumb, had spent much of the winter at Longleat being introduced to the new order but still, as far as Health and Safety were concerned, had to be considered a rookie. Previously, life had evolved around the passion for his horses, which is fortunate because, as far as diet is concerned, at least, and some ailments, elephants are just like horses - with trunks. There was the odd health scare. Locally produced hay arrived from time to time enriched with more than its fair share of local sand from the molehills in the hay field, more than sufficient, in fact, to trigger off the odd bout of colic. A long memory, prompt treatment and the odd night-long vigil was sufficient to contain the problem, but around-the-clock observation was the order of the day for the rhino custodians, too. The search for a rhino calf was intensifying. I'd already taken tissue samples from the tigers and rhino for DNA profiling by the Forensic Science Laboratory to help identify trade in prohibited products and for Munich University to help establish the genetic diversity of the captive white rhino population. Determined now to establish what was going on breeding-wise, we'd been taking regular faecal and urine samples for analysis at The Zoological Society of London. Patterns began to emerge. The rhino were cycling so, rather than lock them up every night in their house, we left them outside and sat in wait like the proverbial 'Peeping Tom'. Sure enough, they began mating, principally at dawn and dusk, the very time they would normally be confined to individual quarters indoors. The rhino watch soon became routine. When it stops, we'll reach for the calendar a year or so hence.

The big advantage with the elephants, however, was the hard work already being done on elephant training. Chaining elephants up is an emotive subject, but you cannot manage our then one ton elephants (and potentially four or five ton ones) unless they are precisely that - manageable. Like a dairy cow in its milking parlour, standing still under restraint for a few routine minutes a day for a bath, foot and skin care, blood sampling and their first tetanus inoculations was ideal preparation for subsequent veterinary care. Andy, meanwhile, was adapting to his new calling like a fish to water. Mike, whose father before him had helped look after the old elephants, was chafing at the bit but, in the meantime, Angela and I had to roll back the years and become elephant keepers of sorts all over again (on top of everything else!) until we could shake out the cobwebs and get the system up and running. We had, however, solved another problem.

For nearly twenty years, we'd been battling to meet what was probably our customers' most persistent complaint; some form of directional signage to the park to replace the long-vanished temporary AA symbols circa 1973 - preferably the standard brown and white tourism signs, standard throughout the country, except here. Eventually, at a cost of some £35,000, we got them erected at major road junctions up to and including the key motorway junctions. Standard EEC signage, though, used an elephant as the standard motif for a wildlife park and we hadn't got any, as customers never tired of telling us. Now, at last, there were elephants at the end of the elephant trail.

Easter 1998 was a total disaster for the entire leisure industry without exception, the worst by far in living memory. The traditional rush to the great outdoors for the busiest weekend of the year was halted by the swirling floods caused by torrential, non-stop rain. For once, the bank holiday news bulletins weren't focused on the motorway jams. Instead, they featured people being winched to safety from the roofs of their caravans by a helicopter - and just down the road, at that. We'd had snowy Easters, cold ones and wet, miserable ones, but nothing to compare with the deluge that engulfed the entire country, including us, over that holiday period. It was a financial disaster throughout the industry and for us especially after a winter of colossal investment - a trying time for man and beast alike. The only consolation in these situations is that the following year the attendance figures are easy to improve upon! If both the new elephants and a pair of white rhino which had arrived from South Africa the previous December had to be treated with kid gloves, the rest of the collection were scarcely less vulnerable. But everything survived, except the finances.

Inevitably, the pace quickened, the sun shone at last and we settled down into the familiar routine of two more bank holiday weekends in quick-fire rapid succession. After one of them, at a routine evening management dinner, a trap was sprung. It wasn't entirely unexpected because I know Wendy Jackson, with whom I work so closely, very well. I knew she'd been up to something, but what a something! As a reward for twenty five years' service, I was off on the trip of a lifetime, it was announced. After all those years looking after a major animal collection and seeing the white-collar guys upstairs go almost at will, finally I was off to Africa at the park's expense. So, too, were Sue and the children. Ivan, our Director of Operations and a native of those parts, would take us together with his wife and children to keep everyone company. In the meantime, there was a wonderful coloured cartoon sketch by our multi-talented resident artist to admire and assume pride of place at home.

There was, though, little time to enthuse or enthral. In any walk of life, the higher up the ladder you climb the more detached you become from the shop floor (or the stable floor!). There's a real danger that you become isolated from what attracted you to the job in the first instance. At 8a.m. though on the morning after the champagne night before it was solidly down to earth once more, of necessity, up to my knees in elephant muck. The pace of life was frantic, remorseless and unremitting. On one occasion, having worked until gone midnight on three successive nights, I found myself, on my weekend off, interviewing a comely, blonde Australian worm farmer who'd walked into the office and asked for a job. I'd pinched myself and checked the calendar. The calls for Mr. G. Raffe and Mrs. C. Lion etc. which flood in to trap the unwary switchboard operator on April 1st had indeed come the month before. Was it a stripagram then? I should be so lucky! I was simply tired and suspicious. There was no let-up. In my celebratory year there was to be no resting on laurels, no relaxing. I was to work harder than I'd ever worked in my life. By mid-September, my diary revealed that I'd been called in on thirty of

Opposite:
The faithful Angela and I share a 25th
Anniversary cake with a small friend.
(Photo D. Clapp, Express and Star)

Below:
David Chorley presents me with my suprise
package for 25 years service.
(Photo Ivan Knezovich)

the thirty four weekends to date and I was losing count. Even this, of course, took no account of the early starts and late finishes. Holidays taken? Nil.

In no time, the end of October was upon us. That last week began in typical fashion - a 3.30a.m. Monday morning start. When the park opened in 1973, our Bengal tigers had come from Kolmarden Zoo in Sweden. It was, perhaps, fitting then that, twenty five years on, Ivan and I should be returning to Sweden in pursuit of our latest venture. Tigers again, but this time even more enthralling - white tigers. White tigers are neither albinos nor a separate species. Most have black stripes of varying distinction and blue eyes, the result of what scientists call 'recessive mutants', where both parents carry a mutant recessive gene. This occurs only rarely in the wild. Only a dozen or so sightings are recorded in the last hundred years, none at all since 1951. In that time, the Bengal tiger population has declined from 40,000 to a low of 1,800 whilst, within that same span, 100,000 have lived and died. Statistically, then, only one Bengal tiger in 10,000 is white. Melanistic specimens are on record but are far, far rarer. So, too, are white specimens amongst the other five tiger sub-species. The world's current Bengal white tiger population of barely 150 originate from that last sighting in 1951 in the former state of Madhya Pradesh, Rewa, Central India - the setting for Kipling's 'The Jungle Book' and still today reasonable tiger country in the Kinha Valley. A hunting party organised by the local Maharaja (ironically for British civil servants) shot dead a tigress and three of her litter of cubs. Fortuitously, a fourth cub survived and was subsequently trapped. It was white. Having escaped the bullets, the hunger and thirst (and a sharp crack over the head in attempting to escape!), this nine month old male was named 'Mohan', the one who charms. By incestuous captive inbreeding, he sired the first litter (4) of white cubs born in captivity, in October 1958. By the time of his death in 1969, he'd sired a further 30 cubs, 21 of them white. It was, then, to see some of his descendants that we drove down the silent motorway.

By breakfast time, we'd cleared Heathrow, by mid-morning we were leaving Stockholm in a light plane heading further north. Ninety minutes later, after landing at Kramfors on the east coast, we were in a car heading further north again. By 2p.m. local time, we were in Junsele, the coldest inhabited place in the whole of Sweden, where, in a similar vein perhaps to the English tradition of building churches etc. in the middle of the road, someone had built a zoo! But, at least it contained a breathtakingly beautiful pair of white tigers with two juvenile cubs. By 4p.m., we were flying south again back to Stockholm, then a further drive a hundred kilometres west to Eskiluna where we finally fell into a hotel - lager in one hand, bread roll in the other - too late and too tired for anything else. There were eight more white tigers to view before lunch the next morning in the town's municipal zoo. So it came about, then, that I the Englishman and Ivan the South African sat down with our Swedish hosts in a Chinese restaurant to discuss buying Indian tigers! Our minds made up, subject to some precautionary pelvic X-rays I'd asked for and the usual veterinary assurances, we were homeward-bound the same evening, arriving on our respective doorsteps at 10p.m.

Severe weather and its associated problems kept me at full stretch for the remainder of the week. Suddenly, it was Friday. I spent the morning darting wildebeest in the park to house them for the winter. Then it was home to change, give a last briefing to everyone looking after the farm in our absence, then we were off. We left Heathrow at dusk but, when dawn broke twelve hours later, I was back amongst the wildebeest, flying low over them in the Namibian bush in a six-seater light aircraft. Ivan, myself and the boys in one, the girls alongside us in another. It was an awe-inspiring moment for myself, Sue (she who hates flying and the heat!) and the children alike.

We quickly adjusted to the African way. Rising at 5a.m. to go on the game drives or to climb mountains in the dark to see the sunrise and be back for breakfast, the next drive or the flight out from the bush landing strips to the next camp. We successfully tracked white rhino and lions in the bush, the desert elephants in Damaraland, witnessed a lion 'kill' in Etosha (much to Nicola's disgust!) and 'did' the Sossusvlei desert in the Namib Naukluft Park which was 110°F by 10.30 in the morning. We barbecued in bush leopard country, rifles on our laps, quad-biked across the coastal sand dunes before breakfast and found time to give the children their first driving lesson in a Toyota Landcruiser far from the maddening crowd. We learnt survival skills, too. Disciplining yourself to kicking everything before you picked it up and taking the rifle when you wandered off behind a tree was important but, ultimately, it was the ability to flick the top off a lager bottle on the bumper of the Toyota that decided how long you'd survive in the heat of the day! We did the evening game drives, too, before coming back for dinner, drinks and the traditional evenings by the illuminated water-holes till long after midnight. To complete the experience, we even saw it rain, which was ironic because while we were away it scarcely stopped, producing some of the worst flooding ever in Bewdley. Bad enough, in fact, to provoke a sympathetic royal visit. Only one fax message was to catch up with us in the entire ten days, the longest I'd ever been away from the park.

One day, as the two families were bouncing down a dusty track from the Sossusvlei desert camp towards the airstrip, we pulled over to allow another landrover to pass. In it was Keith, the park's accountant, and family. Bewdley had come to Africa with a vengeance! There was just time for a snapshot of the three families before going our separate ways. We had a plane to catch, they were desperate for rest and recuperation after a long haul from Victoria Falls. The overriding impression was not just that of a magnificent country, not lightly described as Africa's gem, but of a wonderful people. Even the pilot of a light aircraft would unload one's luggage, bear it off and still thank you, in a manner that could only be genuine, for taking the trouble to visit his country. Somehow, you wouldn't get that in England. The children stuck the unrelenting pace and didn't pass up on a minute of it.

The penultimate part of the stay was in Ongava, the company's own private Namibian game reserve, a thriving example of modern conservation strategy. By combining three derelict subsistence level farms into one unit and convincing the locals that tourism represented their best chance of a future, not least with a promise of first choice of the employment it created, everyone was happy - except the poachers. With the realisation that their future was inextricably tied up with wildlife, the locals watched over it very carefully. It represented security and they already had songs to sing to you around the camp fire at night to prove it. This created a hostile environment into which few poachers dared to tread. The first thing I bumped into was Brutalis, the white rhino we'd helped repatriate back to Africa. We'd never met before, but I felt I knew him rather well. I saw evidence, too, of the first thing he'd bumped into on his homecoming - a now deserted farmhouse. One evening, he'd walked through the French windows into the living room as the manager's family retreated before him up the stairs!

Small by African standards at a mere 125 square miles, Ongava is nevertheless strategically situated at Ombika gate on the southern border of the world-famous Etosha National Park. It offers unashamed five-star luxury and our Namibian guide with the most English of names, one Colin Brown(!), ensured that we enjoyed it to the full. There's often a tendency to hold these chaps who do the safari thing for real in a certain amount of awe. However, I noticed that they, too, took an inordinate amount of interest in what we did with our animals and how. Certainly, when they come over here, they are amazed at the proximity of our animals and flabbergasted by the Eurasian specimens like tigers, which they've heard of but never seen. Again, too, despite the distances involved, we learnt what a small world it is. Twenty five years earlier, we'd discovered a Bewdley in America, we'd had Jeff Cooke's journey 'home' to Worcester, the rendezvous of the three Bewdley families in the desert and now, when shopping in Swakopmund on the Namibian coast, we found ourselves being served by a lady from Hereford! Ivan, meantime, looked after us royally, doing everything humanly possible to ensure that it was, indeed, the trip of a lifetime. The journey home was sombre indeed. We'd all left part of ourselves behind. One thing was decided unanimously without a word being uttered. We will return.

No sooner had the safari suit been consigned to the bottom drawer than the thermals were coming from the top one. It was back to Sweden again, this time to collect the white tigers. I knew from the onset that extracting them at that time of year from such a latitude could well involve an epic of endurance the like of which I wouldn't wish on anyone. So I went myself, accompanied

Our main mode of transport in Namibia. (Photo Colin Brown)

Next stop Sweden for the White Tigers. (Photo Author)

Namibian elephants at a waterhole in Etosha. (Photo Author)

A desert elephant in Damaraland, Namibia. (Photo Author)

Foot inspection for elephants in Bewdley. (Photo Author)

Christopher's first driving lesson - in Namibia whilst, (right) at home the first rumbles of concern over the effect of transport policies on tourism. (Photos Author)

The 'quiet' winters! The new elephant house takes shape. (Photo Author)

only by a cameraman. It involved another 3a.m. Monday morning start. Frustratingly, despite this, the schedule began to slip from the onset with an unexplained forty minute delay in departure from Heathrow immediately putting our connecting flight for the second leg of the journey in jeopardy. As we crossed low over the Danish coast, further inklings of trouble became evident - the ground was hidden in a blanket of snow. As we circled Stockholm's Arlanda airport for another forty minutes trying to land, it became apparent that we'd flown into one of the worst storms the Swedish capital could remember, six feet of snow in twenty four hours! The delays meant we missed our flight north by a matter of seconds.

We waited three hours for the next (and the day's only other) flight out as the blizzard raged. The tannoy fell silent over the deserted lounge as conditions worsened by the hour. It was pitch black by 2p.m. Eventually, though, we found ourselves on our little half-empty thirty-seater being bathed in de-icer by trucks which were themselves being de-iced. The pilot said the minimum operating visibility for the runway lights was three hundred yards. He had remarkable vision - I couldn't see the wing tips. Dimly visible, though, through the darkness was a battery of flashing lights as a phalanx of snowploughs, some ten in all, preceded us as we groped our way to where the snow was marginally less deep. Bathed in the ghostly fluorescent sheen of the anti-freeze, we slithered up the runway once, then twice, before the pilot spun us on a krona, revved and bolted skywards into the teeth of the blizzard. For an eternity, we hung there, held, it seemed, in suspended animation as the propellers clawed at the howling headwind. Eventually, though, the blonde Nordic maiden in whose care we were entrusted ceased her silent prayer. Speech was impossible above the din but, after crossing her admirable chest, she swallowed hard, undid her seatbelt and silently passed a flask around together with a bread roll and a biscuit each. Not much of a last supper, I thought, but as we headed northwards, the method to the pilot's madness became apparent. Paradoxically, perhaps, the further north we went, the more the snow cover diminished. But it grew colder by the minute. On landing, we awoke our faithful driver who'd been waiting six hours and crunched our frozen way northwards, again along deserted roads, for a further two hours. Having long since missed all opportunity of daylight filming, we had to make the most of what we had time-wise. We filmed until 8p.m. in the darkness, ate and fell into a warm chalet at 10p.m. mindful of the even longer day ahead.

It began at 2a.m. when Stefan Jonsson, curator of Parken Zoo, Eskiluna, who actually owned the tigers, finally arrived from Stockholm with the hired van. It had taken him nearly all day and most of the night. It was not an auspicious omen for our passage back. We were up and about by 4.30. The snow had by now caught up with us, reducing the temperature from a potential minus 45°C to a mere minus 20°C. Undeterred, by 6.15a.m. we'd crated the two cubs in the darkness, loaded up, swallowed some coffee and were heading south for Stockholm with our Swedish driver, the cameraman and myself all crammed into the van. The only route out was by road - for some extraordinary reason freight aircraft didn't use Kramfors airfield. It proved to be an epic journey, one that none of us will forget to our dying day - a day that appeared to have arrived. My enduring memory of Sweden isn't the cold, the six feet of snow or the stalwarts who did everything humanly possible to assist us at every turn, but that of plummeting down an icy road at 60mph. headlong into a truck heading north. I thought of Sue where I'd last seen her, curled up fast asleep, and that I wasn't going to see her again. Oblivion beckoned, with both the driver and cameraman either side of me rigid in anticipation of it, but, at the last split second, both vehicles slipped into the same frozen rut, snapped straight and we exchanged wing mirrors with surgical precision, at 60mph. We removed theirs and they ours. It was as close as that. If a cat has nine lives, I suppose those who look after them share them, too. But, there was no time to stand and dither. The day ahead was full of imponderables, not least of which were the road conditions as we headed back into the principal snow zone. One thing, though, was certain - the plane would leave at 6.20p.m. local time with us or without us.

Even for the Swedes, the weather was making the headlines, both at home and abroad. As we battled our way south, the great escape captured the imagination of their media. The 'phone rang incessantly. Everyone wanted to see the tigers and talk to us. Swedish television wanted the film from our cameras, but we refused to stop for anyone or anything. We were well aware that even a five minute delay could prove fatal. As darkness fell again at 3p.m. amidst a sunset across the frozen, snow encrusted lakes as dazzling as anything witnessed in Africa, we encountered what appeared a killer blow. Over twenty four hours after the snowfall, the main road south was still blocked. They'd finally rescued the occupants of the trapped vehicles but, in so doing, over-zealous application of the snow ploughs had destroyed the road. At the police roadblock, they directed us on a hundred kilometre, ninety minute detour, or so they said. An escort, perhaps? No way! They weren't driving in those conditions! The snow deepened as we bumped our solitary way down deserted trunk roads which, by now, resembled little more than a toboggan run - a narrow crevasse in the snow, piled high above the vehicle on both sides, down which only fools chose to slide. Between media calls, the airport kept in constant touch, checking our progress but getting more anxious by the minute. Far from checking in three hours prior to flight time, after a six hour journey it was more a question of whether we would get there at all. They advised us of the weather conditions and the roads ahead, suggested detours and talked us in like an aircraft itself landing blind. It took us precisely twelve hours to the minute non-stop door-to-door to cover those four hundred miles. We slid into the cargo terminal with three minutes to spare, the Heathrow-bound Boeing 767 with a full compliment of 250 unwitting passengers being held back for us on the icy runway. All paperwork was dispensed with as we hurtled through the handling bays but we made it, we thought. With the tigers now aboard, the passenger terminal proved to be another breakneck journey away on the other side of the airport for our long-suffering driver, Stefan - only to be refused boarding ourselves! A blunt exchange of views resulted in a personal escort. We sprinted through the departure lounges as the accelerating roar of the jet engines which threatened to take our tigers away reached a crescendo. Still clad in thermal clothing and burdened with the luggage and the camera unit, it was perhaps the feat of the day but, again, we made it, only to sit on the plane for an hour and a half while they negotiated a fresh take-off slot. Thankfully, the passengers remained blissfully unaware both that there were two tigers in the hold beneath them and that the two dishevelled passengers thrust so belatedly into their midst at the eleventh hour were responsible for the delay. Poor Stefan, though, still had another hour and a half's drive to reach home. We became firm friends, and whenever I go to Sweden his door is always open.

Heathrow itself was equally infuriating. Having been closeted with the tigers all day, I was denied access to them for two hours on the grounds that they were suddenly a rabies risk, notwithstanding the fact that the accompanying veterinary certificate held that their country of origin had been rabies-free for over a hundred years! After generating a further mountain of paperwork from bleary-eyed nonentities, I managed to resume contact with my charges in the quarantine area, but I had to fight my way through a throng of admiring cat lovers first. So much for the rabies regime. We eventually extracted them from this nonsense at 11p.m. and headed straight into the bank of impenetrable fog that had enveloped the M40. It reduced progress to a crawl, so it was gone 2a.m. before familiar voices were heard from the ghostly figures emerging from the darkness of the Bewdley night, resplendent in their crisp, new, white quarantine suits. Like servicemen who are given a number on signing up, the keepers are given a radio call sign which they will keep. 'Giraffe 1' was there. So, too, was 'Elephant 2' together with 'Lion 2' and 'Lion 11'! We had been, seen and conquered all the trials and tribulations that the weather could throw at us in nearly twenty four hours' non-stop travelling, but we were back.

It was gone 4a.m. before the cubs were tucked up into their newly-converted quarantine unit and I could go home. I laid the duty-frees outside the children's door, Christmas style. Sue was where I'd left her forty nine hours before and precisely how I'd imagined her to be half a lifetime ago as fate threatened to intervene earlier in that interminable day - fast asleep in a soft, warm bed. I'd had one set meal and four hours' sleep in the interim, but I was home. She stirred briefly as I slipped in beside her, our arms linking instinctively, both finally able to relax.

Little did I realise it, but the difficult part was still to come as our antiquated quarantine laws bit hard. I had a CITES certificate authenticating the tigers' origin as captive bred in a controlled environment. The were micro-chipped, too, just in case someone confused a white tiger with something else. The health certificate confirmed the absence of rabies in Sweden for over a hundred years. Yet, despite the fact that, quite clearly, we weren't dealing with stray cats and dogs which had been roaming the streets in some far off exotic land, we'd had to reluctantly accept the need for quarantine, notwithstanding the fact that the animals were once more (out of obvious necessity) secure within another controlled environment. The rabies regulations, in fact, permit the display of quarantined animals in captive situations provided suitable safeguards exist. The most obvious, of course, is a 'stand off' barrier to prevent any physical contact between the interned and their admirers. I argued that in our 'drive through' safari situation the protocol was, in fact, reversed - the visitors being enclosed in their cars with the animals enjoying their freedom of movement. Local MAFF officials were pretty relaxed about the proposed regime when I went over it all with them on New Year's Eve. After all, the only way anyone could contract rabies if there were a risk, and everyone at MAFF accepted unequivocally that there wasn't, would be by leaving their vehicle and going walkabouts into the tigers. If that were to happen, rabies would be the last thing on anyone's mind! But, to our horror, their powers that be at HQ in Tolworth overturned the local advice. The white tigers would have to remain under wraps for six months until June, three bank holidays on and half way through the season.

The risk was non-existent but, apparently, the problem to the bureaucratic mind lay in the public's perception of what quarantine should be seen to be! And all this on the very day, coincidentally, that the government launched an international initiative aimed at conserving tigers. Talk about a red rag to a bull! Could they not look in their own back yard first, I enquired? Armed by now with a certificate from the Swedish Ministry of Agriculture itself to the effect that all Swedish territory had been rabies free for a hundred and twenty years, I went to our MP. If ever there was a worthy cause, this was it. After all, hadn't I travelled home with the tigers on a passenger jet containing 250 passengers? Where, then, the rabies threat? To compound the nonsense still further, an Indian lion was being transferred from Dudley Zoo, a mere fifteen miles away, back to the very Swedish zoo that our tigers had originated from, without quarantine! David Lock, our new Labour MP, threw himself into our cause

Namibian sunrise, Damaraland.
(Photo Author)

Swedish sunset, North of Stockholm.
(Photo Author)

while I snapped away at the ministry's heels for the next two months.

Heads shook in universal dismay at my apparent naivety in not seeing a lost cause. These laws are, after all, carved in tablets of stone and are not negotiable. The stakes, though, for us could scarcely be higher. We were already building the tiger reserve apace at a truly prohibitive cost - in time for the traditional pre-Easter opening. The marketing men were beavering away, the TV commercial was being shot, the new stationery (resplendent with white tigers) was printed and even then being mailed out to schools and coach companies. I noted that Sir Elton John, too, was railing against the quarantine rules and wrote to him to enlist support - but continued to phone Westminster three times a day as well. I pushed incessantly for a personal meeting with the then agriculture minister. Geoff Rooker, a Midlands MP himself, had to understand the implications of such matters on the regional tourism and leisure industry, the animals' welfare and, besides, what about the job losses! Eventually, MAFF conducted a face-saving Health and Safety review and buckled. They were very impressed by the fact that the wardens in the cat sections carried guns, but never enquired what, if any, ammunition they had! It was, though, a landmark policy reversal which meant the white tigers would, in fact, see the light of day well before the longest day. It was nearly March and, although Dave Chorley was in America when he received my news, the sigh of relief was almost audible. It was the country's first ever 'drive though' quarantine.

As usual, there was little time to savour the moment. Construction continued apace during what is popularly assumed to be the quiet out-of-season interlude, not just on the new tiger facilities but on a new monkey exhibit as well. The monkeys have always damaged cars and always will, but we were becoming concerned that the issue was becoming a bit more than a joke. Certainly, coach operators thought so and were having serious reservations about their pride and joys being routinely vandalised. The park layout, though, meant that avoiding the monkey area meant missing out on the lions - and the new white tigers. So, we built a new road loop to accommodate a new monkey reserve which could be bypassed without missing out on the cats, the third major development (with the elephants) in barely twelve months.

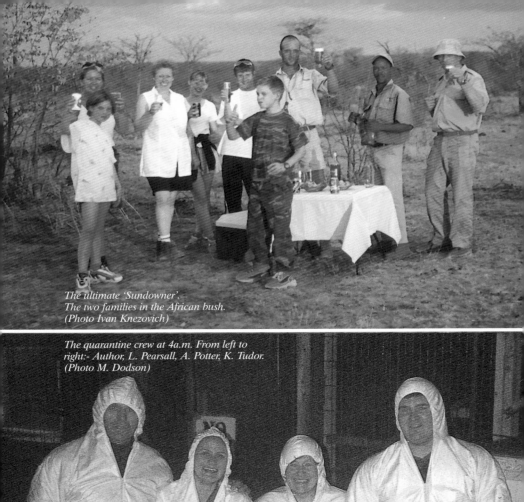

The ultimate 'Sundowner'.
The two families in the African bush.
(Photo Ivan Knezovich)

The quarantine crew at 4a.m. From left to
right:- Author, L. Pearsall, A. Potter, K. Tudor.
(Photo M. Dodson)

In retrospect, 95% of vehicles still preferred to run the monkey gauntlet so we were probably wasting our time, other than to provide people with the choice and ourselves with a cast-iron disclaimer for any vehicular damage, but we weren't to know. It meant breaking fresh ground, though, in every sense of the word, for the area we expanded into was an SSSI (Site of Special Scientific Interest). Hitherto sacrosanct by conventional criteria since the park's inception, it did, though, occupy 28 acres of our entire 195 acre site and was the only geographical direction into which we could expand. However, it had been totally neglected by English Nature and its predecessor, the Nature Conservancy Council, and had, I considered, long since lost all pretence to being heathland, the reason for its original classification. I instigated an intricate arrangement utilising a heathland restoration programme I'd commissioned from the Worcestershire County Trust between ourselves, the Wyre Forest District Council, the Forestry Authority and English Nature. Under the agreement, the area could be used by the monkeys whilst being managed in a manner likely to encourage heathland regeneration, about the most threatened form of habitat in the county. Potentially, everyone stands to be a winner.

Construction ground on throughout an exceptionally wet winter amidst the inevitable delays and unforeseen hiccups incumbent in such matters. One morning, for example, an eighty year old World War 1 three-inch trench mortar fell out of a JCB bucket beneath the nose of a startled dumper driver. Having cleared the area, I investigated and, not for the first time, found myself awaiting the bomb squad. A sensible precaution, though, for having removed it from the dumper, it was felt prudent to destroy it. A local bobby (whom I'd known for over twenty years) and I tossed a coin for the privilege of pressing the detonator. I lost, but still had a grandstand view as it went up. It was live.

The following day, I walked into another explosion..... at home. I'd recognised the omens immediately I walked through the door but was still caught off guard. The children had locked themselves in the bathroom, the dog was under the bed, the cats in the airing cupboard. "What's this about you defusing a bomb?" demanded Sue, waving an evening paper beneath my nose. My protestations of innocence were entirely genuine at first - life was so hectic I'd actually clean forgotten all about it. Christopher's assurances, though, echoed beneath the loo door. "Don't worry, Mum, it's safe. The bits are in my bedroom!" The bomb squad, though, weren't so reassuring. They couldn't sweep the area for other ordnance. We simply had to call them if we found any more!

There were other potentially dangerous situations to defuse that winter, too. There was a BSE scare that took months to resolve, the salmonella which I found had accompanied the white tigers and their integration with some home bred cubs of similar age, all of whom would catch mange from a tiger introduced from another collection. There would be another trip to Sweden, another pair of white tigers, young elephants still being domesticated, the little matter of a major animal collection that couldn't be ignored simply because we were too busy elsewhere, and the first rumbles of concern over the effect of transport policy on tourism outside the major conurbations. There was another battle royal to be won against the DETR as well. During 1997, I'd been advised by this august body of yet another EEC directive. Once again, 'commercialism' reared its ugly head. In essence, Article 8(1) of Council Regulation EC No. 338/97 forbade any Annex A species being used for any commercial purpose. i.e. purchase, offer to purchase, acquisition for commercial purposes, display to the public for commercial purpose, use for commercial gain and sale, keeping for sale, offering for sale or transporting for sale. However, all this could be bypassed by applying for an Article 30 of Commission Regulation EC No. 939/97! Basically, it appeared little more than a 'super' zoo licence, but that didn't stop them enquiring for details of any existing zoo licence that we might have (as if we could survive a day without one!) or stop the endless quest for mindboggling trivia that drove us (and even them!) to distraction. Ultimately, the stumbling block proved to be the requirement that every Annex A specimen i.e. tiger, elephant etc. on view to the public had to be micro-chipped for identification in perpetuity. Quite how the public could make the distinction was never elaborated upon. Even if they visited with a transponder in their pocket to register the numbers implanted within the animals, they'd scarcely get close enough and, besides, the transponder was proving problematical. Running it over

David Chorley (the managing director) one day, it flashed up 'No ID'. This was immediately interpreted as 'No Idea!'. It was then passed over Wendy Jackson, our long-suffering secretary, whereupon it flashed up 'Ready'!

Meanwhile, I'd refused this missive. Not being entirely out of touch with progress, I'd been micro-chipping specimens for some time, as and when the opportunity arose, but could see no justification whatsoever for having to sedate animals simply to comply with this requirement. I gave a written undertaking to do so whenever the animals concerned were handled, but this wasn't good enough. The JNCC, the DETR's advisors, wouldn't back down. We couldn't have our Article 30 until every eligible animal had its chip. Both our vets (The Vale Veterinary Group together with Taylor and Marshall for the reptiles) supported this contention but, ultimately, I called in the cavalry. The endorsement of my stance from the International Zoo Veterinary Group's Andrew Greenwood clinched the argument. Our Article 30 certificate arrived within days. It had taken two years but, if that is what it takes to stand tall and be counted amongst the biggest and best, so be it.

All this, though, lay in the future at the end of another exhausting day in a momentous year of unforeseen twists and turns. More immediately, though, in just four hours I had to be back at work or else someone would lose their day off. Time enough, though, to dream. For two days, my toes had itched as the Namibian sand had eked out of my boots into the Swedish snow. Doubtless, in years to come, I'd give some geologist a migraine calculating how it had got there. Subconsciously, perhaps, it triggered memories of my first encounter with a big cat. Lying beneath an ancient car, wiring up an ailing exhaust system to get it mobile, I'd felt a boot being removed, then the sock, then the rough rasping tongue, then the hot breath. Sensing a practical joker, I'd rolled over onto my stomach, only to find myself staring at four rather large paws! The original safari concept had evolved around a field full of lions through which you drove and then went home. The idea has come a long way, both in the variety of species we now keep and the thought that now goes into keeping them. I hope I've contributed something.

Outside, the full moon glistened white in the bright blue night sky, like a football. Eerily, its rays sought out a white number four reflecting defiantly from an ageing track suit top in the wardrobe. My mind drifted back to a fateful leap on an August afternoon nearly thirty years before, as if it were yesterday. The penalty miss still rankles but, that apart, I guess things hadn't worked out too badly. As for the consultant's advice to forget farming? Well, we've got our own farm now; acres of rolling hills, woods, pools, streams and meadows. Here live our cattle, sheep, horses, deer and llamas, not to mention nine cats, three dogs and two raucous teenagers. It's a funny old world, isn't it?